LIVERPOOL CAPTAINS

A Journey Of Leadership From The Pitch

LIVERPOOL CAPTAINS

A Journey Of Leadership From The Pitch

Ragnhild Lund Ansnes

deCoubertin
B O O K S

First published as a hardback by deCoubertin Books Ltd in 2016.

First Edition

deCoubertin Books, Studio I, Baltic Creative Campus, Liverpool, L1 OAH
www.decoubertin.co.uk

ISBN: 978-1-909245-42-6

A CIP catalogue record for this book is available from the British Library.

Cover design and typesetting by Thomas Regan at Milkyone Creative.

Printed and bound by CPI Group (UK) Ltd, Croydon, CR0 4YY

To Elvira, Elias and Jostein: my favourite team.

CONTENTS

FOREWORD

Roy Evans

EVERY LIVERPOOL CAPTAIN IS DIFFERENT. EACH HAS HIS OWN personality and makes different decisions in order to stamp his authority and make the team successful depending on the situation.

It is always simpler to be captain for a successful team, when you can go out and win trophies. When the going gets tough, the captain's responsibility can feel more demanding, and even weigh you down. That goes both for the teamwork on the pitch and the relationship with the manager off the pitch.

That is where things have changed the most over the years. Fifty years ago, the captain would take charge and make changes when he saw that things were not working properly. These days, the managers want to kick every ball. Yet the captain still plays an important role. The manager has no opportunity to pass on messages to individual players. So the captain is an essential connection and an important communicator. That requires special skills: the ability to get a message across, to motivate your team and to restore energy even. And last, but not least; respect.

The captain does not always have to scream and shout to get his messages through. The important thing is that the other players listen to him and that his message reaches its target. A good captain must always be very close to his players, and enjoy their respect. He does not necessarily have to be friends with everyone off the pitch – that is practically impossible – but when the players go out on that green mat, everything else must be put aside. At that point it is all about giving your best performance for the team. And that means everybody. Not least the captain.

One point has often been discussed: can the role as captain ever influence the player carrying the armband in a negative way? For some, it may do, for others it does not matter. And for some, the duties off the pitch may be the most demanding. I feel convinced this book will touch upon that.

As far as the performance on the pitch is concerned, I would like to emphasise that the captain's role comes second to his personal performance in the game. You always expect most of your captain. He must lead and perform at a top level. After all, that is how he earned the captain's position, through years of hard work. And that is why he can never let the responsibility as a captain undermine his own performance. If he does, he cannot go on as captain.

I am sometimes asked who I rate highest of all Liverpool captains. That is a very difficult question to answer. There are so many great players and strong personalities who have been captains through the years. And there are a lot of others who could have been captains, but never were. Take the 1965 team that won the FA Cup for the first time: Ron Yeats was the captain; but practically every man was a potential captain.

Ron Yeats, indeed, was captain when the great days at Liverpool started. Ian St John was there too. The two of them have had their names written into Liverpool history in capital letters. Others who deserve a mention, in my opinion, are Alan Hansen, Emlyn Hughes, Graeme Souness and, not least, Steven Gerrard. He will always be up there as one of the greatest; he achieved fantastic things even though the team was not always the best. Steven grew to know all there was to know about being a captain. And everybody respected him. When he spoke, everybody listened.

When I was manager, John Barnes was an excellent captain. He always had an opinion, and was always on the lookout for improvement. Barnes was passionate and very dedicated. Paul Ince was another leader with special abilities. He may not have been liked by all, but I believe he had almost everything a captain needs. The players looked up to him. He always gave 100 per cent, and would take no nonsense. A role model.

My conclusion is that all of our captains have done an outstanding job for the club – even though they have played at different times and at varying levels. Some of them have collected a lot of trophies, some did not win any. That is football. The captains cannot be blamed. I am certain they always did their best, and that they were proud of their teams.

The role of the captain is really important, especially at a club the size of Liverpool, where the expectations are huge. It is vital, not least for young players, who need someone to lead on the pitch, someone to set the standard. A captain is there for the team first, and less for himself. It certainly requires a bit of an ego to become captain, preferably a strong one, but it must never overshadow his work for the team. That was never a problem with the captains of Liverpool when I was there. The team has always come first. That is why we remember them and appreciate them.

Roy Evans
2016

RON YEATS
SHANKLY'S MILLION-DOLLAR MAN

*'Big Yeats was one of the Kop kings. King-size player, a born leader, and great to have
around wherever and whenever.'*
Ian St John

MUSIC BOUNCES OFF THE WALLS IN THE DARKNESS OF THE
Liverpool Echo Arena, the city's waterside concert venue. Red and blue lights take
turns in shining their way through the vapour created by the fog machine on the
dance floor. We are here to celebrate the winners of Liverpool's 2015 Players' Awards.

The blue light hits a shiny object that turns out to be nothing less than the honorary trophy of the club: its Lifetime Achievement Award. The trophy is floating across
the floor, held by the hands of a giant from Liverpool's history. He has danced for
so long now, on this warm May night, that the back of his white shirt is completely
soaked. He greets us with a big, hearty smile, this giant of a man who was first
brought to Merseyside by Bill Shankly more than half a century ago.

He became an important piece of the puzzle that elevated Liverpool out of the
doldrums and into the First Division and then on its path to becoming the most
successful club in English football history. Ronald Yeats would also go on to be the
second longest serving captain in the history of the club, a mile ahead of the man in
third place: Emlyn Hughes.

When he was appointed Liverpool manager in 1959, Bill Shankly came to

Anfield on the condition that he, and not a committee as had traditionally been the case, got to pick the team. Shankly promised to build Liverpool up to become a bastion but only if he alone had mastery over his squad. Ron Yeats was an important part of his rebuilding plans: he had been captain of every team he had played for, and was almost immediately – five months after arriving on Merseyside – chosen by Bill Shankly as his leader.

Shankly immediately nicknamed Yeats 'The Colossus'.

'Take a walk around my centre-half, gentlemen, he's a colossus!' Bill Shankly grinned happily at the press conference in 1961, imploring with enthusiasm and conviction that reporters should 'go into the dressing room and walk round him!' Shankly compared Yeats to a 'mountain'.

On this day in May 2015, Ronald Yeats, centre-back for ten years and captain of Liverpool for nine years, has been honoured along with Ian St John, striker, best friend and room-mate through his entire career at Liverpool. There is not a dry eye in the house as Yeats and St John come on stage to accept their trophies. St John is, as ever, quick with his repartee, but of a sudden goes quiet, just as he is about to start his acceptance speech. The master of words, who still works in radio for good reason, is now looking out over the tables and sees current LFC players and their wives, and former stars like Robbie Fowler, John Barnes, Steve McManaman, Alan Kennedy, Phil Neal, Mark Wright, David Fairclough and Phil Thompson, to name but a few of those who turn up for the club when the Liverpool family comes together. Then he looks upwards to the stands: there are thousands of people who have bought tickets to honour this year's LFC prize winners. The vocal Scot, who scored shedloads of goals through the 1960s, has gone silent. He draws a deep breath, then finally speaks.

'The two of us were privileged who were allowed to join the Bill Shankly revolution,' St John says. 'This big guy and me have known each other for more than sixty years, ever since we played for Scotland Schoolboy International. The first time I saw this colossus of a man, I thought he was the coach! We've been best mates and room-mates for many years, and we're still Liverpool fans.'

The wordsmith is out of words. Tears are starting to well up as he looks over the crowd. But then the giant at his elbow begins to speak, and I hold my breath. I know these days it can be difficult for Ron Yeats to find the right words. All those years of heading the super-heavy leather ball out of defence, or scoring headers from a set piece, has weakened his memory. He suffers from Alzheimer's disease, like so many other players from those days, and over the last year some memories have disappeared.

It is safe to say that Yeats, born on a cold November's day in 1937, has sacrificed a lot for Liverpool FC.

✦

A few days earlier, Ian St John had taken me to visit the man who set the high standard for leadership on the pitch for Liverpool FC. The two friends have not seen each other in the past year. St John has been battling cancer, and one of the operations hurt his knee, making him less mobile. His once supple body had been instrumental as Liverpool climbed into the top division and won their first FA Cup in 1965, led by Ron Yeats.

'I feel very honoured to be able to say I've captained all the teams I've played for,' Yeats begins. He is freshly shaven, and side by side with St John, 'the Saint', on the sofa. We are in the living room of his tastefully decorated house, and his wife Ann is in the kitchen, making us all coffee and tea.

It was not immediately obvious that Yeats would almost go straight in as Liverpool captain. He succeeded Dick White, who in his turn had taken over the captaincy from Ronnie Moran – the boot room legend who became an important part of Liverpool's coaching staff after his active career. Usually the honour of the captaincy is bestowed on someone after long and faithful service in the red shirt, as one of the best and most experienced on the team. But Shankly had a lot of faith in his fellow Scot. Yeats had captained Dundee United at a young age, and, standing 6ft 2in tall, had the physical stature of a leader. After five months at Liverpool, Yeats was appointed skipper.

'It was a nice gesture by Shankly to make me captain,' Yeats says before I ask him about his leadership qualities. 'I was big and strong and set the standard for the game. When I played well, that is.'

'But you weren't afraid to shout at us on the pitch!' St John slips in.

'No.' Yeats smiles. 'If I needed to!' he adds. 'But there rarely was a need to shout, we were such a good team. They knew how to score and win games.'

Roy Evans says the Liverpool team of the 1960s is the best team he ever saw.

Ian St John breaks into one of those big, hearty smiles.

'Did he really say that? That's so nice of him to say,' Yeats replies, almost with surprise. 'Roy is a good guy.'

Even old football legends, it seems, thrive on praise and acknowledgement – even long after their playing careers have ended.

Shankly had first seen St John and Yeats in action when they played against each other on different army sides while doing their national service. His plan was to build his new team around the pair.

Shankly convinced the board to buy St John first. He had already made a name for himself, setting a Scottish record for the fastest ever hat-trick. Two minutes and thirty seconds was all he needed to net three for Motherwell against Hibernian in 1959. Players like St John do not come cheap. When Liverpool paid £37,500 for him in 1961, he was not only the most expensive player they had ever bought, they actually doubled their previous record to get him. A price like that might well put an excessive pressure on a player, and football history is full of such examples. But St John was unfazed by any expectations.

'Feel the pressure? Far from it! We got to play football and we thought it was absolutely fantastic. Imagine, getting paid to play. Even if it was minimum wages, we got paid to do something we loved, in front of supporters who appreciated us. It was wonderful. And no pressure at all. That's something you put on yourself, if you go around saying: "We've got to win, we've got to win!" But Shankly sent us out with a completely different message: "Come on lads, go out on the pitch and have fun!"'

Ron Yeats smiles so his eyes narrow. You can tell he is reliving some of Shankly's messages in his mind, while nodding and smiling at his friend who continues to talk about Shankly's instructions: 'Enjoy yourselves, keep the ball moving, and when you're not moving, hold on to the ball and just remain positive; and don't forget to have fun during the game.'

St John is also full of praise for Liverpool's fans: their supportiveness and importance in making players look forward to games. The interaction between the supporters and the players was a crucial success factor, he says. The more they enjoyed playing, the better the football, which in turn gave the fans even more reason to be happy watching the games. An enjoyable symbiosis. That is how you play good football, Shankly told them: with joy.

St John got off to a brilliant start, scoring a hat-trick against Everton on his debut in the Liverpool Senior Cup Final before a crowd of more than 50,000 at Goodison. The Reds lost the tie 4–3, but it demonstrated that he was worth the record sum Liverpool had coughed up for him and also helped convince the board that Shankly was on to something when he wanted to invest heavily in his other chosen Scottish player.

Ron Yeats was happy about that. He was still in the army, stationed in Aldershot. He played for his army side, as well for Dundee United and Scotland's Under-23 team and would regularly travel over a thousand miles per week between the army, his professional team, the national team and his family. Yeats was not keen on flying, and would regularly throw up on board while travelling between Aldershot and Scotland. All the while his wife and two little girls were living in Aberdeen. It was extremely tough for a boy with travel sickness.

Yeats had first played football as a five-year-old in Aberdeen's bomb craters and dirt roads during the Second World War. He gives a lot of credit to his football-mad teacher, Miss Allen of the Causewayend Primary School, for his becoming a footballer, although his father had played to a high standard with the armed forces too. Miss Allen was beautiful and soft-voiced, and knew a lot about football. In the 1940s, she got Yeats into the school team, and regularly came to see him in their games. She also ensured Ron got into a new school team when the family moved and he changed schools.

Many years later, after Yeats had been appointed captain of Liverpool and was at the height of his fame, he was strolling around the streets of Aberdeen. Suddenly he came face to face with a lady who smiled at him. 'I knew you'd make it, Ronnie, and I'm so happy for you!' Yeats recognised his old teacher immediately. To him her words meant as much as all the praise from important personalities in Scottish and English football.

When Shankly arrived at Liverpool in 1959 he started a massive rebuilding process in every aspect of the club. He began by preparing a better training field, then moved on to improve Anfield, both for players and fans. He wanted them to have better conditions and be proud of their team, and that meant the home arena could not look like a shabby, giant toilet. He saw to it that the pitch was improved, he had water installed and restroom facilities added. The apprentices, including a young Tommy Smith, were responsible for keeping the facilities spotless, in addition to cleaning the senior players' boots – as well as their own training duties.

The most important part of the upgrading job was to improve the quality of the squad. The first time Yeats spoke with Shankly, he asked if Yeats knew where Liverpool was. Yeats thought it was a geographic question, but he was wrong.

'We're in the First Division of the English league,' Shankly said, answering his own question.

'Oh, I thought you were in the Second Division, Mr Shankly?'

'Yeah, but we'll play in the First Division after we sign you, son!'

His memory may be fading, but Ron still remembers this conversation vividly. From that day in 1961, Ron knew that this was the man he wanted to play for.

'Shankly made me feel like a million dollars,' Yeats says, smiling at me with the eagerness of an impressionable young man.

✦

Both Yeats and St John grew up in poor homes in Scotland, Ron in Aberdeen, on the northeast coast, and Ian in Motherwell, an inland steel town further south, between Glasgow and Edinburgh. While Ron's neighbourhood was full of craters and bombed-out houses after the Second World War, St John dryly remarks that he wishes theirs had been bombed too – it was in such a state of disrepair it ought to have been demolished. They lived in miserable conditions and poverty was omnipresent.

Yeats grew up in a family of six, the third in a flock of three boys and a girl. Both parents worked to make ends meet, his father in a slaughterhouse. 'I guess they both worked way too much,' he says now.

Before joining Liverpool, and even as they made their way as young players in the Scottish leagues, both Yeats and St John worked in 'civilian' jobs to provide for their families in Scotland. When Yeats played for his local team Aberdeen Lads' Club as a teenager, he trained as a mason at his uncle's firm. He had left school at fifteen, and the thought of making a living as a footballer did not cross his mind. At the time, he believed he simply was not good enough.

The masonry firm soon went bankrupt and so Yeats followed his father to the slaughterhouse. Working as a butcher's apprentice was not for the faint-hearted. Yeats had to rise at three in the morning to be in time for work. They were long days, and football training came afterwards. Life took a turn for the better when he could kick Leeds shins instead of pulling shins of beef. His time at the slaughterhouse kept him out of trouble and away from the temptations of teenage life. There are few opportunities to go out for a drink and a dance if you have to get up in the middle of the night to go to work. That was how he kept in shape. And it paid off. When he was seventeen, Yeats was picked to play for Scotland Under-19s against England, Wales and Ireland representative teams. It was in one of these games that his and St John's paths first crossed.

Life is full of coincidences, marginal turns and roads taken. One small step could lead you in the exact opposite direction. Serendipity and fate eventually led Yeats to Liverpool. Yet his career could have taken a completely different turn and he could have stayed in Scottish football instead of the English league, if Bill Shankly's brother had snatched Yeats when he was manager for Falkirk.

Yeats was still a teenager when he married Margaret and they were expecting their first child. As a slaughterhouse apprentice the young family man only made £4 15s (£4.75) per week, and the outlook was modest, if not bleak, for the young family. That is why they were happy to see him presented as a possible Falkirk player in the paper, and he was invited for a try-out. But it coincided with a rare off-day for Ron, or maybe the pressure of expectation made him under-perform. Falkirk reserves lost 3–0 and the young defender struggled to keep up, felt out of his depth, and had a sore knee.

It turned out he needed cartilage surgery, and as soon as he recovered from the operation he was a much better player. It did not take long before two representatives from Celtic contacted him, and told him not to sign for anyone else before he heard from them. Yeats had high expectations, but as the weeks passed he heard nothing, and hope faded. When Dundee United approached him and offered him a contract, Yeats accepted it on the spot. The ALC received an £80 transfer fee, and Ron got £20. It made him feel like a millionaire.

Christmas 1957 was only a few weeks off, and the £20 jackpot – a month's salary in the slaughterhouse – magicked away any financial worries in time for the festive period. Indeed, it was enough to pay for presents to both sides of the family. Later, Yeats learned that Celtic's two scouts had been in a tragic car accident, killing one of them and severely injuring the other. Had it not been for that crash, his prime years as a footballer might not have been at Liverpool.

Yeats continued to live in Aberdeen, about seventy miles north of Dundee, and still worked at the slaughterhouse. It was tough, especially on match days. He would have to get up at three in the morning, go to the slaughterhouse in a suit and change to working clothes, work as fast as he could to slaughter ten or twelve animals before nine o'clock, and then get washed and changed back to his Sunday suit, catch the 9:20 train to Dundee and sit there for an hour and a half, worrying that he would be late for the game. For away fixtures there could be even longer train rides. Dundee United were in the Scottish Second Division and everybody on the team worked part-time: players, managers, coaches and those with other responsibilities. The club, though, was financially sound thanks to its membership-based organisation and as many as 80,000 to 90,000 members.

In his second season at Tannadice, Yeats was appointed captain. He was only 21 and still a slaughterhouse apprentice on the side, something appreciated by the home fans, who would shout, 'That centre-forward is just a hunk of meat, Ron. Parcel him up!' Yet when he did not play as well as the fans had come to expect, he was told off good and proper: 'Tak' 'im awa' to the slaughterhouse.'

At the end of that season, United decided to hire a full time manager. Yeats had finished his apprenticeship and was a fully trained butcher by then, but had been called up for national service and sent to Aldershot, where he was made a physical trainer. Fortunately, each battalion were allowed three professional footballers who could continue playing for their teams, as well as playing for the army team, and this helped Yeats develop as a player. Playing against other army teams he met other Scots who were already professionals in the English league system. This taught him a lot about the uncompromising English league, and gave him much harder competition than any of the boys in the Scottish Second Division where he usually played with Dundee United.

Yeats was young, ambitious and ready to take on the world. The year was 1961. Yet another season was drawing to an end at Dundee United, who were now in the Scottish First Division. It was time for new wage negotiations, and Yeats was frustrated. He knew very well what his army mate, Alex Young, made at Everton, whereas he could not afford a house of his own. He was also starting to get tired of travelling between Aberdeen and Dundee.

His self-confidence grew as press rumours would have it that Hearts, Manchester United and Liverpool were all interested in signing him. But it was Liverpool that were quickest to move. In spring 1961, Margaret Yeats read in the paper that her husband was moving to Liverpool. Bill Shankly had signed Big Ron.

Both Ian St John and Ron Yeats were born in the late 1930s, and were toddlers when the Second World War broke out. They can still remember sirens going off to give warning about air raids. Both recall running to the nearest shelter: the fear, the chaos and the lack of food. In one of the bomb raids, Yeats' childhood home was bombed to smithereens and they lost everything they owned. Both of their fathers were conscripted; St John's father never returned. He was six years old when he lost his dad. Luckily, other father figures appeared in his life. Teachers who cared that little extra, football trainers; dedicated men.

In 1961, when St John and Yeats were 22 and 23 years old respectively, they met the most important father figure of them all: Bill Shankly.

'Shankly's ambition was to be best,' St John says. 'He demanded that we always strove to be the best we could. Never second best, never settle for mediocrity. He set the standard incredibly high for us. He never tired of telling us to aim high. He expected us to give our best in both match and training. If you didn't give a hundred per cent in training – perhaps you'd been out the night before and had a few beers – he could tell immediately. He didn't like it and would be at you at once.'

A good father notices you. A good father dares to discipline you, in the hope that it will help you improve. A good father cares about you. Shankly was the father figure of both of these men.

'I had a guy like that on my boys' team, he helped me to a higher level, and that helped me progress to become a professional footballer,' St John adds. 'And then there was Shankly. Our new father figure. Whenever he spoke, we listened.'

Ron nods, and confirms that Shankly was like a father to him too.

'He was a wonderful man.'

As captain, Yeats did not have to do a lot of talking before games or at half-time. Shankly took care of that.

Ron continues: 'Before a game he would give us instructions about what to do, and his half-time instructions were spot-on. He was very clear on where we had to do better or what we needed to focus on. He inspired the team with his well-chosen and tactical words, and his extreme charisma.'

Shankly's management skills, his coaching staff and the new captain from Aberdeen soon brought results. After just one season in the red shirt, Shankly was proven right in his prediction that Liverpool would make the top division with Ron Yeats in the team; after eight years in the Second Division, Liverpool were promoted.

There are books filled with great Bill Shankly quotes. He was certainly both charismatic and eloquent, and knew how to use big words to attract people's attention and inspire his players. But even though he was well known for his press conferences and his speeches to the public, he could be brutally honest in communication with his players. Shankly strongly believed that you should aim at being honest in all aspects of life, and live up to the expression: an honest day's work for an honest day's pay.

St John says of this ethic: 'Shankly couldn't stand people who were given a chance in the starting eleven, but who didn't give everything they had. He hated people who were dishonest. He even said that if he'd been a street sweeper in Liverpool, it would have been the cleanest street in the city. That was his view of life: it didn't matter what you did, as long as you were the best at what you were doing. We should always strive to be the best we can be, and always be honest. Always do our best even if working with menial tasks. That was the message he drilled into his players.'

St John and Yeats are convinced that this perspective on humanity helped build a team of thoughtful, considerate and compassionate people – good team-mates. Shankly's message was clear: work for each other, help each other, pull together, turn someone's bad passes into good passes. That way, as team-mates and friends, you could change bad days into good days for the rest of your team. That way you could lift a bad game and make it a good one, when someone took that extra responsibility for a mate who was having a bad match or two. It was a matter of running that little extra, encouraging your team-mates, fighting for two. Not wasting any time yelling at people or accusing them. Next time it could be you having an off day, in need of some extra support.

St John smiles his crooked, friendly smile, the one that makes his eyes narrow to two slits, as he thinks back. 'In life, as it is in football, it's first and foremost about how you treat other people. Shankly was incredible at this. He'd set himself high standards in life, and he lived by them. He'd worked down the mines in Scotland and learned how important it was that everybody gave all they had, and worked for each other. He was a fantastic role model and man. He could have been a politician and a better prime minister than any of those we've had till now!'

Shankly went by many names: 'Mr Football', 'Shanks' and 'Mr Liverpool'. But for his new Liverpool players he simply went by 'The Boss'. He kept a little black book in a desk drawer in his sparsely furnished office at Anfield containing a list of all the players that lived up to his high standards – and who would be good enough for Liverpool. This was the Shankly bible: a small book that helped him keep track of players that were on their way into – or out of – the team; a bible he had started using when he was manager of Carlisle. This bible was crucial for making lists of who would have to go and who he wanted as replacements in the squad, from when he took over as new manager for Liverpool.

One of Shankly's good ideas, five months after signing him, was to appoint Yeats as his manager on the pitch by making him captain. The manager, though, did not give his captain any special instructions. Yeats' job was to make sure everyone was OK, and that everybody did the best they could for the common goal.

St John was well pleased with the leadership of his new captain. His great ability and contribution really did lead the team in battle. Yeats worked tirelessly, but would never point a finger against any of his own.

'Ronnie was a brilliant tackler and good in the air,' St John says. 'In addition, he was feared by our opponents, and played a kind of football that set an example for the rest of us.'

Yeats used to charge forward on corner kicks. When St John saw the ball approach, he would think, this one's mine! But his captain would shout, and come charging in to head the ball instead. Yeats scored quite a few goals that way; sixteen in total, none of them penalties. Neither he nor St John took penalties. The old forward describes penalties as 'an odd business'.

'You need to have a few regular penalty-kick takers, who aren't afraid to miss,' he says. 'I was so worried I might miss that I didn't want to take any. And our games were never decided on penalties. What do you think, Ron, looking back at the first rounds in the European competitions? The matches were settled by the toss of a coin if there was no decision after two legs and a neutral replay...'

With that, Ian laughs heartily by my side, and Ron joins in. Ian brings back memories of matches where the captain's intuition and a fifty-fifty chance of calling heads or tails would decide whether you won the game and went through to the next round. As captain, it was Yeats' responsibility to call heads or tails if the cup tie had not been decided even after extra time and a second rematch.

Liverpool had a good season in 1965, and English supporters at the time had started to discover European football tournaments. There was quite a bit of money for the clubs in these competitions, and they also gave the clubs a lot of esteem, which was an added motivational factor.

Sometimes the coin fell on the right side for Ron and Liverpool. In the quarter-final of the European Cup they met FC Cologne, and both the home and away games were goalless draws. A play-off was then held in Rotterdam, and ended with another draw: 2–2. The match was now to be determined by the toss of a coin – or, more precisely, by tossing a round, wooden platter with one white and one red side. Ron was scared of what lay ahead. He had already lost two toss-ups that day: at the start of the match and at the start of extra time. He went for the obvious red side, and won. He jumped a whole yard in the air when it was announced that Liverpool would be going through.

That was a stroke of luck, yet St John has no doubt that Liverpool were successful first and foremost because Shankly's players were in such a good shape:

'People say players today are so fit. I'll tell you who was fit! Believe me, fifty years ago Liverpool Football Club had the fittest players ever!' he says.

Really?

'Without a doubt. We played matches in Europe, flew home and played matches in the league and in cups. Nobody was rested. You played, went home, played again. You played the entire game and added time. And both the pitch and the ball were heavy as lead. I don't think today's Liverpool fans realise what we had to go through. People say football players' fitness level has developed over the years, and I'm sure it has, but trust me, we were in incredibly good shape. And definitely the fittest team in the league.'

While players today make astronomical sums of money, and clubs outbid each other to snatch the brightest talents, clubs were less greedy in relation to their profits in the 1960s, Ian St John believes.

At the same time, when it came to pay negotiations it was the duty of the captain to negotiate as best he could on behalf of the entire team. Yeats' successor as captain, Tommy Smith, practically served as a shop steward. Ron, while less forceful, had similar duties. When Liverpool won the Second Division title in 1962, salaries jumped from £30 to £40 a week. With relatively modest weekly wages, the bonus plans were important. One of them was the crowd bonus, a reward for the players based on how many supporters were attracted to the stadium. With Liverpool promoted to First Division, that job was pretty well taken care of. Because Liverpool's home record was strong, more and more people started flocking to Anfield. The supporter bonus meant one pound extra for every 1,000 fans over 28,000 supporters present, to each player. On the best days, 50,000 were let in through the gates of the stadium. Ron played a key role in negotiating this supplement.

In 1961, indeed, England became a very attractive country to play in for professional footballers from both Scotland and Ireland after the maximum wage of £20 per week was abolished. Johnny Haynes, the England and Fulham captain, made the headlines when he was awarded a £100 per week salary by his chairman, comedian Tommy Trinder.

In 1962, the Liverpool players received – in addition to the crowd bonus – an added four pounds in victory bonus. So Liverpool stars earning up to £74 pounds per week were among the best paid in the league.

We have been talking for a couple of hours, travelling back in time. Ann, his second wife, comes in with mugs of coffee and tea. Ian breaks into song: 'You're just too good to be true!' Ron laughs heartily.

The two best friends have shared holidays, and their children practically grew up together. As players they used to room together before games. St John was lucky, because he got to share a room with a man who was always up early to make tea. Ron used to make tea for the entire team, so he definitely did not think too highly of himself just because he was the captain.

'Ron was in a league of his own when it came to making a good cuppa, and he'd never let me make my own,' St John says.

That's incredibly kind of him. What did you do in return for him?

'I tried to score goals!'

'Yes,' Ron smiles. 'You did!'

They were not just room-mates; they were partners in crime out on the town too.

'After games we would go out and have a couple of beers,' St John continues. 'Shankly always told us to be back at a certain time. But sometimes the two of us would be back much later than the appointed time. Shanks didn't drink alcohol, so sometimes he'd give us a proper earful when we were late. He didn't like us drinking alcohol at all, even though we didn't drink much. But he liked Ron and me, so he'd never leave us out of the team even if we'd been a bit naughty the night before.'

The boys would lie in their beds chatting into the night.

'At that time I shared rooms with Ron more often than I did with my wife!' St John remembers.

Laughter rolls over the sofa once more.

✦

The more I hear about Shankly's team from the 1960s, the more I wish I had seen them play in front of a chock-a-block Anfield with more than 55,000 spectators in the ground. For nine years and through 417 matches, Ron Yeats was team captain. In the club's history, only Steven Gerrard has led the team in more games. Great football ability is obviously an important factor for a captain, so what does Ron think were his strengths on the pitch?

'Probably my size. That I was tall, and good in the air. And I was good at winning the ball and giving it to players who were better passers than I was.'

And you must have been good at reading the game?

'Yes, I could read the game well,' he concludes. 'And I made sure nobody I played against would get a single kick of the ball around me!'

Ian interrupts: 'Ronnie was an excellent tackler. There were so many times when we thought the opponents' forwards would get past him, but Ron stopped them. Always tackling on the ball. He very rarely caused a penalty for the opposing team. He wasn't the type to pull shirts, tug at people's arms or yell. Besides, we had Gerry Byrne and a young Tommy Smith coming into the team after a while, both hard as nails, just like Ron.'

Was Ron a vocal captain, yelling and ordering you about?

'Ronnie was a very encouraging captain. Some captains bark at their players, but he would encourage us instead: "Come on, lads!" Of course, if we gave our opponents more room than we ought to, he'd let us hear it, there was never any doubt he was the boss on the pitch.'

A captain needs the players' respect, regardless of the era they play in. This was never a problem for Ron.

'All the players respected him, and he did a really outstanding job as captain all those years he served at the club,' St John says. 'He came practically straight in and took over after Dick White. It was one of those rare occasions. Normally you'd need to rise through the ranks. Hah, I was just about to say that it was an excellent choice to give Ronnie the armband, but then there were no armbands at the time!'

Being responsible for a team like this in the uncompromising English top league for as long as nine years is an honour for the very few. Not everyone would have been able to handle it either.

Did you think about the pressure it was, being responsible for a team like Liverpool for so many years? Did you sometimes think it would have been good not to have that extra responsibility?

'No, no!' Ron says, shaking his head vigorously. 'I didn't mind being a captain. And if somebody else had been chosen for the job, that would've been fine too. I never asked for the job in the first place, you see. But Shankly wanted me to have it, and no matter what job I had been set to do, I wanted to do it to the best of my ability. And I think I managed to do that as captain too.'

Ron rarely gave any instructions to his team-mates at half-time or after a match. Shankly was the boss of those. But there was always room for both captain and players to voice their opinion.

'We had an open dressing room,' Ian explains. 'If anything needed to be said, if maybe someone in the opposition was causing trouble, or if something worked really well, we'd say so.'

'At half-time I'd let Shankly talk,' Ron reasons. 'He'd give short and accurate feedback and let us know what we did well, and where we needed to improve; like if we gave some of the opposing players too much room. His half-time pep talks were brilliant, because he knew the game so well, and was so desperate for us to win as a team.'

Shankly had a strong winner's mentality, and it shaped the squad. Not only did this lead them into the top flight, they won it at the second time of asking too. Then on 1 May 1965 they took home a great trophy that Liverpool had never won before: the FA Cup.

'We went to London a couple of days before the final, and Shankly took us to the splendid London Palladium theatre to see a comedy show, as part of the preparation,' St John remembers. 'He wanted the trip to Wembley to be both memorable and enjoyable, and he wanted to lift any sense of panic we may have ahead of the important match. So he took us to the theatre to give us a great night out.'

To keep the spirit up on match day, and to reduce nerves, Shankly invited singer Frankie Vaughan and comedian Jimmy Tarbuck from the Palladium into the dressing room before the match. That provoked plenty of joking and laughing before the seriousness set in. Leeds boss Don Revie could not understand what the havoc around the Liverpool dressing room was about. Leeds kept the door to their dressing room locked.

England's national arena was filled to capacity.

'Leeds were a difficult side to beat,' St John continues. 'They were a very good team, just like us. And they were tight at the back, just like us. We wanted so strongly to win, but it was a very tough match.

They had Bremner and several other great players, Yeats recalls suddenly. He is back on the wet Wembley pitch.

'Not to forget Jackie Charlton and Hunter. They were a very good team, and under Don Revie they were the next big team to make a breakthrough in Europe.'

Rain was pouring down and the pitch was waterlogged. After just three minutes, Liverpool's Gerry Byrne broke his collarbone after a collision with Leeds captain Bobby Collins. Yet Byrne continued to play, despite the pain. They had no substitutes and they were in the final to win it. Shankly and the rest of his staff kept the seriousness of the injury from their opponents. On top of it all, the game went into extra time and Byrne played the extra half hour as well. It proved to be Byrne who assisted the 1–0 goal that Roger Hunt headed in, three minutes into the first half of extra time. Billy Bremner scored the equaliser in the 100th minute, and the teams were back to square one. But then Ian Callaghan surged up on the right side and passed to St John. The two Leeds players on the goal-line could not prevent an acrobatic St John from heading in to make it 2–1 in the 111th minute.

In the dressing room afterwards, Byrne needed help to get dressed. His pain was agonising.

'Gerry should have had two medals,' Yeats says.

'He should have had them all!' St John adds, and they both laugh.

'You know, it annoys me no end how pathetic players today can be, they roll around pretending to be injured. And then Gerry played the final including extra time with a broken collarbone. Players today are big, strong lads, they ought to search their conscience and see how ridiculous it is to fall down like that when someone barely touches you. And when they do six rolls on the pitch, you know they're not injured… And then sometimes they will stop and look for blood, as if they were boxers! Ridiculous. Nobody touched their face in the first place, so why look for blood there? They should be made to watch themselves on film. As punishment. Every Monday morning.' St John has raised his voice a trifle and rubs his bad knee in frustration.

'It's not a man's game any more.'

Then he looks up at his friend and smiles cunningly.

'Will you tell the story about the Queen?'

At the time the May 1965 final was perhaps the most momentous occasion in Liverpool's 73-year history. Finally, the Liverpool fans would not have to take the Evertonians singing, 'We've won the FA Cup, and you haven't!' 'Ee-aye addio' roared over Wembley. Ron Yeats was ready to climb the steps and receive the yearned-for trophy from Queen Elizabeth herself. During the last minutes of the game he had been wondering what to say to her. A few days before the match he had received a phone call from Buckingham Palace, and been instructed – should Liverpool win – not to address the Queen until she had talked to him, and that he had to say 'Yes, Ma'am' and 'No, Ma'am'. Yeats had corrected the palace staff member by saying, 'You mean when we win the cup, not if!'

Extra time had been played in pouring rain on a heavy pitch. The players were shattered as they walked up the steps to the royal box at Wembley. Ronnie wiped his hands on his clothes before he reached the Queen, who was ready to present him with the trophy.

'You must be exhausted,' Queen Elizabeth said to Yeats.

'I'm absolutely knackered!'

'I'm certain that you are,' the Queen said, and gave him the cup. The men on the sofa are now roaring with laughter, thinking back to the conversation fifty years earlier.

Yeats was the first Liverpool captain to receive the FA Cup. He was so tired he had almost no strength to lift the trophy, but he did. And as he raised it and looked over at the sea of supporters, the shouts of joy that met him sounded as if it came from a million people. It was the sound of life itself, the passion of the Liverpool fans. This was their reward. And Yeats felt how proud he was of them. He almost wanted to throw the shiny trophy into the crowd, to give them their share in it. It was his greatest moment as captain and as a Liverpool player.

'Winning the FA Cup and having the trophy presented by the Queen was my proudest moment,' he says. 'And I felt we deserved to win.'

The jubilant scenes and the crowds that gathered when Liverpool welcomed their heroes afterwards speak volumes. It looked like there could not possibly be room for one single person more to squeeze into the thronging crowd they drove through on the open-top double-decker bus, all the way until Yeats lifted the cup on the City Hall balcony. Not even the Beatles managed to create such a frenzy in the city.

What a journey Ron Yeats and Ian St John have had. Winning promotion from the Second Division, winning the First Division after a couple of years, and then winning the club's very first FA Cup. How could this happen?

The old captain knows: 'We had a lot of good players, there's no doubt about that. And we all played for each other. And that was really important, I think, that we played for each other and helped one another. The players were like brothers, you see.'

St John expands: 'We were a very close-knit group. And the game was very different back then, we didn't have a huge staff and a massive coaching team around us, like they do today. We were a small squad, and the players played every week, all season. No substitutes. So if you were injured, you'd continue playing. And we were the same team year in, year out, playing sixty-odd matches every season. That way we became very close.'

Football in the 1960s has left its legacy too. An alarming number of former players now struggle with dementia. It cannot be a coincidence that so many former professional footballers from the 1960s and early 1970s struggle with the same diagnosis as Yeats: Alzheimer's disease.

'The football itself was incredibly heavy,' Yeats says, 'especially when it was wet. When you headed it… Most of the times you headed it you'd just think Jesus Christ! It's almost impossible to imagine.'

'The ball was like a medicine ball, like the big, heavy balls from PE,' St John adds.

Yeats becomes serious. 'You just had to make sure you hit it with your forehead. If it hit any other part of your head… Oooh, the headaches you'd have after a game…'

St John helps him out. 'They never understood that back then. Today people realise the serious consequences of blows against the head like that. And remember, back then the ball was played a lot more up in the air. The wings would send cross-

R. LUND ANSNES

passes, and as attackers we'd often crash our heads into the defenders'. There could be elbows involved too, and I was often accidentally hit by goalies. Knocks like these have caused problems for a lot of players.'

It's damaged the memory of a lot of players...

'I was invited to a trade union meeting in the US about this a couple of years ago,' St John replies. 'They're identifying and discussing the delayed injuries in football. In Europe, people are worried about this. If doctors' research shows that football gave a lot of us health problems, the clubs would have to pay a lot of money in compensation. I've taken this up with the Professional Footballers' Association in England, where I presented them with the fact that a number of players in our generation suffer from dementia. After a while I got a reply, they'd discussed it, but since women our age suffer from dementia too, they said it was hard to substantiate. There was nothing they could do for us.

'It's true that women our age suffer from dementia too, but in the same numbers as men in our industry? I'm not talking about men in our country in general who get Alzheimer's. I'm talking about the percentage of our little group of professional footballers from the 1960s. I believe this is an occupational injury, a health condition caused by our job as footballers. When boxers receive those heavy punches to the head, they need to rest. That was never an issue in our time.

'To be honest, all the big names among players from the 1950s and 1960s are suffering from memory lapse or dementia in varying degrees. They need compensation to pay carers, people to help and assist them in their everyday lives; for hospitals and treatment. They ought to be compensated to get the best help they can for their condition, and be able to lead a dignified life in the years they've got left, but it's not happening.'

I think a lot of people out there don't know that many of their old heroes struggle with dementia.

'On our team, Geoff Strong got it. He died. Ron has it, I've got symptoms, and Tommy Smith has been hit hard by Alzheimer's. And this was just our team. I could have listed a lot more players from other clubs at that time who suffer from the same. Football and the clubs have billions flowing through the system, from television rights and sponsors. So it's not about a lack of funds.'

And you helped build Liverpool Football Club to a top team. You should get something back, after sacrificing your health for the club.

'Yes, I agree. There should be a system for employees with occupational injuries, who have their health damaged in the industry they work for.'

18

✦

Liverpool still runs through Yeats' veins. He returned in 1986 as a chief scout, a job he held for an impressive twenty years until he retired in 2006. And he says his proudest signing was Sami Hyypiä. Another leader and captain material. For thirty years of his life Yeats served LFC. How has the club changed him?

'It's difficult to answer that,' he says. 'I've always been strong and all, you know, and I've enjoyed my time at Liverpool immensely, I admit. I still go to see the games at Anfield, and sometimes now, when I'm at a game and watch them play, I think, I wouldn't have done that! It's easy to become a little sarcastic when you're not playing yourself any more. But I always want the best for the team. I'm hopeful for new triumphs. I still enjoy very much watching the team play.'

So you're still a fan of Liverpool FC?

'Oh yes! Before a game I'm always nervous on behalf of the team, and when they lose it gets to me. Then maybe I think what I would have done differently. But I keep that to myself.'

Ron Yeats smiles.

✦

We are back in the Echo Arena in May 2015. Two friends with greyish-white hair stand side by side, one half a head taller than the other.

Steven Gerrard played his last home game at Anfield the weekend before. He gave speeches at the stadium, in press conferences and at the banquet after his last match. Tonight, Gerrard is practically out of words. Maybe he feels that the overwhelming focus on his person has emptied him of expression, at the same time as he cannot thank the fans and the club enough, for what they have given him.

But the old captain, Big Ron, still has a few more things to say. Now, in front of thousands of people, in the limelight, he finds both his words and his sense of humour. He smiles and begins to speak.

'You all talk about Steven Gerrard. I think I'm only a little behind him as a player. In everything he does, he is a wonderful captain, but not as good a captain as me! I was captain for ten years for such a great team. I've appreciated every minute of my time with the club.

'It gives me great joy to be able to say: I was one of you.'

2

TOMMY SMITH

THE ANFIELD IRON – THE WORDS THAT DISAPPEARED

'He would go into any battle, and loved it… He gave me strength just by the way he held us all together by his hardness.'
Phil Neal

'IF YOU GET ANY CLOSER TO THE BALL WHEN I'VE GOT IT I'LL break your back!'

The noise of a capacity stadium goes unnoticed. Because right now, Tommy Smith has done as he usually does: made himself respected by vocally threatening the opponents' most lethal striker.

Football is a psychological game. Liverpool's captain looks mean. His notoriety precedes him, and he has just confirmed yet again the myth of his nickname: The Anfield Iron. As a sixteen-year-old on the reserve team, he broke an opponent's leg. Playing midfield when Liverpool reserves met Newcastle, Smith flew into a tackle, and it ended with a long-term injury.

'Suddenly I was back in my school days,' he says. '"Smithy broke someone's leg out there!" It wasn't my fault! He broke his own leg! If he hadn't jumped in it would never have happened! I made up all kinds of excuses. I was sixteen years old and had broken a player's leg. I contacted him later and found out he was going to be all right. But I remember the looks I got on the pitch against Newcastle: I don't want anything to do with that guy. So I learned early that it was smart to frighten people

I didn't like.'

Tommy Smith grins. It is a sunny day at his home, in spring 2011. He was born in the closing months of the Second World War and always attracted troublemakers like flypaper.

It is 2 September 2013 – exactly one hundred years since Bill Shankly was born. The day is celebrated with a photography exhibition in the *Liverpool Echo* building on Old Hall Street in Liverpool's city centre, where a gigantic card has been set up for people to write their messages of congratulations. Later that night, the card fills up with greetings and autographs from players who have served the club since Shankly's days up until today. A gala dinner is being held in one of the best hotels in town. Shankly's family and the 1960s team – Shankly's men – as well as more recent Liverpool legends, have all been invited. And with them, nicely dressed dinner guests around small round tables decorated in white. The hall is packed.

In the VIP room, there is a reception with welcome drinks for the Shankly family and Liverpool's former players. Tommy Smith is there along with Ian Callaghan, Roy Evans and Ian Rush, chatting over drinks, each one impeccably dressed in suit and tie. I get a welcome kiss on the cheek from them all, as is tradition here in Liverpool. It is a couple of years since I last met Smith. That was at his home in Crosby while writing a previous book.

Since then, Tommy has withdrawn from the limelight. Once he was the king of nightlife and owned a nightclub; now he is rarely seen in public. His wife, and love of his life, Susan, was struck by Alzheimer's disease a few years back. Tommy was once a master speaker and well regarded *Liverpool Echo* columnist – he gave a fearless and forthright look on football over twenty years' service. Now he has quit much of his work to nurse Susan. She was the one who gave us such a warm welcome two years ago, and made coffee and tea. Back then Tommy was busy telling us about all the fights he had been in, both on and off the pitch. When he mentioned all the different metallic parts that have replaced worn-out body parts (two knees and an elbow), and how these parts had started to disintegrate and cause trouble, Sue jokingly slipped in: 'The Iron Man has started to rust!'

Sue went up to the first floor to get some photos that Tommy wanted to give us, but came back down again with a lost look on her face, and without the photos. She had forgotten why she went upstairs. With that, her husband, The Anfield Iron, broke off from his stories about kicks, fights, head-butts and threats to comfort his wife, and let her know it was OK that she had forgotten. He patiently reminded her of her mission and she returned a few minutes later with a photograph of her husband. It shows Tommy crouching behind an impressive collection of trophies and medals laid out on the grass.

Two years later she was much worse. Alzheimer's is an illness that slowly deprives a person not only of their character, but also the ability to communicate and take care of themselves. What is left is a body that may look fine, but is otherwise inhabited by someone who no longer knows the difference between day and night, who does not recognise their closest family, and who completely loses any sense of direction, belonging and language. For a lot of Alzheimer's patients, restlessness, despair, frustration and anger move in when words, control of one's own life, and understanding of basic needs fail. It is not the same for everyone. Alzheimer's has different effects on different people. But the disease changes them, changes their personality and may render them completely dependent on care.

On Shankly's birthday, Tommy gives me a kiss on the cheek and a firm handshake. I ask him how it is going, and he replies that it is a tough and difficult time.

'I think my wife's illness is rubbing off on me,' he whispers.

He tells me it is heartbreaking to see Sue become gradually worse. How she forgets more and more. That she disappears, day by day.

When Tommy goes on stage on this Shankly anniversary, to tell a few of the many good stories from his long life with Liverpool Football Club, some words fail him. And he struggles to remember the point of some of the stories. He, who was tough as nails all those years on the pitch, laughs a little nervously and shakes his head when he cannot find the right words to finish his story. Finally he finds someone who can, and passes the microphone to him.

The night is brought to an end with a touching tribute; all former Liverpool players side by side on stage, young and old, sing, 'You'll Never Walk Alone' at the top of their lungs, in honour of the boss, Bill Shankly.

Through Bill Shankly, Tommy Smith got to experience his life's big dream: playing for Liverpool FC, a team that played their games in Tommy's neighbourhood. And Shankly chose Tommy as his captain to succeed Ron Yeats, who had helped lead the club for nine years.

✦

In the last fifty years, only five prominent Liverpool captains have come from Merseyside. One of these was Tommy Smith. As Ron Yeats' successor, the challenge was huge. Smith had captained occasionally in one-off matches before, but in the summer of 1970 he was called into the manager's office. Shankly asked if he would consider becoming captain permanently, and barely managed to finish the sentence before Tommy said yes.

'I felt it was a huge honour and a great privilege,' he says. 'It was a role that took a lot of responsibility, and I was ready to do my very best.'

Shankly chose a local boy in every sense of the word. A fearless man and third-generation Kopite, Smith grew up at number 9 Lambeth Road – practically a stone's throw from both Goodison Park and Anfield. He had stood on the Kop throughout his childhood; albeit usually only the last twenty minutes, because his father could not afford tickets. So Tommy used to wait until they opened the gate in anticipation of full time.

He had literally fought his way through life. There were quite a few who wanted to pit themselves against the strong and sturdy Tommy and he would often end up in fights without looking for trouble at all. He wonders now if he gave off some kind of 'Try me if you dare!' vibes. He was strong as an ox from a young age. He was also equipped with a temper, and a sense of justice that often manifested itself rather cogently. Tommy could take a lot of stick, but he could not tolerate being spat at. If you were mean enough to do that, you were guaranteed a thrashing.

His most used phrase at the time, often repeated later in his football career, was: 'Don't mess with me, or you'll have to call an ambulance!'

One of the first pieces of advice Shankly gave him when he came to the club as an apprentice was 'Don't take shit from anybody.' He made a note of that, and has lived by it his whole life.

He was an only child, and a leader even as a child. 'Tommy wasn't born, he was quarried!' Shankly joked. Not only was he picked to play for Liverpool Schoolboys – the team for all the best players in every school in Liverpool of the same age – he was also selected their captain. And it was on his way home from training with Liverpool Schoolboys one night, aged just fourteen, that he received the shock message. He got off the 33 bus to be met by his cousin Rosie, who told him that his father had died from double pneumonia. His dad, the big, strong, popular man, had been taken away. Tommy could not believe it.

He had to learn early to take care of himself, just like Ian St John, who also lost his father too early. Now he could not ask his father for advice, or threaten to call for his dad if the going got tough in the rough neighbourhood in which he lived. He also lost the advantage of being part of a two-income household. Eventually, they had to move to his mum's mother, as she could not support Tommy alone in their own home.

A small family of three had become two; it was a difficult time. So when a letter from Shankly turned up in the letterbox, saying he wanted a chat with the young football talent, to Smith it was like a gift from heaven. At this time there were no agents. Tommy took his mother with him to meet Shankly, who had become Liverpool manager only six months earlier.

'Tommy was like a thirty-year-old at fifteen,' says his best friend Chris Lawler, Liverpool's right-back. They were apprentices together and they painted the Kop and the rest of Anfield and the dressing room facilities several times, among other chores for the club.

One can only imagine the scene when fifteen-year-old Tommy and his mother came to Anfield for their first meeting with Shankly: Tommy red-faced, afraid that his mother – who knew little about football – would embarrass herself, and him. He listened intently to Shankly's description of what an apprenticeship with LFC involved: he had to be willing to sacrifice every holiday to clear up and do maintenance at Anfield. Christmas and Easter was high season for football, and he would have to help get the stadium ready for the games and clear it up afterwards. In the summer holidays he would help paint the premises and keep the general facilities in repair.

But in return, Shankly promised to take good care of Tommy, and give him an extra food allowance every week, so he could eat well. And he would get the chance to develop as a footballer by playing on the A, B and C teams.

'I think Shankly felt a little sorry for my mum and me,' he concedes.

When Shankly had finished talking about what lay ahead for young Smith, and asked whether he and his mother accepted the offer, Mrs Smith started to talk. Her son felt waves of embarrassment through his body, and he wished the floor would open up and swallow him, when his mother asked a football-related question!

'Mr Shankly, Liverpool have never won the FA Cup, have they?'

'No, Mrs Smith, we haven't.'

'Let me give you some advice. If you let my son play, you'll go on to win the cup!'

This was to be an extraordinarily prescient promise.

Smith signed on as an apprentice and the years of hard work and training started. One of Tommy's first duties was to work in Bill Shankly's private garden on Bellefield Avenue, which overlooked Everton's training ground from the back of the house. That way he got a chance to get to know the boss a little.

'I painted the Kop three or four times,' he remembers. 'And we dug up the Kop for better drainage, we painted the dressing rooms, we painted everything. I was working full time with only two weeks' holidays.'

For this, he was paid £8 a week.

'My mother got paid a pound a week for food. And I ate it all!'

Smith had been thrown in to play with the reserves already as a sixteen-year-old. When he was finally given a chance to play for the first team, he had to be patient before he earned a permanent spot, because the first team played well, and made it impossible for Tommy to squeeze into the first eleven. But in 1964 he was right by their side when Liverpool won the First Division for the first time since 1947. When the title was secured, Ron Yeats ran a lap of honour around Anfield with a cardboard trophy, waiting for the previous champions Everton to hand over the real deal.

Just like Ron Yeats and Ian St John, Tommy too felt that Bill Shankly became like a father to him.

Bill Shankly was a mystery, and a man of contrasts. He readily embraced new ideas, but at the same time kept to tradition. Sometimes he could be stone cold and insensitive, at other times he was genuinely warm and considerate. He seemed so experienced in the ways of the world but, at the same time, football was all he knew.

He believed football was a game of hearts and minds. He would say: 'Some people think you play football with your legs, but that's wrong. You play football with this,' and point to his head, and then to his heart. He used to encourage players to engage in discussions because he felt that would increase their passion for football.

Smith and Lawler managed to secure permanent spots on the team in 1965, in time to play in the FA Cup final against Leeds, where Ron Yeats as captain had the honour of lifting the FA Cup for the first time in Liverpool's history.

In the Wembley dressing room after an exhausting final, Shankly went over to Tommy, put his arm around him and said, 'Smithy, your mother must be one of the best visionaries in the world!'

Half a century later I ask Tommy about this.

It must have made an impression on Shankly that a mother did the talking. That probably did not happen that often?

'Absolutely, but she had to, since my father died,' Smith replied. 'I think it was the only time she was in Shankly's office. Impressive that he remembered what she had said five years earlier…'

Smith was part of the team when Liverpool won the FA Cup for the first time, and, twelve years later, their first European Cup. He was also captain when the team won the UEFA Cup.

His proudest moment as captain, however, came in 1973, his third and final year as captain. We are back at an Anfield filled to capacity, as many as 56,000 people squeezing together in the hope of celebrating Liverpool's first league title in seven years. The Reds were playing Leeds, and had to win to all but guarantee pipping Arsenal to the title.

The first half was goalless. In the second half, a corner to Liverpool: Leeds cleared, but Kevin Keegan got his head on the ball and Peter Cormack booted the knock-down straight into the back of the net.

'Anfield exploded and I could practically feel the league trophy in my hands,' Smith recalls.

Five minutes before full time, Kevin Keegan secured the victory with a second goal. When they received word that Arsenal had only managed a 2–2 draw in their game, the party was on.

'I was in the clouds, and very, very proud,' Smith continues. 'I was the captain who led Liverpool to win the league. It felt monumental. Yet again Liverpool were the best side in England. Only Chris, Cally and myself were left from the previous Liverpool team that had won the league. I was deeply moved.'

There was still a theoretical chance that Arsenal could overtake, however. Liverpool would have to lose their last game, and Arsenal had to win their last two by 31 goals. The Londoners' chances were so slim as to be practically non-existent.

The following Saturday, Liverpool played Leicester City at home. The match ended goalless, and Tommy Smith accepted the trophy. Shankly, in his dark-grey suit, red shirt, tie and handkerchief, accompanied the team on the lap of honour around Anfield, all this to the deafening cheers and chanting from the supporters. When the team stopped in front of the Kop, a supporter threw his scarf down at them. A policeman kicked it away. He was quickly reprimanded by Shankly.

'What are you doing? That's someone's life you're kicking in the dust!'

The manager walked along the Kop with the supporter's scarf around his neck. In between all the players, kids and adults alike swarmed around him. The Kop honoured the boss and the league winners by singing 'You'll Never Walk Alone'. Shankly clenched his fist and raised his hand in the air, a scene later immortalised in bronze on a plinth outside the stadium. The Kop replied by giving an ear-splitting cheer in the middle of the song.

The captain had faith in the team this season of 1972/73, but there was still a small voice in his head nagging him.

Smith recalls: 'It was saying to me: Could this really happen to you? You've got a fantastic family, a good life and a good career. These are facts. Do you really think you're so blessed that your dreams come true too?'

'I certainly silenced the voice on that day!'

In May Liverpool brought home the UEFA Cup as well, after the final against Borussia Mönchengladbach. They had a 3–0 lead after the first match at Anfield, but the return game was tough and Liverpool struggled to stay in the game. At half-time Shankly organised the team more defensively, and Tommy was told in plain words to shut down his area of the field. The captain worked his legs off to control both midfield and defence.

'I knew I had to do everything in my power to drive the team onwards, and heighten morale and performance. Gradually, the game swung our way.'

When the match was over, and a 2–0 defeat had ensured their success, Smith was so tired that he barely managed to lift the lead-heavy UEFA Cup trophy with the marble base.

'Afterwards both Shankly and Fagan said that I'd played my best game ever in a Liverpool shirt,' he recalls. 'I don't know about that, but I admired and respected the two of them enormously, so I appreciated the praise a lot.'

The captain is a role that gives a player a standing, a prominent place on the team, a pat on the back, extra glory, symbolic power: he is a chosen one among the chosen. Yet the captaincy can also create discord and enmity in a team. The world can seem such a sweet place when you receive the honour of the captaincy, and it can feel a crying injustice when you are relieved of that responsibility while still on the team. It is a knock to your self-esteem, a source of conflict and a shift in the balance of power. Ultimately it is a challenge to your own ego.

Liverpool FC is no exception. Changing captains has sometimes caused problems. Tommy Smith knows this all too well. In July 1973, Bill Shankly approached Tommy and asked him to come into his office for a chat.

'Tommy, son, I've decided to appoint Emlyn captain of the team. You will still be club captain, but from now on Emlyn is the team captain. OK?'

'I wasn't OK with that at all, but the decision had been made,' Smith reflects.

The biggest problem was that he and Emlyn Hughes did not get along at all. They were very different.

After the initial shock, I actually felt a bit of a relief at not being captain any more,' Smith admitted in his autobiography. 'Just like my predecessor, Ron Yeats, I had taken my responsibility as captain very seriously. There had been a lot of work:

organised visits to hospitals and schools, replying to letters asking for autographs, and requests for personal appearances by first-team players to charity events, golf days, cricket matches, as well as dealing with players who had problems. There had been daily and never-ending extra duties as a captain, on top of being leader on the pitch. I honestly felt some relief in being free from some of these tasks, but I did wonder why Emlyn had been chosen.'

Tommy simply did not like Hughes. His attitude, and some of the choices he made while on the team, saw to that. So it was particularly bitter to lose the captaincy to him. An icy front formed between them.

'In any workplace, there may be this one person that you simply have no chemistry with, and a football team is no exception. When players do not get along, the least a manager can ask for is that they respect each other as footballers. That was the way it was like with Emlyn and me.'

In August 2015, two years after Shankly's centenary, there is a new anniversary – another one to remind us that time flies, and that the glory of the past moves ever further back in history: it is 50 years since Liverpool FC won the much desired FA Cup trophy for the very first time.

We are in the Connie Club, a stone's throw from Penny Lane. Ian St John, Chris Lawler, Tommy Lawrence, Ian Callaghan and Tommy Smith are side by side in front of a black drape with a replica of the FA Cup. A fortunate few in the backroom are allowed to go and sit between the heroes of 1965 and have their photo taken with them.

Afterwards it is time for the legends to tell their stories. But there are only four chairs set out next to James Pearce from the *Liverpool Echo* – one of the journalists who follows Liverpool FC closest. Only Cally, the Saint, the Flying Pig (Lawrence) and the Silent Knight (Lawler) will be sharing their stories. The Anfield Iron is in the back of the room, dressed up in a checked blazer, hands folded. He was always gifted with words. But he has lost so many words recently. He lost his wife Susan only a few months ago, and it was a terrible blow to him.

Grief had become all-consuming. For 54 years it had been the two of them; and all of a sudden he was alone. Within weeks of her death, Alzheimer's took charge of Tommy too. It was like a dam burst inside him.

In only two weeks the children noticed a considerable change in behaviour in their seventy-year-old father. More and more words disappeared; he was confused, forgetful. Different. He had all the symptoms of an illness that the family knew all too well already. Now Tommy was struck too. He had stayed strong for the love of his life. When he no longer had to look after Sue, the illness took over. It is fascinating how a body can keep afflictions at bay out of love, protection and responsibility for someone.

Not needing to be strong for his wife any more, change happened quickly. He still recognises people, and he talks in few, short sentences. And he is well aware that things are not functioning properly.

A few weeks later, Chris Lawler and I visit Tommy Smith in his house in Crosby. He still lives in the same small detached house where I saw him and Sue together. Today we are let in by his daughter Janette, who gives us a friendly smile at the door, and serves us coffee. She lives about a mile down the road and visits her father every day.

Janette says that he had called her at four in the morning; he thought it was daytime. I have brought a lovely photo of Sue and Tommy that I have had enlarged and framed. They are laughing at the camera in the sun in the back garden. It was taken the last time I was here, two years ago.

'After my mother and Sue died, I've…'

Tommy searches for words, but cannot find any. He wipes away a tear with the back of his hand and strokes his hair.

She was a beautiful lady, and you were so good together.

I give Janette an identical photo.

'Thank you so much, I love it. We haven't got many photos of them together from the last few years,' Janette says. Together with her brother Darren, she shared her father with a whole city. Absolutely everybody knows who Tommy Smith is: a highly respected citizen of Merseyside, recognised on every street corner.

'We belonged to the red part of the city in the most literal sense of the word,' Janette says. 'I remember how everything we owned was red. We had a red car, and everything we bought was red. We weren't allowed to buy anything blue! If I needed a new coat, it had to be red.'

Janette is on the sofa, smiling and looking over at her father in the armchair from time to time. We look at photos from a happy childhood.

'I remember going to Anfield with him as a child, and we would suddenly be pushed away, he created such a commotion in the crowd when he arrived. We could be wandering down the streets in the neighbourhood and people would suddenly come up to dad, asking for his autograph. After he became captain, the crowds could be so big that we sometimes had to fight our way back into our own house. Often when we went to Southport for a meal at a restaurant we just had to leave and go home, there were so many people wanting to talk that we simply could not eat. It's probably nothing compared to what the current Liverpool players experience, but I remember clearly what it was like for us.'

You grew up in a family where Liverpool FC was a huge part of everyday life. What was it like?

'Everything was red. Football would be on the telly. But for us, the red football madness was normality. We didn't go to that many games. Wives didn't go to as many games back then, but we got to see some. And the club arranged Christmas parties every year, where Father Christmas came and gave us kids presents. It was a very nice time.'

Did you get more attention from boys as you got older, having such a famous dad?

'Oh no! They were all terrified of him. He had completely the opposite effect. I remember well this one boy, he had walked me home. He caught sight of Dad, who was working in the garden, and he just took off! I tried to call after him: "It's OK, I'm here!" But all the boys I met were terrified of my dad. Except my husband.'

The memory is undoubtedly a little comical, but I can also understand Janette's admirers. Tommy Smith is scary-looking. He is heavy-set, has scars on his face that prove he's been to battle more than once in his life. His appearance would probably be intimidating if you met him in a dark alley and did not know who he was.

With as long as sixteen years in Liverpool's first team, the club became the most natural part of the world for the Smith family. And today, a part of that world came to visit, one of those who watched little Janette grow up.

What's it like, seeing Chris Lawler again today?

'Every time I meet Dad's old team-mates, I have to introduce myself,' Janette says. 'I've obviously grown up, and am a mother of two boys. Every time I say who I am, Dad's team-mates light up, and say they're happy to see me. It's really nice. The players are like extended family to us.'

Since Tommy cannot talk much any more, Chris is here to help his friend tell the story of his life. Ian Callaghan suggested Chris for the job, since he is the one who knows the old captain best, and was closer to Tommy than any of the other players. It is ironic that he was chosen, if you read what Tommy had to say about his best friend in his autobiography.

Chris was the first friend I made when I came to the club as a fifteen-year-old in 1960. He was a year older than me, and I had met him many times playing for the Cardinal Godfrey College School Boys against St Teresa. We became fast friends and room-mates when we had both played our way into the first team. The funny thing about our friendship is that, despite all the years we played together, and shared a room, we never had a proper conversation. Chris is the most quiet man I have ever known. He was an amazing defender, and always up for a laugh and a joke with the rest of the lads, but he practically never spoke. He is a man of very few words.

For the first time, the tables are turned. Now the formerly quiet one will help his formerly so vocal pal and captain to speak. After all these years, the Anfield Iron and the Silent Knight have switched roles.

I knew Tommy was ill; several of his former team-mates and other former Liverpool players had told me. That he would most likely not remember much. But it surprises me just how badly he has deteriorated. How quickly the illness has developed. Smith is in a burgundy wing chair, his favourite. Lawler is on the light-grey leather sofa next to him. We turn the television off, and turn time back to 1970.

When Tommy was appointed the next captain by Bill Shankly after Ron Yeats in the summer of 1970, Yeats was one of the first to congratulate him with the promotion. He also gave him some advice.

'Remember that no matter what goes wrong during a match, it's never your fault. Not even when you're the one who made a mistake,' Yeats said.

'Why?' Smith asked, bewildered.

'Because you're the captain! If your team concedes a goal, look for the player who looks most guilty, and blame him!'

'Does it work?'

'Well, it's worked for me for nine years,' Yeats said with a smile.

When Smith played against Liverpool's arch-rival Everton for the first time as captain, he was partly to blame for Everton scoring twice. Both times he gave Chris Lawler a proper scolding, as he looked most guilty. And Tommy knew that he would not talk back. So he accused Chris of bad communication. Chris swallowed the accusations and did not say anything to his friend and captain at all. He just ran back and got ready for the new kick-off. At 2–2, none other than defender Lawler barged forward and scored the winner in front of an Anfield that celebrated wildly. When Tommy ran up to Chris, hugged him and congratulated him on a great goal, the scorer remarked dryly: 'I didn't say what I was going to do this time either!'

All these years later, they both laugh heartily at the memory. Tommy is right here with us, even though his words are stuck. But he understands everything we say, and remembers more than he manages to express.

'And 3–2 was the end result,' Chris says with a smile.

'We beat them 3–2,' Tommy echoes.

He talks carefully, as if he has to make an effort to express himself.

'Here I am, scoring the winner, and you blame me for the goals against us!' says Lawler. 'But even though you blamed me, I didn't say anything. Even though it wasn't my fault.'

Then Chris turns towards Tommy: 'It was a good game, wasn't it?'

Tommy smiles gently as Chris continues.

'There are so many stories to tell. Like when we played Arsenal in August 1967. I'll never forget. You were captain, and Bill Shankly wanted you to win the toss-up, to have the advantage of the wind in the first half. But we lost the toss, Arsenal got to play with the wind behind them. Tony Hateley scored an own goal, and we lost 2–0. Afterwards Shankly looked at you sternly and said, "Tommy, what did you call?"

'"Heads," you replied. And Shankly yelled back at you: "Tommy! You should always call tails!"'

When we talk about Shankly, Tommy manages to express his first full sentence. It sends chills down my spine.

You were the second of only three Shankly-chosen captains.

'Yeah.'

After Ron Yeats himself, you were appointed as successor. That's quite a compliment!

'Yeah.'

He talks slowly, but his eyes sparkle:

'It was great, you know.'

He smiles at me.

What do you think Shankly saw in you as captain material?

'Hard... erm...'

He wants to speak, but once again his words are stuck. Chris takes over and begins to explain.

'Tommy was a young man with great confidence,' he says. 'He was mature and early developed. He really knew what he wanted in life, he was very ambitious.'

An intelligent man, with good confidence and a great plan, would you say?

'Yes.' Tommy confirms this himself, smiling in his armchair.

Chris is certain that their family backgrounds helped shape their personalities. Not least when it comes to their communication skills. The family situation of the two best friends were complete opposites.

'We were fifteen siblings in the family, I was last but two, while Tommy was an only child. My brothers were so dominant, I didn't get half a chance! So I became the quiet one in the pack. But Tommy could say anything he wanted since he was alone. That way he was shaped to take the floor and the lead from when he was very young.'

Lawler was also a local lad. He grew up in a small house with only three bedrooms for seventeen people. The family had to take turns eating, and the youngest had to wait till last, and see what was left. His father worked in the dockyard, but only had an income on days he was commissioned to work.

What type of leader was Tommy?

'He was direct, brave, vocal, temperamental, and led by example. And he was determined to make everyone understand just how important it was that Liverpool won all their games.'

Then Chris asks, 'Do you remember Steve Heighway, Tommy?'

'Yeah.'

'He came to the club from the university,' Chris explains. 'His attitude was a little "easy come, easy go". We'd been to London, and Arsenal had beat us. On the train going home, Tommy and I sat together, with Steve Heighway and Brian Hall nearby. Steve was having a laugh, and Tommy got furious. We'd just lost a game, and the rest of us were down in the dumps. Tommy leaped out of his seat, grabbed Steve, and said: "You know what, this is what we do for a living! We all have our debt to pay!"

'We got a bonus every time we won, and Tommy didn't like his attitude when we lost. So he looked after us, and made sure we all had the right attitude at all times.'

Janette has been listening to our conversation.

'Darren and I used to hide when Dad came home after a loss,' she remembers. 'We knew instantly when they had lost, as he would slam the door shut. Then we would hide behind the bedroom door; we knew we had to leave him in peace for a while. He was either happy or furious after matches.'

What were his happy homecomings like?

'Then he would often have stopped on his way home to buy us presents; small gifts or sweets, to celebrate.'

Looking back, Janette, what's your proudest 'Dad' moment?

'It has to be when he scored in the European Cup final in 1977. We were at my nan's house, she looked after us. She was too nervous to watch. My brother was upstairs watching, but came running down to watch the replay with me when Dad scored.'

It was 1–1 between Liverpool and Borussia Mönchengladbach in the Olympic stadium in Rome when Tommy Smith scored in the 64th minute of the game during his 604th appearance for Liverpool. He scored 48 times for the club in total. Near the end of the game Kevin Keegan was brought down, and Phil Neal scored from the penalty spot (as he would continue to do for many years), securing Liverpool's first European Cup.

'I was around ten at the time, and absolutely everyone I knew had seen my dad score when Liverpool won the European Cup final for the very first time. I was on cloud nine in school the next day. I was so proud of him.'

That match is also Tommy's strongest memory from his time with Liverpool, along with their first ever FA Cup victory in 1965.

Your father was known to be hard as rock. How would you describe him as a father, compared with his image as a player?

'He's really a very soft man. He couldn't bear to see us cry, he would do anything to comfort us.'

Janette looks over at her father.

'You're a real softie, aren't you? Ha-ha, the look he's giving me!'

Here's the truth at last about the Anfield Iron!

'My dad simply loved shopping,' Janette continues. 'I remember once when Mum was having a rest, she'd been so busy, Dad took me shopping. He bought me this fantastic coat and a couple of pairs of high-heeled shoes, and I was only around eight. We had such fun on these shopping trips.'

So you'd rather go shopping with your dad than your mum?

'Yup.'

This big, tough, intimidating guy loved shopping and his family. Or rather – he was both. On the pitch he was undoubtedly rock hard and unyielding, nobody can take that away from him; off the pitch – in private at least – he was a different man: doting, committed, a big softy.

Tommy, there's been a lot of talk about how aggressive you were on the pitch. You had this fire within, a burning desire to win with Liverpool. Every time. Was this aggression only with you on the pitch, or was it there all the time?

'On the pitch. It was on the pitch. I never feared anyone. I just…'

Again, he is searching for words.

'Sorry. Goodness!'

'Just take your time,' Janette encourages him.

We're in no rush. Is it difficult when you want to say something and can't find the words? It must be frustrating?

'It is.'

How do you get on with your daily life these days?

'A friend of mine, Frankie Allen, comes here and picks me up, helps me out with different things. Do you remember Frankie?'

Yes.

'He visits you a lot, and takes you to events and dinners. The more active you are, the better you speak,' Janette adds.

'Yes. Because I struggle sometimes… You have to write things, it's just the way it is.'

'Write cheques?' Chris jokes.

'Oh no, he can still do that quite easily,' Janette laughs, looking at her father, the king of shopping.

We reminisce about the day when Liverpool secured their very first FA Cup victory, and nobody had thought about what reward they would get from the club if they pulled this off.

Chris takes over: 'Not a lot of people know this, but we didn't have a bonus scheme for winning. Winning or losing would not have made any difference financially. So captain Ron Yeats went up to see the director on behalf of the players, and asked him what we would get for the victory. He came back and said the club was so pleased with the team that every player would get a £1,000 bonus. But since the two of us were new on the team, we only got half of that. There was nothing we could do about it.'

That wasn't fair?

'No, it wasn't fair, but none of the other guys cared. Even though we could have bought a car with that money!'

I turn to Tommy in his wing chair.

No wonder you turned shop steward when you were appointed captain!

He smiles from his seat. Above him hangs his MBE, awarded for long and faithful service to football.

Tommy was very active in his time as captain, also helping his team-mates off the pitch. He negotiated bonuses and would speak to the club management on behalf of the players; always unafraid and goal-oriented. And he was in his element when he helped arrange the traditional Christmas party and other social gatherings. He would often set them up in his own pub, the Smithy in Billinge, St Helens, that he owned in his prime as a footballer. (Later, after his retirement from playing, he bought and refurbished the Cavern Club.)

While he showed a lot of care and consideration for his team-mates, the true focus was his wife Sue. Both made sacrifices for each other over fifty years of marriage. They had to postpone their wedding the summer when he was twenty, because he – at short notice – had been included in the first team and a pre-season tour of the US.

'Mum was a real softie too, just like Dad,' Janette says. 'We were a very, very close-knit family. When I had children, we used to travel places together, to the US and elsewhere. And both Mum and Dad were excellent baby-sitters for their grandchildren.'

When Sue was struck with dementia Tommy continued to pick up his grandchildren from school on certain days, as well as taking care of his wife.

'Dad always looked after her well. He actually had to stop working as it took all his time caring for her when she got worse. It was tough for him to give it up, but he never hesitated. He cared for and helped her tirelessly. But as she gradually deteriorated, he eventually realised that he could not leave her alone even for a short while. It became exhausting for him.'

He was so patient with her, he helped her explain or describe things every time she forgot something. And then she died, terribly sad, and everything changed.

'Yes, he changed. In just two weeks he was completely different. It went so quickly.'

In a short time he's been struck with the same illness that took your mother away. What's that like for you?

'It's just really hard. Frustrating, and very sad. It's the only way I can describe it.'

A lot of people don't know about your father's condition. And on the outside he looks the same. What's it like when you're out among people?

'It's difficult, but we try to go to places where they know him. They're very kind to him. That helps.'

And how does he get by on a daily basis?

'I try to be here as much as I can. Someone has to be here every day. We don't have to be here all the time, but we have to look after him, and just take one day at a time.'

Do you ever worry about him when he's here on his own?

'Oh yes! But we try as well as we can to look after him, we're only a mile down the road. It's difficult, but we manage the way it is now.'

There hasn't been much talk about this publicly in football, but so many from your father's generation are suffering from Alzheimer's. Ron Yeats is struggling. Geoff Strong died. It can't be a coincidence that so many players from that generation have the same problems. How do you feel about them having literally given their whole body to football?

'I think, if you asked them, they would never have wanted their football careers or their life with the club any different. In boxing there are a lot of safety precautions, they haven't had that in football. Being a footballer today is a different world, the balls are so much lighter. But still, when my boys play football, I flinch every time they head a ball.'

In addition to Alzheimer's, your father has rheumatism, he's got an artificial elbow and two knees, and he told me earlier that some days he struggles to get out of bed. Do you wish now, knowing what has happened to his health, that he hadn't played football?

'No. Because football and Liverpool has been his entire life. He couldn't not have played. But I do think they should do some research into the connection between football and dementia. And continue researching Alzheimer's, to find new ways to slow the illness down.'

Should there be better compensation schemes? There's so much money in football now.

'Yes, there is, but money wouldn't make Dad well again. Perhaps instead they should donate money to research?'

What about financial support for nursing and care?

'The FA provides some support, but it's very limited what you can get.'

With better support schemes, you could have had more help for the daily care for your father, on days when you cannot be there.

'That would have been good. They should definitely look into that for the future.'

And finally, Janette – how would you describe your dad as a player, and as a father?

'As a player, I agree with Chris: an ambitious player with an extreme will to win. And as a dad: a real softie.'

Tommy Smith sees us out, like he has always seen his guests out. He takes my hand and gives me a handshake that is less firm than before; then kisses me on the cheek as goodbye.

As we drive off, I see Tommy in the window in the hall. He is looking at us open-faced, but his eyes are sad. He lifts his big hand and waves at us. I wave back and feel a lump in my throat, thinking: I'll never be able to chat with Tommy Smith again. He's gone. Just seventy years old. Football stole him and all his words and stories with its heavy, wet leather balls.

3

PHIL THOMPSON
LOCAL PRIDE

'Phil Thompson was Liverpool mad, it was his club, his city.
The captaincy was his dream job.'
Graeme Souness

IT IS NOVEMBER 1970. PHIL THOMPSON HAS BEEN THROUGH A
trainee period with other very talented players, and they are all competing for the
same thing: a professional contract. He is sixteen years old and worried sick; it will
soon be decided who is allowed to continue. Players reach the critical point where
futures are determined; they both look forward to and dread their seventeenth birthday in equal measure. Either you are given a contract, or you are out of the club. And
for this youngster, there is no bigger dream than becoming a professional footballer
for Liverpool Football Club.

But Thompson is injured, and if there is one thing the boss cannot stand, it is
injured players. Bill Shankly does not even talk to them. They are like air to him.
So Thompson's dream is in grave danger. And it is the only dream this tall, lanky
teenager has. He is so thin and long-legged he is perfectly moulded for running. He
won the cross-country race while representing the North of England at thirteen, but
was drawn into football after changing teachers in school.

He has overcome a lot of obstacles on the way, but this time it is serious. He has
a stretch injury in his thigh, and now he is walking around the training pitches to

recover after his injury. The moment of truth – his birthday – is only two months away. Will the injury deprive him of a chance to play for the red club that he has followed his entire life, in this city split between red and blue? Families even, torn between red and blue, like his own.

He receives physical therapy, but it takes time for the pain to ease. His body does not repair as quickly as he wants it to. As if competition was not hard enough as it is. Five apprentices all dream about staying. But there will not be room for all of them. While he walks around the pitch as part of his convalescence, the boss comes over to him. The actual man who enjoys such enormous respect, and who will decide on the young man's destiny. And the strange thing is, he starts talking to him, even though he is injured.

'Do you sleep well, Phil? Do you get enough to eat?'

Phil Thompson nods, his heart skipping a beat for fear of what comes next.

'Thommo, twenty-first of January is your birthday, isn't it?'

'Yes,' Thompson replies, surprised the boss knows his birthday, and even more that he is talking to someone who is injured.

'We've discussed matters, and we like the way you behave on and off the pitch. Everybody is extremely happy with you. I know that being an apprentice is a hard and uncertain time. So I want you to calm down. Don't tell anyone else, but we want to sign you on your seventeenth birthday, so you needn't worry.'

Thommo was the only one of the five who got to stay…

It would take a lot for someone to exceed Phil Thompson in the enthusiasm and energy he possesses as a voice in football. Footage of him in studio during matches has gone viral on YouTube – a suit-clad and seemingly calm and collected adult who completely loses it when important results go Liverpool's way. He will shoot out of his chair as quickly as a spaceship launched into orbit. The chair falls to the ground, while he stays in the air for a second, hanging there like Superman, jumping up fist first. Happiness mixed with passion and love. Primal screams so loud and raw that you know this is the real deal.

He is from Kirkby, a tough neighbourhood in Liverpool. Today the area is home to Liverpool's Academy. These days, when Thompson keeps up his weekly workouts at the local training centre to stay in shape, he looks straight over to the LFC Academy, that will hopefully foster new local talents like himself.

Shankly once made the humorous comment: 'Thommo, you must have bluffed a lot in your childhood!' He got the nickname 'Pinocchio' because of his long nose. He grew up with a father who had the same job and fate as many other Liverpool dads: he worked on a ship, and was away for weeks on end. At home, Mrs Thompson was alone with seven children. The kids had to fend for themselves a lot of the time, because their mother had no chance to pamper them. Phil Thompson is convinced that the responsibilities they had from early on in life helped shape him for the Liverpool captaincy.

'We had to take responsibility from when we were quite young, and that definitely helped shape me to become a leader,' he says. 'We were given a lot of responsibility because there was only our mum to look after us much of the time, and she was away at work a lot. We got home from school and had to fix our own lunches. We didn't have much. We weren't very well off. Three bedrooms for the nine of us. But mum was there to build us up. She really did everything she possibly could for us, to give us what we needed. And because of that, I had a fantastic childhood.

'Growing up in Kirkby was rough. You had to keep your head about you. Sometimes you had to talk your way out of trouble, sometimes you had to fight your way out. That was my childhood. You had to fend for yourself.'

He had four younger and two older siblings, and they all learned how to look after one another.

'And that's what it's like on the pitch too. Maybe I learned team mentality and team ethics at home. You take care of the people around you. And you don't just take care of them on the pitch, but off the pitch too. It's the same way for a captain. When captaincy comes your way, you have to look after the team outside matches too. You plead their cause to the manager and coaching staff. You raise subjects on behalf of the whole team.'

Dissatisfaction, wishes, squad opinions. Thompson wanted to do the best he could for his team-mates when he was given the honour to become Liverpool captain.

'Sometimes you put your head on the line there, on behalf of the team, but it's also great fun to be captain. That's why losing the captaincy after three years was such a dreadful thing.'

I meet Phil Thompson at Anfield on a lovely, sunny afternoon in January 2015. Phil turned 61 only days earlier. A few light clouds are reflected in the 'Welcome to Anfield' sign above the ticket office, as the sun is making its way down behind the brick houses across the street. Bill Shankly welcomes us with open arms, with a scarf around his neck and in classic, creased trousers, all set in bronze. The low sun throws a golden light on the statue and on the black-and-white photo from inside the stadium that hangs on the wall behind him. We stop and gape at the sight: the statue's shadow hits the wall so perfectly, it looks like Shankly is in the stands, alive and kicking, surrounded by the warm sunlight, a near-sacred halo around him. The golden sky. Thompson breaks the silence.

'Wow! Look at that!' he says. 'That's giving me goose bumps, it's like he's here! The man I can thank for all my years with Liverpool FC. What an incredible sight!'

We find our way up into the Boot Room, the first-floor restaurant within the walls of Anfield. It is a modern addition to the premises where Phil has often told stories from his – and the club's – heyday.

There is absolutely no doubt, Philip Bernard Thompson timed his years as a first-team player well. Seven league championships, one FA Cup, six Charity Shields, two League Cups, one UEFA Super Cup, two UEFA Cups and two European Cups, speak volumes. This is not a beginner's trophy list, this is serious stuff. In thirteen years, he won twenty-one trophies.

Thompson's dad, Owen, was an Everton fan and tried to win the children over to the blue side, with sweets, exotic gifts from abroad, and even money. But he did not stand a chance. After all, Owen had married a woman who was a regular at Anfield. Through the 1950s and 1960s, June would dress up and go to matches with her twin sister May. She got to see Bill Shankly come in late in the 1950s and start the job of renovating both the team and the stadium. She had seen Ron Yeats lead the team out in countless matches. She had seen his best friend, Ian St John, tear down the oppositions' defences. She had seen supporters grow in numbers through the 1950s and 1960s, as the Reds steadily climbed the league table.

When she had children, she brought them along to the games. That was how her son, Phil, had a front-row view to watch his heroes return from the FA Cup triumph at Wembley in 1965; his heroes making a lap of honour; the much wanted trophy causing the eyes of the puny eleven-year-old to sparkle.

Did your parents stay married?

He breaks into a laugh.

'Yes, they did! When I became a Liverpool player, my dad changed from blue to red, like so many others – Jamie Carragher, Michael Owen and Robbie Fowler – who went through the same change. Dad was a great support for me.'

The derby matches with Everton are among Liverpool's most anticipated games every year, and the biggest of all for Phil.

'A lot of people think the Manchester United matches are the biggest, but it's not for me. It's because I grew up in this city. I was lucky enough to experience that Everton didn't beat us for seven years in a row! That's a long time, and it meant the world to me.'

Phil Thompson from Kirkby, number three in a row of siblings, just like Ron Yeats and Ian St John. He thinks of himself as a likeable lad, and there are many of us who can confirm that he is, full of enthusiasm, energy and smiles. He is always there for his friends, his team, his family, for the former LFC players' charity, for TV channels – and for writers trying to understand the captain's role in football. He was rarely bossy at home, but sometimes he could explode. He wonders if he suffers from 'middle child syndrome'.

'Looking back, I think I've got a streak of the bully in me too. I was usually a nice kid, growing up, but if I was pushed too far into a corner, no matter how big or heavy those pushing scrawny little me were, I would fight back. I would crack.'

His temper could certainly crack under his desire to win too.

'I've always wanted to be the best, and sometimes I may have pushed other people too far because of my burning desire to win. But there were more of us who hated losing. Especially the players from the 1978/79 season, that I feel was the best ever Liverpool team. We were all driven by a winning instinct. Graeme Souness, Kenny Dalglish, Jimmy Case, Terry McDermott, Ray Clemence: we all hated losing. We'd fight like mad for ninety minutes. That could help explain why we scored so many goals in the final minutes of a game back then. Just like Manchester United seemed to do under Ferguson.'

I am sure that his instinct, his determination and drive were drilled into him while he was a young apprentice at Liverpool. Character and winning instinct were nurtured in the regimes of Bill Shankly, Bob Paisley, Joe Fagan and Ronnie Moran. The Boot Room gang could see that the local lad, Phil Thompson, stood out in competition with a lot of other young talents for the apprenticeship.

'They saw how my character and charisma developed, I think that's why the captaincy ended up with me.'

Emlyn Hughes's time as captain was over after six seasons. Being captain of Liverpool was Thompson's greatest dream: to have the honour of captaining the team of his heart, the team from his home town. And he did have hopes to be appointed captain when Emlyn Hughes's time as boss on the pitch came to an end. But instead of appointing Thompson, Bob Paisley chose Kenny Dalglish as the new captain, even though it was uncommon to choose an attacker as skipper.

Dalglish did not stay in this role very long. After captaining a few games, he asked to step down.

'I don't know what happened, but rumours claimed Kenny didn't like captaining, that he didn't want the captaincy, it didn't feel right for him.'

Why not?

'I don't know. I never got around to asking him. But maybe he felt that he was too far away from the rest of the team to be captain, Kenny is a smart fella.'

A few matches after Kenny had been appointed, the team were playing Arsenal. Only an hour before the game, Bob Paisley came over to Phil and said, 'You will captain today, Phil.' Thompson was filled with joy and pride.

'Wow! I thought, this is my destiny – Liverpool captain. It was meant to be.'

His friends, Terry McDermott, Graeme Souness, Kenny Dalglish, Phil Neal and Ray Clemence, were all really happy about the choice.

'I remember particularly well Phil Neal coming over, saying: "You wanted the captaincy so much. You deserve this. It was written in the stars." It was a fantastic, wonderful moment of my life.'

Thompson could not wait to lead the team out on to the pitch for the first time as Liverpool captain. Making sure they kept up the ritual of every home match; going over to the Kop first. He could hardly wait to go over to the famous stand and wave at his brother, Owen, who stood where the two of them used to stand together, cheering for the Reds. Thompson wanted to make sure that he reached the Kop first on this very special day, because at that time the team did not go out as a group. The players went out one by one as they were ready: sometimes on the prompt of the referee's whistle, sometimes a little earlier. And sometimes the team went out even earlier, to warm up for a few, short minutes in front of the Kop.

'There was never a long warm-up session on the pitch before a game,' he remembers. 'You warmed up a maximum of five to seven minutes, just before the match started. That was it. For some it was just a quick sip of brandy or a quick stretching routine. Or just a couple of minutes sitting on the radiator!

'It was around ten to three, and I was dying to get out on the pitch. I told the lads, "Come on, let's go out now! We've got to get out on the pitch!" And everybody tells me to calm down. It's only ten to three. When there's just six or seven minutes left till the match, I say: "OK, lads, time to go out!"

'We wish each other good luck. We walk down the steps. I touch the This is Anfield sign. Walk up the wooden steps to the ground. Step out on the pitch. Sprint over to the Kop and stare to see if I can find my brother in the crowd. When I reach the penalty area, everybody in the stands is laughing. I think, What's going on? I turn around and realise that Kenny Dalglish, Ray Clemence, Terry McDermott and the rest of the team are still in the tunnel. They've let me run out on my own, while they stayed in the tunnel, and now they're practically pissing themselves with laughter. I'm the only fool standing all by myself in the middle of Anfield.'

It was a fantastic moment, and it says two important things.

'First of all, they knew how important this moment was to me, and they wanted to let me enjoy it to the full. At the same time, it shows the way we loved to fool around as a team. We could joke about anything, disregarding who got the brunt of it, as long as it made us laugh.'

They won Thompson's first match as captain, against Arsenal.

'So it didn't matter that they'd made fun of me. It was how I was introduced as captain for Liverpool.'

Did you feel extra pressure or nervousness that day, because you were the captain?

'I was always nervous and always focused. If there was one thing I always saw to, it was that I made sure everybody else was focused too. As a local lad, every game was important.'

Was it a tactical masterstroke of Bob Paisley, waiting till one hour before the game until appointing you as captain?

'Yes, I'm sure it was good for Paisley, but I didn't get to tell the big news to my mum and dad. And I didn't get to tell my brothers and sisters. There were no mobile phones at the time, and I couldn't call them at home, because they'd already left the house to go to the match. It was just an hour and fifteen minutes before the match that the team line-up was handed in and the new captain was announced.'

Phil Thompson. The local lad from Kirkby. New captain of Liverpool FC: a natural and popular choice to everyone on the team. And not least to himself. A typical leader, the vocally strong and football-smart Thompson, who bled for his shirt. If you ever want to use such a description for a footballer, then Phil Thompson deserves it. Moreover, he had learned a lot from his predecessors, Tommy Smith and Emlyn Hughes. It was all about getting the best out of your team-mates. But he definitely felt that the responsibility of the captaincy weighed him down

'Yes, I did feel the burden of the captaincy. But luckily it was an easy job too, since I played with such incredible players. They were all top-class players on an international level. Still, as captain you need to show leader abilities. I felt I had to be the one shouting loudest, to ensure that we were doing the right thing on the pitch.'

When Thompson took over as captain in 1979, he felt an overwhelming personal responsibility to do his utmost to lead the team to the best possible result. In football today, the manager is the one with most of the responsibility. Managers get kicked out of clubs almost before they have time to furnish their new homes, unless they deliver as expected right away. Neither captain nor team is to blame if results fail.

Was the captain's influence stronger in your day?

'I think a lot of captains in foreign clubs don't take on the same responsibility as English captains do. Our captains are the exceptions, when you look at it like that. This goes back generations. But of course, things are always changing. I don't know if captains today do this, but we had a committee, made up of the most experienced players, who used to sit down and decide things. We looked at what we wanted of collective benefits, bonus plans and things like that.'

Almost like a trade union?

'Yes, that's how we got organised. We called it the players' pool and it usually consisted of the most experienced players, usually six of us. We'd discuss what the players were going to do off the pitch too. We decided when the team were wearing the same clothes or playing with the same type of shoes. It was about cup final clothes and cup final bonuses. We decided. Money we made from special happenings went into this players' pool. At the end of each season we distributed the earnings and spent it on the players. The captain played an important part in this. Sometimes there were more of us settling matters, sometimes it was just me and my committee members. We sat down and decided what would be the best for the team. So the captaincy was a varied role. I've no idea if this still exists today.'

Modern football is much more individualistic, which makes Thompson unsure if a players' pool would work as well.

'With all the personal contracts around today, and the enormous amounts of money in football, a lot of players wouldn't want to share their massive income with those of their team-mates who make less. We were much more of a collective back then than players are today.'

Thompson was like a trade union leader, making decisions on behalf of the workers. That way, he was strongly involved in a lot of tasks off the pitch too. On the pitch, he played chess with his team-mates.

'The most important matter for a captain is communication. I controlled Alan Hansen and Alan Kennedy, the players around me. Moved them around as chess pieces. Ordered them about vocally. Ray Clemence operated in the same way. He was older and wiser than me. He controlled his zone in front of the goal, the team zone.'

Thompson could hear Clemence bark out commands. He could look to his right, and Clemence would shout: 'Left shoulder, left shoulder! Someone has to watch the middle. Cover up, cover up! Watch it!'

'Clemence communicated with us all the time, and that taught me good habits, just like he did with Phil Neal, Alan Hansen, Emlyn Hughes and Alan Kennedy,' Thompson says.

Throughout the game, he communicated with the players in front of him, in midfield, players like Graeme Souness, Jimmy Case and Terry McDermott.

'Their eardrums were practically ruptured after every game, because I'd yelled at them so much!'

Thompson gesticulates eagerly when he talks, and his eyes gleam with passion. In his mind, he is back on the pitch playing chess. A wonderful, strategic game, with live pieces: eleven of them, with an X Factor of a leather ball, and eleven opponents.

Ronnie Moran had followed him up and trained him in the reserve team. He had constantly been yelling: 'Open your eyes, Thommo! Open your eyes!' And Thompson had learned the important ability to read a game, and being ready ahead of the next move in the game. To avoid checkmate.

How was your voice after your matches as captain?

'I had none! I would have taken on the same responsibility as my leader-type predecessors – Emlyn, Smith and Callaghan. They were all very vocal. Shouters. That being said, Smith probably shouted more than Cally. As a team we needed these strong, vocal communicators.'

This was both apprenticeship and inheritance. The communication course was the school of life. The captains had it in them. The sense of responsibility, the commitment and the talent for the organisational. Not to forget the great football understanding and great playing talent.

'The Liverpool FC players who made captains were first and foremost very good players, but they also showed great communication skills and a great sense of responsibility.'

Phil Thompson has no doubt that having great skills as a player is even more important than personal aptness to succeed as captain. He points to Alan Hansen as a good example of this. During his playing career, he was a man of few words. He did not really become vocal until he started working on TV. Hansen led the team by being an outstanding player, with great positioning, calm playing and tons of experience. The younger players who played with Alan were helped through simple and clear instructions.

But how does Thompson think it is today? Did Steven Gerrard have the same freedom to shape players and contribute to the tactical aspect, or are the managers today in total control of the game, for example?

'I think managers today have more control over the game than when we played.

And much of the reason is that we were a good side with incredibly talented players. We could play and make decisions even if we were shouted at from the sideline.'

In training at Melwood they were often more or less left to themselves. They would do their regular warm-ups, then play seven- or eight-a-side on the pitch, often on their own, through 40 to 45 minutes, while the coaching staff played the apprentices.

In Thompson's time, the team mainly consisted of players with English as their mother tongue, even if sprinkled with dialects of Irish, Scottish, and various regions of England, of which Scouse could be challenging to understand. Today, teams consist of players with many different languages. A lot of them do not speak English when they arrive in England. They neither understand nor speak it naturally. That obviously poses great problems in communication for the modern captain.

'That must be a big challenge to the captain,' Thompson says. 'Especially when you're under pressure, and you want to communicate with the players on the pitch, try to make them do what you want them to do. I wonder what it's like having to change language from your mother tongue to English so quickly. And I don't understand how Steven Gerrard and Jamie Carragher have managed to communicate, because it's easy to lose one's head in the heat of a match. And I don't know how these foreign players understood Carra at all, his Scouse accent is even stronger than mine!'

The Boot Room period was over when Roy Evans stepped down as manager in 1998. The joint-management with Gérard Houllier had not worked, and Thompson was brought in as assistant manager. For the first time since Shankly in 1959, the manager of Liverpool had not been recruited from within their own ranks. Moreover, it was a foreigner, a Frenchman, who was picked to lift the club once again to an international standard. And with him, players of many different nationalities started coming in to Liverpool.

'We had a lot of foreign players in the squad, but we tried to get as many of them to learn English, because it would be of great help for them on the pitch. But we tried to keep instructions as simple as possible: "Man on", "Behind you!"'

The captains that have served Liverpool have had different strong points, and hence their biggest influence has been in different areas. Where was Phil Thompson's biggest influence as captain? On the pitch? In the dressing room? At half-time? In training? Off the pitch? In 'civilian life'?

'I'd like to think that I was a good captain because I felt responsibility for the players in all of those settings. But I still think my greatest impact was in match preparation – making the players understand that all matches were equally important. We had to do everything to win, no matter who we were playing. Not all of our players were Liverpool fans. They came from all over England, Scotland, Wales and Ireland. Looking around the dressing room, I could tell by their faces that some of the players, when we were playing smaller clubs like Coventry, Southampton or Bristol City, weren't as hungry for a win. If you haven't got that hunger, your performance will drop. Obviously this wasn't the case with the local players, like Terry McDermott, Jimmy Case, Sammy Lee and David Fairclough, they wanted to win every single game. And nobody needed extra motivation for the big games, against Manchester United, Everton, Arsenal or Chelsea. They were motivation in themselves back then.'

A lot of Thompson's team-mates have given him credit for making them understand what it takes to be a Liverpool player. Which was exactly what he felt was his most important role on the team, not just during his three years as captain, but in the years before and after that.

'I felt that I was in a position to make this my job. A lot of my team-mates were from other teams and had played for big clubs. And yet, Liverpool were different. You came here to stay. You fought every match to prove you deserved a place on the team. I didn't play well every week, but it was my right and my duty to tell players what to do, and how to behave. Drive them on.'

There is no doubt that you need to be born with leadership abilities to be a good captain. But is it the same type of abilities that you would need to be a business boss? I put the list of still-living captains in front of Thompson and ask him if he believes the people listed there would have made good business leaders?

'Definitely! The way we operated in our time would have made us good business leaders because we were pretty tough, but still quite fair. We tried to organise for the collective, not just ourselves, because it's not all about me – neither in business nor in football. We made sure everybody shared our ideas on what we thought would be best for the team, rather than best for you. It was all about having a tight bond between management and players to get the best result possible and work for a common aim. As soon as the distance between management and workers – or players – is too big, you fail. That's why working to create such tight bonds is very, very important. This is also true for the bond between management and other employees of the club or company.'

Just like his predecessors, Gérard Houllier also thought it was vitally important to treat everybody at the club with the same respect, no matter what responsibilities they had. He taught Thompson that, as a manager, you cannot enter a room and say 'good morning, good morning' and smile at some, and then turn around and throw out a 'morning' without eye contact, or with a limp handshake, to others. Houllier was concerned with the type of signals that kind of behaviour might give. It creates divisiveness. Thompson, who learned a lot about leadership and communication from Houllier during the years they worked together, says his boss often used business life as an example when it came to building a sense of team and team spirit. One of his examples was that he held up eleven pencils in a bundle, then tried to break them in two, while he said: 'Look at this, together we can't be broken.' Then he took one pencil out of the bundle and snapped it in half: 'Look how you're all on your own. You're so brittle, you may break.'

'It's a brilliant image of unity; strong and fascinating,' says Thompson.

During the past ten years of Liverpool's history there have been plenty of examples of how the team has played tremendously well and won big games, but lost or struggled against assumed weaker opposition. When Thompson was assistant manager, and later caretaker manager during Houllier's heart trouble, he saw players do fantastically against Manchester United.

'But no matter how good it feels to beat Manchester United, and no matter how long you can relish such a victory against the arch-rivals in Manchester, you cannot win the league just by beating them,' he admits. 'You must perform well against all teams, even against presumed weaker opponents.'

Thompson's first season as captain, 1978/79, was a fairy-tale campaign. One of the many seasons in the 1970s that will bring many a reader to tears just thinking about it. It was such a successful one, where Liverpool won the league for the eleventh time. But his strongest and proudest moment as captain came in a different year. There is one trophy that outranks all the others: the European Cup. And this was in a time when only the league winner got a chance to play in Europe's premier club trophy.

'I don't think anything can surpass the European Cup final in 1981,' he says. 'Parc des Princes, in the city of love. Real Madrid against Liverpool. The all white against the all red. Nothing is more romantic than that!

'My predecessor, Emlyn, had had the honour in 1977/78. Now it was my turn. I was desperate to lift the big silver trophy, because I'd been a Liverpool fan since I was tiny. It was one of the biggest days of my life.'

Real Madrid, a dreaded super-team. The Spaniards were the most successful club in the history of the European Cup. And yet, the match in Paris was not brilliant or full of great entertainment value. It was, instead, trench warfare on the sporting field. Fortunately for Liverpool, Alan Kennedy managed to score the only goal of the match, ten minutes before full time, and victory for Liverpool in the European Cup for a third time became a reality. Now it was just a matter of sending Madrid up first to collect their silver medals, and then organising the winners, Liverpool, who would take gold. Captains go first.

'It looked great when Emlyn lifted the European Cup for us in 1978. He was a Liverpool fan when he lifted it, because he'd played for us for such a long time, and he was such a passionate player. But he hadn't been a Liverpool supporter since childhood. So for me to go the grades from childhood to lifting the trophy for the club as captain – that's my proudest moment of all. Champions League, the European Cup, whatever you want to call it. It is the proudest moment you can experience as captain. And now I had done it. It was very, very moving.'

Liverpool had practically made a habit out of winning the European Cup. This was the third time Phil Neal, Ray Clemence, Ray Kennedy, Jimmy Case, Terry McDermott and Liverpool had won 'the mother of all trophies' in five seasons. And it was Thompson's second. It was a demonstration of power in European football.

Friday morning, after the team had returned to Merseyside, when the Liverpool press arrived to take photos, the trophy was missing, having been taken by Thompson to Kirkby. The captain had simply put the trophy in the boot of his car Thursday night after the final and taken it to his local pub to keep the party going and to share the triumph with the neighbourhood. There were many who stared in disbelief at Phil Thompson showing up at the Falcon, where they were all celebrating Liverpool's European Cup triumph.

Sometimes the wind turns at a moment's notice. And so does the joy of captaincy. In May 1981, Thompson was on top of the world. But at the start of the next season, the squad was barely recognisable. Bruce Grobbelaar had replaced Ray Clemence as goalkeeper, and the team had problems in defence. They struggled to get used to Grobbelaar's very different and somewhat peculiar style of playing. It was a long learning process. Bruce needed to get used to his defenders, and they to him. They conceded a lot more goals than they had in the past and this frustrated their temperamental captain. On Boxing Day Liverpool lost at home to Manchester City and slumped to twelfth position. It was beyond belief that the triple European champions were sinking like a rock in the league table. It was a critical moment and Bob Paisley needed to do something quick. One thing he could do was change the leader on the pitch, in the hope that performance would improve.

In team meetings, analysing their matches, Thompson often took the blame for goals conceded. Bob Paisley saw what was happening – that his skipper took the blame for mistakes he had no control over – and he realised the captaincy was weighing heavily on him.

'Let's give the captaincy to Graeme for a while, see what happens,' Paisley said.

'No you won't!' Phil was fuming. 'Why are you kicking me out, Bob?'

'First of all, I think it will be good for you, that you will get back to your best form. Secondly, you take on too much responsibility. You blame yourself for every goal against us at the moment. You're letting the responsibility weigh you down.'

The New Year had just begun. Liverpool's players were on the bus from Melwood going to play away against Swansea in the third round of the FA Cup, a tough match. Thompson was seething. He had not exchanged a single word with Souness, whom he felt had stolen the captaincy from him. And he was especially hurt because some players on the team had known about the change before him.

'I hated losing the captaincy,' he admits more than three decades on.

They were ready to go out on the pitch, but Thompson was still fuming with anger and disappointment. It was a cold war between him and Souness. Before Thompson became captain, he used to be the last one out on the pitch. Now he was ready to once again fall back into that habit, instead of having the honour of leading the team out. He was at the end of the row, waiting for everybody to pass him. Joe Fagan came over and grabbed him by the arm.

'Phil, listen, I know that…'

'Never, ever, tell me how to behave when I'm out on the pitch!! When we're at war on the pitch I'll fight by his side, but don't tell me what to do in my private life! It doesn't affect my game!'

Fagan pulled his hand back. Phil is certain that he had guessed exactly what Fagan was about to say: that he would have to put away his personal agenda and concentrate on what was happening on the pitch. The players went out, it was a tough game, but they crushed all Swansea resistance and won 4–0.

'It was a difficult match, but we still won convincingly with Graeme Souness as captain, and I played my best game in a very long time,' he says. 'But I was still angry. I was an angry young man on the pitch, who still did what Bob Paisley wanted. And that led to an unexpected side effect: a burning wish flared up, a desire to get better. I improved my game overnight to show Paisley he'd made a mistake giving Souness the captaincy.

'In fact, this was leadership at its best. Making tough decisions for the best of the collective and the club. And you know what, when I had time to think about it, I realised he was right. It made me see that I had indeed taken on too much responsibility when I shouldn't have. I had blamed myself even when it wasn't my fault. [After losing the captaincy] my performance went from a six to an eight or nine in every match. That's psychology for you! And it had another good side effect: we went on to win the league, even though we came from twelfth place!'

How long did it take you to get over your loss of the captaincy?

'I wish I could say I was so professional I got over it right away, but I didn't. Souness and I didn't talk for months.'

How did it influence your role as motivator on the team?

'I held back a little. It wasn't my job any more. But still, captain or not, I was one of the senior players with the longest experience, so I had a motivating role nonetheless. I read the game, I talked to the others, moved players around. It was difficult for me to let it go after Souness became captain. On the pitch I was still the same, shouting and giving orders. But in the dressing room and in training I had changed. I lost some of my bite for a while. And my relationship with Souness was strained for quite some time, but then things returned to normal and we went back to being friends.'

Their friendship turned sour again when Souness returned to the club as manager in the early 1990s and fired Thompson, who was reserve team manager at the time. The notice of dismissal said he yelled too much at the reserve team players, and that he impeded their progress.

'It was the legacy from Joe Fagan, Ronnie Moran and Roy Evans,' Thompson reasons. 'The way I worked was their normal form of communication. I inherited it from the Boot Room boys.'

Liverpool FC was your life. How long did it take before you reconciled yourself with the fact you had lost your job at the club?

'I never did. Liverpool was part of me. I was dejected, depressed. I didn't go to matches at Anfield. That was hard in itself. I had a shop in Liverpool that I worked hard in, and after a while I started working for *Sky Sports*, who had just started airing Premier League matches. It was great to get to see lots of football with them.'

It took a few years before he returned to Anfield. It was a difficult time for his whole family.

'When I lost my job at the club, I decided to tell my kids what had happened that weekend, before they went to school on Monday. They were only seven and ten years old. It really hurt when Souness fired me, and it was painful for my family and my sons. And it was unbearable to hear what they'd gone through in school because I'd been fired. They cried, they were broken-hearted. At that moment I decided I would never talk to Souness again.'

What haunted you later?

'Insecurity was the worst. Especially a few years later, when I found out that he had questioned my loyalty to the club. I thought: How and why could you doubt my loyalty? I was speechless. I just had to try and move on in life. Feeling that someone mistrusted me, Phil Thompson, hurt a lot. And not least did it hurt my family, who had also enjoyed being part of Liverpool FC. I love Liverpool FC, from a coaching perspective too, and I thought I was there to stay for many, many years as a coach. I was passionate and loyal. It was heartbreaking to have somebody doubt that.'

Later he got the chance to come back and be assistant manager to Gérard Houllier.

'I don't think anyone could have been more loyal than me,' Thompson insists. 'When I was caretaker manager, while Gérard was ill after his big heart operation, I told the press outright that I was only looking after his job until he got back. A very good and loyal partnership grew up with Houllier. That's how it was: we were good friends and loyal coaches.'

It would take fifteen years to break the silence with Graeme Souness. The breakthrough came at the funeral of Sheila Walsh, the club secretary who had served under Souness, Roy Evans, Joe Fagan, Kenny Dalglish, Bob Paisley and Houllier. They all attended her funeral. The ex-managers were on the front row, including Thompson, who had been in charge for six months while Houllier was out because of his heart trouble. Before the ceremony, Phil and Graeme met. They shook hands out of respect for Sheila.

'When we left the church, he came over to me and shook my hand again. He said: "We have to start talking again. We've behaved like schoolboys all our life."'

Thompson accepted his hand and said: 'Yes, we have.'

4

GRAEME SOUNESS
A LEADER IN GOOD AND BAD TIMES

'Souness was the engine of the team, the cogwheel... probably the best captain
I've ever played under.'
Phil Neal

DECEMBER 1981. SHOOTING EXERCISE AT MELWOOD. GRAEME
Souness leans against the goalpost and teases the players who are testing their new
goalkeeper, Bruce Grobbelaar. Souness is struggling with an injured ankle but still
comes to training. As training continues Bob Paisley strolls over to him. He has an
unexpected proposition. 'Would you like to be the new captain?'

Souness was not expecting that. Liverpool have been flailing in the league and a
3–1 home defeat to Manchester City on Boxing Day has left them in twelfth. But
there had not been the slightest hint about a change of leadership.

'Yes, of course I would, but I think a couple of others are in front of me,' Souness
replies, still leaning against the post. He is thinking primarily of Kenny Dalglish
and Phil Neal, who are both older than him and have been there longer. He believes
Paisley should consider them first.

'No, no! I want you to be the new captain!' Paisley says, adamantly.

'What?! OK, yes, I'd love to be captain.'

Many of the former Liverpool captains interviewed in this book consider Graeme Souness to be Liverpool's greatest captain and, indeed, the greatest midfielder in Liverpool's history.

Having been fed steaks as pre-match meals and rehydrated afterwards in the players' lounge, Souness – at the height of his powers – moved to Italy and picked up a lot of new ideas, helping him understand what it takes to make footballers more athletic. He brought these back with him when he returned to Merseyside as manager in 1991. With that arrival came new training methods and new diets; ways to make you a better footballer, ways that were a little too innovative for Britain at the time. Not least a traditional club like Liverpool.

Souness does not do half measures. He throws himself fully into projects or not at all. He has always expected others to embrace the same attitude.

An extremely popular Liverpool player, he was not viewed in the same way as a manager. Graeme Souness seldom gives interviews about this period, a time from which his reputation has never fully recovered.

It is 10 January 1978. Graeme Souness is 24 years old and has just arrived at Liverpool for the first time. A few months earlier they had lifted the European Cup for the first time. He had been signed to replace a club hero, Ian Callaghan. Unlike others, such as Terry McDermott and Ray Kennedy, there is no 'trial period' where he is expected to bide his time in the reserves. Both of those players had a year to adapt to the club: part first team and part reserve before they were moved to senior status on a permanent basis. But Souness is straight in there, replacing the man who has played more times for Liverpool than anyone else. The prospect of this happening did not intimidate Souness.

'I was so happy and excited, it turned me on that I was going to play for such a glamorous team,' he says. 'But I wasn't going to feel inadequate playing for a team like that. I never sell myself short.'

No, you seemed to have such great confidence…

'I've asked myself where this confidence comes from. There is no obvious reason for it. I was the youngest of three brothers, so there was always a support group for me if you like, growing up. As the youngest you're always getting the best treatment. You're the baby, the bairn, as we say in Scotland. My mum and dad always called me that, the bairn.'

The boys are four years apart. Graeme was born on a spring day in 1953. His mother was very strict, but his father followed his youngest son closely, and made him feel very, very special. That built confidence. And his mother taught him discipline.

'As the third child, I think my mother tried to make good the mistakes she'd made bringing up my big brothers. Not that she did anything wrong with them, they're good guys, but it was as if she'd practised on them on how to bring me up. I had a great childhood, and I believe being the youngest is the single biggest reason why I had such an inner calm and belief in myself.'

But there were more advantages to being the youngest. It meant he always had someone to play football with in the street outside their prefab home in the Saughton Mains area of Edinburgh, a house that was supposed to be temporary because of the shortage of houses in Scotland after the war but ended up his home throughout his childhood.

'I had the advantage of always having someone to play with who was better than me, because I got to play with my older brothers and their friends. Whatever sport you're in you'll improve if you have to play against somebody better than you all the time. They will pull you up to a better level. So again, I was lucky to be the youngest.'

A lot of footballers who have made it as professionals have been in the same situation: they have had older siblings to challenge them, Ian Rush for one. His big brothers let him play with them, and they did not go easy on their kid brother, he had to join in on their terms. That helped a little boy to become very good. The regimen is the same for so many aspiring players: training a lot when young; playing with those a little older; training, training, training – for hours every week. Then maybe you can make your dream come true one day.

Souness's father had also been a great football talent, with a good left foot. A fracture in his leg put a stop to any football career, but it was something to be grateful for: his leg broke only two weeks before his regiment was sent to France during the Second World War. While he could not make it to the front, many of his fellow soldiers never returned.

At fifteen, Graeme signed an apprentice contract with Tottenham, after playing for his local club North Merchiston. Tottenham got an unusually self-confident Scot in their team. When the young Souness saw the level of the other players, he could not understand why he couldn't get a chance in the first team. At seventeen, he would always go over and look for his name on the team sheet that was put up every Friday. Alan Mullery, the captain, would be on the list, of course; and Martin

Peters too – he had won the World Cup with England. And the rest of the first team. But no Souness. He kept knocking Bill Nicholson's door asking why his name was not on the first-team sheet. But no one ever told him to be patient, or wait until he got his chance.

Tottenham loaned him to Montréal Olympique in 1972. It gave him a chance to prove that he really was good, it was not just his opinion of himself. He responded by playing himself into the NASL All Star team. Feeling that Tottenham did not seem willing to give him a chance, in December 1972 he accepted without hesitation an offer to join Middlesbrough.

Souness stayed there for five years, and helped the team to promotion in his first full season – the 1973/74 campaign. He matured into an outstanding midfielder under the tutelage of another legendary hardman taking his first steps in management – Jack Charlton. Yet Souness's own experience of not being taken seriously as a young player at White Hart Lane bore a lasting impression. Two decades later and beyond he went on to give a lot of young players that chance when he was given managerial responsibility in the English top flight.

The year before Souness joined Liverpool, waves of shock had washed through Liverpool supporters when Kevin Keegan, the club's first genuine superstar footballer, had announced he was leaving to join Hamburg. His departure precipitated a period of rebuilding. Kenny Dalglish became the new number seven, bought from Celtic for what seemed the staggering sum of £440,000 in summer 1977. Alan Hansen, the Partick Thistle defender, was signed for £110,000. Now they had a Scottish star player in attack, and a Scot who was a calm and safe passer, who knew how to dribble his way forward out of defence (a trait which sometimes made the fans wish he would make simpler clearances). All that was missing was a new midfielder, and with Souness's arrival the following January the Scottish influence would be complete.

Souness slotted in immediately. His first months at Anfield were a resounding success. As well as entering the first team immediately, his first goal for the club, an elegant, long-range shot against Manchester United, was voted Liverpool's goal of the season. After only half a season in a red shirt, he was part of the Liverpool team that retained their European Cup.

The three newly acquired Scots quickly hit it off. They teamed up in the dressing room, and quickly gained respect and became a dominant part of the team both on and off the pitch, because they were great players and strong personalities.

That day in December 1981 when Souness was asked to take over as captain, the situation was different from the continued success he had so far encountered in his four years at Anfield. The team was in a crisis, down in twelfth place in the league. Yet with Souness as captain, the fortunes of the team shifted. Looking back now, he swears he did nothing different to his predecessor Phil Thompson, aside from being the first one on the pitch instead of the last. Yet somehow he led his team from mid-table to the League Championship in half a season. So something must have happened. Something crucial.

Although now, all these years later, Thompson says Paisley did the right thing, that his performance had dropped, and that he took on too much responsibility as captain, at the time he was left heartbroken and furious by the decision to strip him of the captaincy. Souness, however, was without remorse.

'That was none of my problem,' he says now. 'I can honestly look back and say… that I never thought about how disappointed he must have been. Maybe it sounds harsh or insensitive, but I can't recall giving him a second thought.

'He's a local boy. This was the club he'd played for since he was fifteen or something like that. Maybe the responsibility was too much for him. I only got to the club when I was a man. But any way you look at it, our manager did the right thing.'

He remains adamant that nothing changed in him when he became captain.

'I didn't go through any obvious changes, no. The only difference was, I was the first one out the tunnel, and I wore the captain's armband. Did it change the way I played? I don't think so. Did it change me as a person? Did I become more vocal? I doubt it. Did I change in the dressing room or in training? I think the answer to both is no. Back then we didn't fully understand the responsibility of becoming captain, and what it actually meant to be captain for one of the most important football teams in the world. In that area football has changed dramatically. In my time, even though I captained both Scotland and Liverpool, I was never asked my opinion in the dressing room or in meetings. That was coach and manager territory.'

But didn't you give messages to the players?

'No! When I got the responsibility all Joe [Fagan] said was, "Do your own job." If that went well, and I had time, I could help the others. But I had to do my own job first.'

When pressed again, he finally admits one small change: as captain he had to deal with criticism amongst the other players if Liverpool had played a bad match. Although that did not happen a lot during his captaincy, the turnaround after he took over as leader on the pitch was spectacular. Liverpool went on to an incredible, point-collecting run that would have knocked the wind out of any opponent.

Can you explain this? How could such a turnaround happen? Was it how you led and inspired the players with your own performance and attitude?

'I've no idea! I can't remember changing anything.'

So there it is, Souness still insists that he did nothing. No changes to the game. No changes in communication. So it is all still a mystery…

The Scottish influence on Liverpool at this time was tremendous. There were many strong personalities on the team, but the three Scots, Dalglish, Souness and Hansen, were among the loudest voices in there.

Liverpool's coaching staff had noticed, of course.

Imagine being a fly on the wall back then when the three Scots ruled the legendary changing room area. What would we have seen?

'Criticism was severe,' remembers Souness, 'as was the humour; nothing was out of bounds, perhaps except when the younger lads were pulled into it. Since Liverpool was the best club in Europe – arguably in the world – the dressing room was a harsh place where you were on your own. You had to fend for yourself. And us three Scots became a unit, so we weren't easy to pick on.'

There must be something in your character or personality from a very young age that makes you the kind of leader who can set off a turnaround like that, with such strong personalities in the team. In addition to confidence, what was it that made you such a great player and captain.

'You'll have to ask somebody else that.'

But what do you think? The will to win?

'Yes, I think everybody will agree to that. I probably disliked losing more than most.'

Hating to lose is an incredibly strong motivation in sports. You give that little extra when you have no energy left, you work harder when you fall behind, you never give up. And you never expect to lose. You need to really hate losing to have the mindset of a winner.

'All the greatest footballers have really hated losing.'

And if you want to be the world's greatest footballer, you cannot just hate losing, you must also love playing. Look at Luis Suárez. Every time he was taken off the pitch to be rested ahead of the next game, he looked despondent.

'All the top players I've come across have loved to play. That doesn't mean they loved all the training without a ball, but as soon as a ball was involved, everybody was happy.'

Confidence, then, the will to win and a love for the game – these are all important ingredients. But I am still trying to figure out what else is needed to become a captain and player of Souness's stature. But Souness is not giving anything away. He is tough as nails when the conversation turns to his role as captain, because of his solemn conviction that he was no different as a captain than as a player.

'Please don't try…' he says, surprisingly modest, and gives me a smile. It prompts me to laugh. Perhaps his initial short answers reveal Souness's modest side and, indeed, a contrast to his public image.

Well, you're obviously stubborn too, and stubbornness can be a driving force to perform well, but can it also be a challenge when you're a leader? That you want one thing, and are determined to see it through, even if the rest of the team wants something different?

'It stems from my childhood. I was spoiled rotten, and got used to getting my way, and it sticks with you the rest of your life.'

He smiles.

What about your temper, you've always had—

'… a ridiculous temper, yes.'

How has it been, living with that?

'I'm over it now. I'm older, wiser, and on medication. The medicine is for my blood pressure, I've got heart trouble. No, I think you learn from your mistakes. If you don't, you're a fool. I was foolish and stubborn. It helped me in my time as a player, but not so much as manager… I was extremely confrontational.'

Doesn't that mean you also have a strong sense of justice?

'Not everyone will see it like that.'

From your point of view, I mean. Presumably you wanted to prove you were right?

'No, I like to think of myself as a team player. I was the type of player who was asked to look after the younger players. Boys who were more technically gifted than me, but who lacked the experience. I always stood up for my team-mates, and they for me. We were a proper team back then.'

That probably also answers the question of why Bob Paisley chose you as captain. You think about and care about the whole team. You see, I'm trying to find out what makes someone good captain material. I find you all have some things in common.

'We do?'

Yes – the will to win, and caring for others…

'Well, I don't think you'll meet a single footballer at a certain level who hasn't got a strong will to win! But some feel it stronger than others.'

Another common denominator for a lot of the Liverpool captains is an excellent debut. Traditionally, the best player on the team was chosen to be captain, and the best often got off to a good opening game, building confidence for the season and helping the debutant on his way.

Graeme Souness got off to a good start. His debut was against West Bromwich Albion away, and he played convincingly in a game they won 1–0 with a goal from David Johnson. But his first home game was not so good: Liverpool lost 2–3 against Birmingham.

However, losing did not become a habit for Souness. Far from it. His six years at the club were very successful, as he picked up five league titles, three European Cups and three League Cups. Liverpool had triumph for breakfast, lunch and dinner.

'In our days, winning was natural. It was both expected and taken for granted. Joe Fagan and Ronnie Moran were far ahead of their time as coaches,' he says. 'They were constantly on to us, especially Ronnie. He made us work even harder by telling us we were good, but not as good as former players or teams had been. Ronnie was in your face and very direct, while Joe was a little more subtle. We were so keen to prove that we could be just as good as former players had been.

'Obviously we were, but the coaches wouldn't let us feel like it.'

Although he was Liverpool's most successful manager, Bob Paisley is regularly mimicked by the footballers who played under him. They share stories about how he struggled to string words together in coherent sentences. Souness describes him as quiet; that his actions spoke louder than words. Paisley, he says, did not want to get in an argument; he might even let someone think they had won the argument, but then they were sold at the end of the season.

'He was ruthless, because he had to be. At the same time he was a smiling sort of grandad to all. Nice and quiet.'

Paisley was known to be clumsy with words, but Graeme saw him change from being nervous talking to more than one person to practically relish talking to a crowd in his last few years. He eventually turned into a comedian when faced with an audience. Words came easier with practice.

What did you learn from Bob Paisley's leadership?

'We knew he watched players like a hawk. If they had two bad games in a row, he'd study them closely, try to figure out what was wrong. Today they'd be stomping their feet if you play two bad games in a row. Transfer talks start, agents come in, the player is the talk on *Sky Sports News* and in the papers. Luckily it wasn't like that back then. Paisley would rather try and get to the bottom of why a player wasn't performing well.'

Paisley gave surprisingly little instruction to his captains. He never gave Souness any orders to pass on to the rest of the team. They were simple, almost trite comments, like: 'Go out and see if you can win the toss today,' or 'If you're having a good day, help someone else.'

This was the mantra for everyone on the pitch. If you have a good day, let it benefit your team-mates, put in that little extra for them.

Souness needed little instruction on how to accept and lift trophies because it was a process he'd become accustomed to so quickly. But when I ask him what it feels like to walk up those steps first, as captain, and lift the trophy in front of a sea of people, his answer surprises me.

'There was no difference going up first, as captain, nobody was better than the next man. You made a career at Liverpool, you became a senior player and it was expected that you were just like your peers. When Ronnie [Moran] was upset with us he'd call us "bigheads". In Liverpool it was expected that you didn't think you were bigger than the team, and that you were considerate of your team-mates.'

It finally dawns on me why he has been so short and reserved in his answers to questions of his captaincy. He played at a time when Liverpool's players were drilled with the notion that they were all equal, and equally important. They all stood up for each other, and fought for one another. It was the 'Liverpool way'.

'I would hate if a former team-mate of mine said I changed when I became captain, or said the captaincy made me a different person,' he admits. 'I would have been incredibly disappointed with myself in that case.'

What would you say is your proudest moment as a captain?

'Winning trophies. But still, even though I won the European Cup three times, once as a captain, we won the league all three years when I was captain. Three years in a row. Winning the league gives you a different type of recognition to winning the European Cup, the FA Cup or any other cup. Winning the league means you've worked incredibly hard and dealt with the difficult periods of the season better than any other team. It means the big personalities in the team have fought extra hard and dragged the others with them.'

Just imagine: league champions three years in a row, with the same captain; a captain who ended his Liverpool career by leading his team to a European Cup triumph. With nothing left to win with Liverpool, he ventured to Serie A – then the wealthiest and best league in the world – where he joined a star-studded Sampdoria team. After two seasons there he was appointed player-manager of the club that once contained some of his childhood heroes – Glasgow Rangers, the team he supported growing up – they had suffered years in the doldrums, but Souness transformed them into the most formidable club outfit in British football.

Regardless of Souness's insistence that he did nothing different as Liverpool captain, leadership remains something a person develops over time. The more you lead, the more responsibility you are able to carry. Having captained Scotland and Liverpool when the latter were the best team in Europe, Souness was exceptionally well equipped for the job as player-manager for Rangers when they came calling in 1986.

Are there any similarities between being captain, player-manager and manager?

'I'm sure there are lots of ways to answer that question, but one thing is crucial: you have to be a football person at a certain level. If you're not a good player, you won't be accepted as captain. It's not enough to be a fantastic guy and have a way with words. The players won't respect you. If you're a top football player, but not a very nice guy, it's just as bad. The players in the team won't want you to be their captain. So you need good playing and social skills. It's the same in management. If you've been a good player, you understand more of the players' challenges. It will give you a head start as boss, better than if you've never played top-level football yourself. But the pressure of a manager is something entirely different. You don't learn much about that as captain.'

How did you manage to keep your mind in both places as player-manager?

'It would be impossible today. There's too much going on. But I was lucky, Walter Smith was my assistant. And again, my personality helped: I thought I could do anything. I was bold, confrontational and I always got away with it… just about!'

He smiles again.

Souness became a star on the team and the boss at the club he had been a fan of since he was little, but at times he was furious. Explosive. At the referees too, which sometimes ended up in a red card. Where did all his aggression come from?

'I was so passionate about winning. I wanted us always to do our best to win. Always. And that applied to everyone.'

Inside Souness there was a constant, burning desire for victory. That often set off a lot of anger and other emotions. Yet despite the volcanic eruptions, he succeeded overwhelmingly in having his mind in two places, and his legs on the pitch for his team. A strategist and an anchor in midfield, in the five seasons he led Rangers, they won the league three times, knocking Celtic off their throne. With Souness in charge, Rangers became Scotland's leading team, but were also at the forefront of a century-long cultural shift. After years of one-way traffic of the best Scottish players going to England for higher salaries and status, some of England's best players started heading to Scotland. In the aftermath of the Heysel Stadium disaster, English clubs were banned from competing in Europe and it led to many star performers exploring their options. At one stage in the late 1980s Rangers had more England players than any English club.

'There was also the Hillsborough tragedy. The Taylor Report determined that all stadiums in the top division had to be all-seaters. As there wasn't the kind of money in football then as there is now, a lot of clubs had to spend money they would normally buy and pay wages to players for, to rebuild their stadiums. At Rangers we'd already had the Ibrox tragedy in 1971, where sixty-six supporters died, so our stadium was already rebuilt. We had a financial advantage on the rest. Besides, all English teams were banned from European competitions [after the Heysel disaster in 1985]. That was to our advantage. Timing means everything in football.'

After his fairy-tale success as boss of Rangers, Liverpool re-entered the stage. The shadow of the Hillsborough tragedy became too much of a strain for Kenny Dalglish and in February 1991 he shocked the world of football by resigning as Liverpool manager.

Liverpool needed a new boss, and tradition dictated that it would be someone who knew the club. Some thought perhaps it would be Roy Evans' turn. But instead, the club chose to offer the job to Souness, who was convincing in Scotland, and already well known and respected in Liverpool. At first, Souness turned Liverpool down. But the board were persistent and managed to convince him.

Yet despite his Anfield roots he brought a moderniser's steak. There was his knowledge about nutrition and new training methods learned in Italy. Under his watch the legendary Boot Room – the space below Anfield's main stand that had served as a sort of strategy den – was rebuilt, and turned into a press room after new media facilities demands when Premier League was introduced.

Expectations were high of the returned former captain and midfield anchor. He made a surprise move by appointing the recently acquired Mark Wright as his captain, despite the many experienced players in the team, like John Barnes and Ian Rush. He gave a lot of young talents their first chance: Steve McManaman, Robbie Fowler and Jamie Redknapp can all thank Souness for their first-team debuts. He also sold off a number of experienced players that he felt were too old, or who did not seem motivated to play for Liverpool. Souness wanted to clear out the mess and build a new winning team. But the results failed to appear.

'I inherited a very old team at Liverpool,' he says when explaining his faith in youth.

The young players got their chances, he says, only because they were good enough and had the personalities to handle the pressure. Disappointments helped make these boys stronger, and they proved early on that they had it in them, that they could succeed. Because elite football is constantly testing you, you have to be able to handle the pressure of expectation, the criticism from fans and the media. And these blossoming talents, despite their young age, largely passed the test.

'The way these youngsters performed, and the careers they went on to make, says it all. It was the right thing to let these young talents get a chance at the club.'

Despite giving the young boys their chance, Liverpool faded under Souness's management. During his time there, as well as afterwards, he was criticised for selling too many experienced players too soon. Liverpool had always had the tradition that the oldest and most experienced players in the club taught, helped and looked after the younger players, in a very practical 'pass it down' manner.

'When I returned to Liverpool, the team had too many old players. They had lived through the Hillsborough disaster and all that followed from it. This was a team going nowhere, a squad that wasn't going to win any more trophies. But I tried to renew the team too quickly, I readily admit that.'

Souness has detailed in other books that he left Liverpool when he was a player because Sampdoria made an offer for him and the club accepted it. As a manager, he not only sold the players he felt were past their prime at Liverpool, he also let players go who did not express a strong enough wish to play for the club, and wanted to move on. Souness hated that: players wanting to leave Liverpool. How could anyone want to leave such a fantastic club?

'When I was a Liverpool player, I would have turned down any offers, including Real Madrid, Barcelona, Juventus or Manchester United. That's how big a club Liverpool was at the time. So when players talked about leaving Liverpool, I was upset and annoyed.'

Out of frustration, he asked players who had hinted they might want a transfer to be gone the next day, rather than telling them to wait until he had found a replacement. That left Souness with too little time to find players who could replace the ones who left. And some sales and releases he regrets.

'I shouldn't have sold Peter Beardsley, Ray Houghton or Dean Saunders,' he admits. 'And I shouldn't have sold Steve Staunton. But as Irish he was considered a foreigner, and back then UEFA put a limit to how many foreigners you were allowed at a club. So that's four I obviously sold off too soon. That being said, Dean Saunders never said that, he didn't want to leave.'

Souness was also criticised for introducing a new nutrition and training regime. A lot of what he wanted to introduce in the squad is a matter of course today, like cutting out huge steaks as a match preparation, and introducing pasta and other foods rich in carbohydrates. He also worked a lot with endurance training and running, to improve players' physical shape, but ended up with a lot of injuries on the team. John Barnes and captain Mark Wright were two key men who often missed games through injuries.

Yet there were good times too; just not with the unrelenting frequency he had known as a player. One important and grand trophy had eluded Souness in all his years as a Liverpool player: the FA Cup.

In 1992 he led the team to the FA Cup semi-final, where Liverpool were drawn with Second Division Portsmouth. But then came the shock: Souness, who had always lived a healthy life and watched his diet a long time before that was common in football, was diagnosed with a heart condition after a routine check-up. Not because of anything he had done – it was rather what he calls 'bad Celtic family genes.' He explains to me that people of Celtic origin have more coronary problems than the average Brit. The pressure he felt as manager of Liverpool couldn't have helped. Whatever the reaons, he needed an urgent operation. It was very dramatic.

In the middle of the shock he agreed to be pictured in *the Sun* when they visited him at the hospital with his girlfriend, on the day of the semi-final replay against Portsmouth at Villa Park on Monday, 13 April 1992. Souness says the agreement was that they could only print the photo the next day if his team won the match.

'I knew that *the Sun* wasn't terribly popular [on Merseyside],' he explains. 'But I was in Scotland with Rangers during the Hillsborough tragedy, I didn't realise the strong feelings Liverpool supporters and the club had against the paper. While I was there, some people on the team had a column in the paper. But I knew they wouldn't be pleased with me for giving the paper the exclusive to my heart surgery.'

A succession of unfortunate circumstances heightened the controversy: The match went into extra time, then a penalty shoot-out, which Liverpool eventually won. In the meantime the tabloid reporter had missed his print deadline. So the exclusive on Souness, the article from the hospital, was printed on the Wednesday instead of the Tuesday that they had agreed on. That meant it was published on 15 April – the third anniversary of the Hillsborough tragedy. It really could not have been any worse: a Sun exclusive with the Liverpool manager pictured in a hospital bed on the most sensitive, painful date imaginable.

That controversy was why it became so important for Souness to show up at the FA Cup final between Liverpool and Sunderland at Wembley the following month, despite his doctor's warning. Souness jeopardised his own health by watching the match from the dugout, though Ronnie Moran was in charge on the day.

'If you look at photos from Wembley, they speak for themselves. I look sick and frail,' he says. 'I realised I'd shot myself in the foot being interviewed by *the Sun*. This was my way of dealing with the situation, to be at the final. But I shouldn't have gone.

'To this day a large percentage of Liverpool supporters dislike me. It's something I've got to live with. I've asked for forgiveness many times. It was the biggest mistake of my life. That's the thing I regret more than anything in my life.'

Liverpool won the FA Cup, and when Rush scored to make it 2–0, he set the record of having scored five goals in FA Cup finals. The FA Cup was some comfort and a triumph in a season where Liverpool ended sixth, their lowest position in more than twenty years.

Everything comes to an end. Even for iconic Scottish superstars. When Kenny Dalglish stepped down, he said being manager was weighing him down because he felt he needed to know the answers to every question himself. Souness felt that it was the responsibility as manager, as the lonely man on top, that got to him. He often lay awake at night wondering if he had made the right decisions: Are we buying the right player? Did we sell the wrong one? Did I pick the right team today? Did I make the right substitutions? Was I too hard on him? Was I not harsh enough?

'I couldn't just leave the office, shut the door and have a break till the next day,' he admits. 'My mind would be on the team and Liverpool twenty-four hours a day. The entire time I was awake, I would feel that responsibility. The feeling that everything comes down to your decisions. It's a lonely old job. Even though I had very competent people around me, in the end it's not much help. Not even when they offer to share the burden with you. You end up carrying it all on your own shoulders. That's how it is being a leader.'

Souness's departure from Liverpool as manager was protracted. He believes now that he should have resigned after the 2-0 victory over Sunderland in the FA Cup final. Instead, he carried on for another eighteen months. Results got worse and after losing to Bristol City in an FA Cup replay at Anfield, he decided to go.

Souness was a player or player-manager at the highest level for some twenty years. He continued as manager for another thirteen years after leaving Liverpool, until 2006 when he was sacked as Newcastle manager. For more than 35 years he was involved in top football but since then he has made his living as a pundit. There has been no way back into club football, though this is not a regret. He enjoys his punditry work with *Sky Sports*.

Perhaps you only have a certain amount of fire in you before the flame dies out? Gordon Strachan introduced this idea to Souness.

'Gordon believes we all have a certain amount of fire in us,' he says, 'and for those of us who started around nineteen, the fire will go out quicker as manager, than for managers like Mourinho or Wenger [both had very limited professional playing careers], who didn't begin to burn theirs until they became managers in their thirties. It's an interesting perspective.'

No eternal flame, then. Based on this hypothesis, one day every leader will have burned up their fire, at least in football. But what sort of leader does Souness see himself as?

'I like to think that I'm a leader who leads from the front, and that I'm a leader who wouldn't demand something from others that I wouldn't have done myself. I'm a leader who lets people know when I'm happy about something, and if I'm not. Clear communication. It's the way I was brought up and that's how I am. That's why I decided eight to ten years ago that management wasn't for me any more.'

Did all the confrontations make it too hard?

'Oh no, that was never hard, that was easy. But football management doesn't work like that today. You can't be as direct, as confrontational. If you fall out with one player, you lose half the dressing room. The players today are much more independent than they used to be. When I was in my thirties I'd won all there was to win. I'd captained both Liverpool and Scotland. But still the coaching staff made the calls, they never asked us for advice. Now you'll have a twenty-year-old who's played something like ten games, giving his opinion on what's best for the team. Football has changed a lot like that.'

In your opinion, have young players in top football today got a problem with perspective? Do they think they're superstars before they have proved anything?

'Of course, that's a big problem. That's what football has evolved into.

Souness says the public has to blame themselves for this development. We are the ones who have put the players on pedestals. People like to elevate these young talents, but tear them down if they do not live up to expectations.

'There has never been a better time than now for professional footballers. It's not the players' fault, not even the clubs. It's the fans who worship these young talents and make them what they are.'

But what about the money, the astronomical sums the players get, even before they've won anything – is that also a problem in modern football?

'Yes, that's another problem. But again it's not the players' fault. People are falling over themselves to give these players enormous sums. It really is a fantastic time to be a footballer. And I can't put my hand on my heart and say that if I was earning £300,000 a week at the age of twenty-five I wouldn't have changed.'

Steven Gerrard was captain for twelve years, he's made a lot of money. How would you compare captaining in his time versus your time as captain?

'I'd much rather have my three years as captain than Steven's twelve. We were obviously a far better team. We won so much and it gave us a fantastic position as a club. It's not about how long you live, is it? It's about how you live your life.'

5

PHIL NEAL
ENDURANCE, COURAGE AND UNITY

*'Phil Neal was a fantastic captain… Even though he isn't a Scouser,
he loves the club with a passion.'*
Ian Rush

PHIL NEAL IS NOT ONLY THE MOST DECORATED PLAYER IN Liverpool's history but also one of the club's hardest working ambassadors, speaking about his experiences at Anfield wherever he goes. He works at Anfield every home game, entertaining guests of the club in one of the hospitality lounges. He also works as a tour guide, chaperoning supporters around the stadium on weekdays. He tells tales about Bill Shankly, Bob Paisley and Joe Fagan as well as all the players he shared a dressing room with and all the trophies he won.

Indeed, the first player Paisley signed after taking over from Shankly was Neal, who he bought from Northampton Town. He could have gone to Tottenham Hotspur at fifteen, but made a promise to his father, who was on his deathbed, to finish school first. Instead he joined his local team, Northampton, who at the time were dropping through the divisions. As the years went by, Phil began to doubt his dream of playing at the highest level.

Finally, at the age of 23, Liverpool scout Geoff Twentyman recommended that the club should sign him. Neal's versatility had impressed Twentyman. During one scouting mission at an away game at Rotherham, Neal had volunteered to play in goal after Northampton's goalkeeper fell injured. His fearlessness was noted.

The message that he should drive to Liverpool and sign came at such short notice that he did not tell his wife, Sue, who was in hospital suffering from hypertension following the birth of their second child, Ashley. Indeed, Sue was not informed about the move until after the papers had been signed.

'I signed them on the spot,' Phil says now of what marked the start of what was to become a highly successful career.

Neal proved to be one of the most consistent and loyal players in the club's history. He would give the next eleven years of his life to Liverpool FC and at the end of that extraordinary period ended up with 23 trophies to his name.

But for Sue, the feeling was completely different. The sudden change of scenery from Northampton to Liverpool put her into an eighteen-month-long depression. It was tough on her, leaving what she had previously known, while at the same time remaining at home with two young children while her husband was away, giving his all for football.

'I wish I'd seen how ill Sue really was. The tremendous pressure she was under, at home with our two rowdy toddlers, without the help of our parents, who lived so far away,' he says. 'My head was up in the clouds, and I just wanted to win more in the red jersey. After seven years at Northampton I finally got to live this adventure. Eighteen months later I was playing for England too. The fact I ignored how sick she was, pains me. It's my big regret in life.'

Despite the fact that Liverpool FC are still Phil's life and job, Sue still hates football.

Every week, sometimes several times a week, for most of the year, Phil Neal speaks about his incredible years at Liverpool. Years that contained more success than most professionals in the history of the game could ever dream of.

So where did the success come from? What made Phil Neal special? Some of the answers lie in defiance and willpower. He gave all he had to hold on to the number two shirt for as long as possible. Thanks to the Boot Room boys, who did anything they could to arrange things for him when he was injured so he could continue playing, he felt like an important man on the team. When he broke his toe, they found him a shoe a size and a half bigger that fitted around the bandaged foot so he could still perform at the expected level. After express surgery on his fractured cheekbone he was told to take a six-week break, but Paisley lured him back on the pitch the following week, with the 'excuse' that he just needed to mark one tiny fellow; 'so it ought to be OK'.

'By including me on every team he picked, Bob Paisley gave me that great feeling,' Neal says. 'Me, an ordinary Northampton player until recently! It was fantastic.'

A hunger for success, for playing time, for not missing out. The feeling of belonging. The feeling of being an important piece of the big puzzle. The feeling of being indispensable. All of this led Phil Neal to an endurance record in English top-flight football, one it will be difficult to beat: for Liverpool he played 417 matches in a row. He managed to play every single game in the First Division for seven years, from 23 October 1976 to 24 September 1983. No forced resting, no stretched muscles, no stomach flu and no fever could ever stop him. And his performance never dropped to the point he was left out of games.

He simply refused to let injury and illness stop him. He has sacrificed more than just a little pain and a lot of sweat during the course of his career. He now 'beeps' his way through all airport security checks; his hip was worn out and has been replaced by a metal one, something he has to explain over and over while metal detectors scan his body before every flight.

Back to the beginning. His debut. At Anfield, no less, a reserve team game against Everton – before the big city derby at Goodison later that day. A lot of supporters had made their way through Stanley Park to see the reserve reds and blues as a warm-up for one of the highlights of the year in the city of Liverpool.

But it would all turn out differently for Neal. As he was getting ready for the reserve team match in the dressing room at Anfield, one of the coaching staff came over and said Paisley wanted him with the first team at Goodison. Great, Neal thought, they'll let me sit on the bench and maybe people at home will get a glimpse of me on TV! He never dreamed that he would be making his first-team debut in the great match.

The year was 1974, 16 November, and there were hordes of people walking to Anfield through Stanley Park. Neal wondered where the car was that would take them to Goodison, but he was told to wrap his football boots in a brown paper bag and put them under his arm. He would be walking across the park to Everton's home ground.

'I almost couldn't get through for all the people asking me if I had a spare ticket!' Neal laughs, thinking back to his short walk from one great stadium to another.

To his massive surprise, Bob Paisley met him at the other end, and said, 'Get ready to play, son!' And that was how Neal made his debut for Liverpool's first team, alongside Terry McDermott. Two debutants in the big derby. Tommy Smith was playing right-back, so Phil Neal made his debut as left-back.

In the dressing room before the game, Emlyn Hughes gave them some encouraging words, in true Shankly spirit, before they entered the pitch. 'He really was the Shankly type,' says Neal. 'He always had an inspiring message before the match, giving us the energy we needed to go out and put in a performance. He was always the last man to speak, we took his words with us, and they would always include a "Come on, we can do this".'

After the match, both red and blue supporters could go to work with their heads held high, because it ended in a goalless draw. And Neal could heave a sigh of relief that his defence had kept a clean sheet.

The tone of voice was always friendly from captain Hughes before a match, but the feeling among some of his team-mates was not always the same. Smith was not on speaking terms with Hughes, who had taken the captaincy from him. Their relationship was at freezing point and it was no secret. Neal, nevertheless, cannot praise his first Liverpool captain enough.

'I loved Emlyn, and I liked the way he handled the captaincy. He was so motivated and hard-working, both in training and matches. It inspired the rest of us. Emlyn loved scoring goals, and was good at boasting both of his own and others' achievements. He was quick with a joke and made a lot of things more fun. All of this in stark contrast to his predecessor and enemy, Tommy Smith, who was a knight in armour and always ready to fight you, armed or unarmed.'

For the first three years on the team Neal did not say much. He listened, observed and learned. By the time Neal himself was chosen as captain he had experienced a decade-long apprenticeship. During these years he had the privilege of learning from Smith, Hughes, Kenny Dalglish, Phil Thompson and Graeme Souness, all of them different as leaders and as instructors. Dalglish only led the team out on thirteen occasions, though.

'Kenny didn't enjoy being a captain,' says Neal. 'He was honest about it. He'd rather score goals and teach Rush and Whelan to do the same.'

Did it have anything to do with shyness?

'Possibly. But he was confident enough to take over as the lead striker after Kevin Keegan, who had made the brave decision to try his luck in German football. What happened next just goes to show what great leaders we had at the club: we won the European Cup for the first time, and Kevin was sold to Hamburg. Kenny comes to us as his replacement. And only three months after we pick Kenny up from Celtic, we meet Hamburg and Kevin in the Super Cup, UEFA's match for the winners of the European Cup and the Cup Winners' Cup. Kenny was fantastic for us up there.

He was a different type of player to Kevin, but then we were a different team. We were so motivated. And we won the match.'

A new captain had to be found. This time, Neal had the pleasure of playing under a local captain with a burning passion for Liverpool: Phil Thompson.

'I admired Phil Thompson because he was a local player, full of passion and mettle. He was a local, and led [from the] front. People forget what a great leader Thommo was. He led us to victory in the European Cup, a trophy he then took off with! He really was an excellent captain, and I still look up to him. He's got the same Scouser courage and energy that Tommy Smith had. They've got so much zest, it's the reason I love being with Scousers, and still live here in Liverpool.'

Neal is convinced local captains have an advantage in the job. It gives them an extra dimension and a higher status.

'For others, it takes time for the fans to fall for you. Even with Kenny Dalglish. But if you're a local player, you've already got your own supporters on the Kop. Tommy Smith, Phil Thompson, they all did. It gave them an extra push forward. The fans were backing them from day one.'

Whether it was in training or before matches, the local players did the important job of getting the other players to understand what Liverpool meant to people and to the city, even in an insignificant match at the end of a long season. It was always full speed ahead and no fooling about.

'Liverpool Football Club is huge. When you come from the outside, like Souey, Kenny and me did, you don't understand the power of such a club. We had to learn that from the local lads. I gave my extra match tickets to Thommo the first five years. He knew so many locals who wanted to come. I was happy to help them get in. They deserved the tickets more than me.'

Thompson never tired of looking for tickets for his brothers and mates. One of Neal's favourite stories from his time at the club is from the final game of his second season at Liverpool, Bob Paisley's second season as a manager. Paisley was under tremendous pressure. He had to win something after taking over from Bill Shankly. They were playing away against Wolverhampton Wanderers. If they won, they won the league; it would be Paisley's first league championship.

But Wolves were not going to lie down without a fight. They needed to win at home to stand a chance of keeping their spot in the First Division (and hope that Sheffield United beat Birmingham City). There was, of course, an unbelievable demand for tickets. Phil Thompson spotted his brothers outside the stadium, and asked Paisley if they could possibly let his brothers and a few mates come in via the dressing room through the back door. Nobody would notice, Thommo assured him.

Paisley was keen not to upset anyone on such an important day, and agreed. In the meantime, rumour had spread among the travelling red fans that it was possible to get in through the dressing room. So when Paisley opened the double door from the dressing room, Liverpool fans poured in. He had no chance of holding back the deluge.

Whenever Neal tells this story, he leans forward, one foot in front of the other, pushing an imaginary double door with his shoulder, and recreating Paisley's agonised face.

A lot of people passed through, while the manager shouted, 'Thommo, how many relatives have you got?!'

The memory from that day still makes Neal laugh. The day would turn out to be a milestone, a turning point for Paisley. Liverpool won and it marked the start of a big haul of league championships and other trophies. It was a historic day for Neal too; he won his very first medal. A couple of weeks later, Liverpool won the UEFA Cup, and in the years to come the club would gather trophies, one after the other.

Until that season when things did not look like working out. The winter of 1981. One of the measures to try and change Liverpool's poor form was to remove Phil Thompson as captain and replace him with Graeme Souness. Neal got to witness his second harrowing conflict between two important Liverpool players about the captaincy. And for the second time, the sacked captain was a local lad. There was an icy front between Thompson and Souness.

Souness and Neal sat next to each other throughout their Anfield careers. They talked a lot, and would still kick each other when England played Scotland.

'Souness was brave, tough, demanding,' Neal says. 'He was an elegant talker, and a cogwheel in everything that went on. He helped out in defence, created width in the game by serving the wings, and threaded the ball through the middle to play Kenny free. He was a driving force on the team.'

Neal describes Souness as a captain with great power and impetus. He was brave, and usually quiet. From time to time, someone still had to be on hand to tell Souness in plain words when big things were at stake. Neal points to the meeting with the 'Butcher of Bilbao', Andoni Goikoetxea, at the heart of Athletic Bilbao, in the second round of the European Cup in 1984. Liverpool did not manage to score at Anfield against the Basques and it turned into an extremely physical night: around a dozen players were involved in a brawl.

Before the return game, when they had to score to progress to the next round, Joe Fagan, who had succeeded Paisley as manager, made his mind very clear, talking to Souness in front of everyone: 'I saw you creating havoc at Anfield. If I see you once come in too late on a tackle on Goikoetxea, you'll be on the bench next to me in a matter of seconds!'

Fagan could not risk a conflict between two players in such an important fixture. In addition, San Mamés was a dreaded stadium to play at – Bilbao had not lost a match at home for two seasons. Every time Souness was in possession, he was met by jeering. But he had a fantastic game and dominated completely, totally overshadowing the butcher. Souness won the duel by a mile and Liverpool progressed to the quarter-final thanks to a goal by Ian Rush.

Neal says it was brave of Fagan to confront his captain like that and in front of the rest of the team.

'There were always four or five senior players who were willing to stick their neck out to help the youngsters on the team. Help them grow to become good people and good players, like Ian Rush and Ronnie Whelan. One day the reward would come in the shape of good players and a tight-knit team. You're playing on a Liverpool team full of England players, but they made sure that you – like them – kept your feet firmly planted on the ground. And all of these players were supporter-friendly. We were at one with the Kop, and they were singing our names.'

It took a while before the Kop started singing Phil Neal's name. But in 1981, they gave him the nickname 'Zico'. And Neal felt it was a big honour to have his name chanted by thousands of supporters in unison.

'It gives you such motivation and purpose, being in a city with people like these. Playing for them is like building a house. First you need to build a foundation wall. That's built during the first six months of the season. And that's how we won so much. We didn't fall off course or lose our sense of direction during those first months. We stuck to our plan and kept focus – and won. And the times we lost focus, we found our way through having a captain who led us back on the right path.'

One by one, important leader figures left Liverpool. Tommy Smith left, and Neal took the right-back position. Then Phil Thompson left. At this stage Neal fell into a leading role on the team. As one of the oldest and most experienced, he helped the youngsters and new players integrate, and made them understand what Liverpool expected of them.

'It's a little like raising kids. I had seven or eight years at the club where I would guide and help players develop.'

For many years, Neal dreamed of becoming captain. So when Graeme Souness left for Sampdoria in 1984, there was finally an opening for him. Neal thought: *I wonder who will be the next captain. Do I stand a chance?* On the first training in July after the holidays, he was called into Joe Fagan's office, and the manager got right down to business.

'You can lead us. You're experienced. You've been here for almost ten years. You've been a good role model, you lead [from the] front, you've achieved fantastic things for us, and you've got the ability to give people feedback and praise, or put your arm around them if needs be. But you can also bark. You deserve the captaincy.'

Phil Neal accepted the job immediately.

'Finally I was appointed captain, after I had watched, learned from and been led by all these other captains who were so different, but who had all been such good role models to us, each in their own way: Tommy Smith, Emlyn Hughes, Phil Thompson, Graeme Souness and Kenny Dalglish. And I'd also learned a lot from both Joe Fagan and Bob Paisley. I greatly respected the way they led the team. They were almost like teachers, you know, when you love geography just because your geography teacher is so good. That's how my leaders at Liverpool taught me to like football even more. They made our lives as footballers even more enjoyable.'

Fagan was without a doubt the most important leader in Neal's career. He was always honest with his criticism, even when sometimes it hurt. Fagan could also be a very charming man. He was attentive, and would dish out compliments at times, both to players and their wives.

It would be an understatement to call it direct communication. The best example of how a thunderous Fagan speech could turn performance radically around came in the Christmas period of 1981, when the team was really struggling. Paisley was building a new side. A young Ronnie Whelan was working on his collaboration with Ian Rush. Bruce Grobbelaar was new in goal that season. But the new squad did not function. Phil Thompson's days as captain were numbered. What happened next, has become one of Neal's favourite stories.

'I tell this story to everybody, whether I'm in Norway, touring Anfield, or travelling with the Liverpool legends. It's a true story, I'm not making anything up. Joe Fagan was Bob Paisley's assistant manager. They were very different types. Bob would talk to us in confidence if we needed a good talking-to, while Fagan was more direct.'

For weeks, Fagan had been worried about the team's development and steadily descending form. They were sinking like a rock down the league table. After losing to Manchester City on Boxing Day, Joe was fuming. They had played the Club World Championship a few days before and lost 3–0 against Flamengo. Nothing was working, and Fagan gave them a right scolding in the dressing room after the match against City. But that was nothing compared to how he berated them after training the next day. Fagan came in and told them Paisley had given him permission to 'speak freely' to the senior players, with the exception of Whelan and Rush, who were new on the team.

'He beat us up, each and every one, in turn,' recalls Neal. 'He started with Souey, then went on to Kenny, before Grobbelaar had a verbal hiding. Then he took the rest of us, one by one, and he told us in no uncertain terms how he felt about each and every one, dwelling on our weaknesses and inadequacies.'

The room was deadly silent while Fagan drew his grim portrait, one player at a time. Neal was told he was more keen on rushing forward than to defend the goal, and all four in the defence were told they were a disgrace to the team. They all sat there, in wide-eyed shock, while he continued the scolding, in detail, player by player. Since he had started with the best players on the team, the rest of them were just dreading what he would say about them.

Finally he summed it all up: 'I'm sick of your excuses. To be honest, you haven't played well enough the last six or seven weeks to deserve the red kit! But now I trust the senior players to get their act together. It's not all lost if you pull yourselves together. I know you can do better. But you need to up your tempo in training and in matches. There are twenty-five matches left to prove it. I won't be having a single meeting with you between now and May. I can't stand any more excuses. No more bullshit!'

On the bus going back to Melwood, the squad agreed that Fagan was right. So sometimes maybe brutal honesty is what it takes to turn results around?

'I'm proud to say that, of the twenty-five games we had left, we won twenty and lost only two,' says Neal. 'We were twelfth on Boxing Day, a few months later we won the league.'

He will not take the honour away from Bob Paisley for leading the team to yet another league championship in 1981/82, but he wants to underline that the lambasting Fagan gave stuck with the players. They often talked about it later. They have also talked about how well he deserved the success he got when he took over as manager from Paisley the following year, and led the team to a triple triumph in the 1983/84 season, Graeme Souness's last year as captain.

'It was great to be able to give Fagan what he deserved: a treble, three years after the dressing-down he gave us. It was great to be part of something that worked so well.'

✦

But one final would destroy it all for Fagan, and rob both him and the club of more success with him at the helm. That would also be the day when Phil Neal lost the joy of being captain.

On 29 May 1985, Neal was ready to play his fifth European Cup final, well aware that the four previous ones had been pure demonstrations of power. If they won this too, Liverpool would get the most sought-after trophy of them all, to have and to hold. And all of that in just eight years.

But this time it was different. He was going to lead the team out, just like Emlyn Hughes had in 1977 and 1978, Phil Thompson had in 1981, and Souness had the previous spring. Now, finally, it was Neal the trophy collector's turn. It would be his mission to lead the team on the pitch to defend the honour won in Rome the year before. He would have to stop Juventus from scoring at the Heysel Stadium in Brussels.

Trouble, however, was brewing on the terraces of this crumbling arena. Twenty minutes before kick-off, the situation got completely out of control, bottles and rocks were thrown in the stands, there was violent, aggressive shouting and fighting. It was complete and utter chaos. The so-called neutral zone was far from neutral, and there was just a small fence separating the Juventus fans from the Liverpool fans – that included hooligans, who had turned up just to cause problems.

And then things took a turn for the worse. A whole retaining wall on the terraces collapsed during the disturbances, with fatal consequences.

First, Fagan was sent out to try and calm the furious masses. The sight of him, as he returned to the dressing-room, is one that Neal will never forget: 'I saw the fearless Joe Fagan with tears rolling down his cheeks. He was such a strong man, but he was in shock, and just sat down in the dressing-room, hiding his face in his hands. He couldn't speak.'

Next, Neal, as captain, was sent out with a microphone, on the same errand. UEFA gave him a sheet with some statements they wanted him to read. He turned them down and said something from his heart instead. The feeling of not getting through was deep and traumatic.

Thirty years later, it is still difficult for Phil to talk about that day, when 39 people died after the wall collapsed, specifically 32 Italians, two French, four Belgians plus one from Northern Ireland. The youngest victim was only eleven years old. Tears roll down his cheeks when Neal recalls that terrible day.

'Back in 1985 it felt completely meaningless that we were going to play a match in the chaos. Kick-off was delayed for one hour. Every second was shocking to us. I watched what happened with my own eyes. Our dressing room was very close to where thirty-nine people so tragically lost their lives.'

There and then he thought: *Why do we have to play this game? I don't want to go out there. I don't want to lead the boys out on the pitch. I don't want to be pressurised like this to lead the team. No!*

'I don't understand why nobody did anything afterwards. No investigation or anything. I just don't understand. Why have I never been asked [by the authorities] what I saw? I've never been asked to give evidence. I've never been asked my opinion. Nobody has been interested in hearing my opinion, and it has worried me all these years.'

After the tragedy, English teams were banned from European competitions. Liverpool received the most severe punishment and were not allowed to compete in Europe for six years, at a time when Liverpool had one of the best squads in history. Neal says he still regrets, as a captain on behalf of the team, that he did not refuse to play the game.

'To put it like that, if we had refused to play, then who'd have gotten the blame?

How much responsibility do you have to put on yourself as captain? Do you think a captain would have been able to stop the match? Is it fair to yourself to feel so guilty?

'Well, I tried. When I learned about the disaster, I said, "No. Let them have the trophy." What I really wanted to say, was, "Can I go and get my family now? I just want out of here. I don't feel like doing anything at all here any more."'

The players' families were seated near to where the dead bodies were lying. The players feared for their safety. It is impossible to imagine what it must have been like, having to play a football match – a European Cup final – while dead bodies were being carried out of the stadium.

The final eventually kicked off, over an hour late. Liverpool played because they feared how the crowd might react if they didn't. But it was inhuman to be expected to put in a performance on the pitch. Liverpool lost 1–0 to a late penalty, but it was a match that should never have been played.

'It was the wrong stadium, picked by the wrong people. It wasn't our stadium, but they blamed Liverpool anyway. We had to bear the brunt for UEFA's wrong choices, and a lot of good players from Liverpool and other clubs lost their chance to play in international top football for the period that Liverpool was banned.'

Neal and Fagan took the experience of Heysel hardest among the Liverpool camp. They had been closest to what happened, and had taken the responsibility of trying to calm down the rioting Liverpool supporters. The day after the final was also challenging for Neal, who had to meet the press alongside Fagan. What do you say after an experience like that? How do you find words that can in any way describe such a horrible, dark day in the history of football?

'I just wanted to dig a hole in the ground and not come out for six months. We knew what had happened. It was horrendous. It hurt so badly.'

For Joe Fagan it was too painful for him to continue his job as manager for the club he had served and loved for so many years. He had thought about retiring before Heysel. After the disaster, the joy and motivation was gone.

Neal was not impressed with the way his own country's government dealt with the Heysel tragedy.

'I'm so sorry for everyone who lost somebody in this tragedy. But the way I see it, Liverpool FC wasn't to blame. I think it was an outrage that Maggie Thatcher said what she said later. She banned English teams from competing in European competitions for five years. Here she is, leading a country, her own England, and what she did just wasn't right. I'm still shocked at what happened. I would have been a better person today if I could have given evidence in an investigation, me and club director Peter Robinson. It's a very grave matter that none of us have had to swear an oath and describe what we saw that day.

'In a way I've managed to get over Heysel, inasmuch as you can ever get over such a horrible disaster. But the fact that so many people lost their lives in that ramshackle stadium is still way beyond my comprehension. I've never been the same after that.'

It also took from him the joy of captaining Liverpool – what was his biggest dream. When Joe Fagan stepped down, Kenny Dalglish was appointed player-manager. For several years, Phil had feared that Steve Nicol would take over his number two shirt, and in October 1985 he did just that. Two months later Neal's adventure with Liverpool was over when he joined Bolton.

'I'd felt under pressure from Steve Nicol for four or five years before I actually had to give up the jersey,' he says. 'That determination made me give everything I had for so many years, and I think a lot of other Liverpool players were the same. Tommy Smith: raw, always willing to fight. Emlyn: just as keen, but a different type of player, happy, energetic. Kevin Keegan: never stopped running. For all our differences, we had two important ingredients in common: courage, and unity. It made us a hell of a team.'

6

RONNIE WHELAN
PERSONALITY SHIFT

'He's got humour, but he definitely wasn't fun on the pitch!... He could do it all.'
Mark Wright

'I'LL ALWAYS REMEMBER AS A KID FROM DUBLIN, GETTING UP early in the morning every FA Cup final day, to watch everything that happened on TV, till the captain lifted the cup at five o'clock. Imagine, then, walking up these steps ahead of Hansen, Barnes, Beardsley, Aldo, Houghton, Rushie. All these amazing players from Liverpool Football Club, and you're one of them. You, the snotty little kid from Dublin, you were never gonna make it, and now you're a Liverpool player. And you're the one walking up the steps who gets to hold that cup up. It's what you dreamed of since you were a kid: and now you've done it. You lift the cup and think again: Yes! I did it. I won that cup. It was great, it was great.'

The year is 1989. Liverpool have beaten Everton 3–2 in the FA Cup final. The Hillsborough tragedy has happened a month before. Captain Ronnie Whelan has taken the trophy home for Liverpool. These are emotional times. In this proudest moment on the football pitch, his proudest moment of captaincy, his closest supporter, mentor and friend is watching. Before he passes away, Ronnie Whelan senior gets to see his son lift the FA Cup, the most famous trophy of them all.

✦

I meet Ronnie Whelan in his lovely, warm home in Liverpool. He's at the kitchen table, facing his first and (so far) only grandchild. The boy is in a high chair, and gives us a big smile. His hair is dark and his eyes almond-shaped. Grandad helps his daughter with the logistics while she is at work. His wife is away playing golf. While he prepares baby food to the two-year-old, Whelan jokes that he is trapped while everybody else is out having fun.

On the wall behind the table is a photographic gallery of the closest people in his life. In the middle – the biggest photo – the entire family is running towards the camera with big smiles. Around them are gold-framed children's portraits; enlarged memories from skiing holidays, cruises and golf; siblings, relatives and wedding magic. It's a gallery that reflects the close-knit environment in the Whelan household.

The phone rings and I am left in charge of feeding the grandchild of a Liverpool captain. He opens up for the food. I wonder if he has inherited his grandad's genes, and if one day he will run out on the pitch as captain for a great football team.

It is not unthinkable. This little guy already has a dedicated grandad who will have a kickabout with him even in the manicured green space outside. A grandad who has the house full of crystal and precious metal, all won in at the highest level of club football: a grandad who has an FA Cup final match ball signed by the team on display in the wall unit. It is a rare trophy, and it is his because he was captain that day.

The little tot's great-grandad, Ronnie Whelan senior, was a respected player in Ireland. He was a forward and an important part of the successful years of St Patrick's Athletic FC in the 1950s and 1960s. Ronnie senior was also capped for Ireland, and it goes without saying that the Whelan family lived for football. His father took Ronnie and his little brother Paul to matches from when they were six years old. From the back of the bus they had an early taste of life as footballers, happily munching sweets offered by the physiotherapist. Little did they know they were glucose sweets, meant to fuel the team's performance. To them, it was their Saturday sweets and the treat of the day.

Whelan senior's clubs became second homes to his boys, who were allowed to potter about along the goal line, and maybe kick the ball a little, before and after matches. The two little ones would drink in the atmosphere and the mood on the way home, with its ups and downs depending on what result the lads brought home. Both boys went on to be footballers after having had their childhood practically soaked in football.

'If you talk to people who saw my dad play in the early 1960s, there are a lot of good things said about him,' Ronnie says. 'My dad was a very, very good player, what in those days was called an inside-forward. He really knew how to play. He had a chance to sign for Chelsea when he was eighteen, but returned to Ireland because he was homesick.'

Homesickness would turn out to be a family trait, and Ronnie junior would experience it too. Had homesickness taken control, his Liverpool career might never have happened.

Was your dad a lead character in the team?

'No, I don't think so,' Ronnie replies. 'Not that I recall, at least, and I can't remember if he was ever a captain. He was a lot like me, laid-back, placid. As a kid I didn't talk or shout a lot. But if something needed to be said, my father would speak out. Joe Fagan was the same. He didn't speak a lot, but when he did, people listened.'

Ronnie no doubt inherited his football talent from his father, and Ronnie senior's mother was also a football enthusiast. Ronnie junior's paternal grandmother was bedridden when all her grandchildren grew up, but she followed their football achievements eagerly, both those of her son and her grandson. Ronnie and his grandmother made a pact: she put money aside in a jar for every goal he scored. At the end of the season she paid him in secret.

Ronnie talks about his great childhood. He went to good schools, had good people around him: Rosemarie, Ann, then Ronnie, Paul and little Janice; Ma and Da. Seven people shared three bedrooms and only one bathroom. It was not easy to provide for seven, so both parents worked a lot. His father started out at the metal factory and later worked at a sports and leisure centre. His mother worked in various shops. The children got new clothes and toys for Christmas. Ma was the strict educator, and Da the playful and funny one. They were a very close-knit family.

'We still are to this day. All my parents' kids and grandkids get together a lot. I miss out on quite a few gatherings since I live in Liverpool. But the family gathers for parties and great occasions. Christmas is huge for the family. Everybody will get together in one house, and there are more than fifty of us. When I grew up, we were never an extended family like that. I would be with one or two cousins at a time, never the whole family. But the family after Ma and Da is very, very close.'

When he talks about his family, Ronnie's face lights up.

Would you like to move back to Ireland?

'I'd go back today. But my wife's parents are here, they're in their seventies and she won't leave them. And our kids grew up here, so it's not going to happen.'

You cannot overstate the advantage it is to a boy, growing up so close to football. Jamie Carragher went with his football coach dad, Jamie Redknapp tagged along with his. It gives you extra knowledge and motivation, spending your childhood in a football setting. You see the dedication, the commitment, the hard training – but also the team spirit and the laughter. Ronnie Whelan cannot thank his father enough for how important he was in helping him reach his dream of professional football.

'We were friends, me and my dad. We got on really well. He was a huge influence on me, on most things I did. He had me involved in football from when I was very young. He was always helping me develop. Whether it was in the garden, telling me what to do: "Use your left foot by banging the ball off the wall for as long as you can." Whatever he asked me to do, I would do to the best of my ability.'

What do you think you learned as a player, and a leader, from your dad?

'The one thing he always said to me was, "If you give a hundred per cent whenever you play, nobody can ever question you." I brought this into my career. Every game I remember, I never tried any less than a hundred per cent. It was always: This is it! We're gonna win this game! I don't know if this is why – ever since I was a kid – I'm two different people on and off the pitch. As a kid I would sit in the dressing room and say nothing, but as soon as we were on the pitch, I'd be pointing, barking commands and telling everyone where to go.'

Ronnie stayed this way as a player through his teens, on the school teams, at Home Farm in Dublin, through all his years at Liverpool and on the Irish national team. He would always be quiet in the changing rooms, incredibly nervous sometimes, but nevertheless bent on winning, loud, vociferous and with a strong sense of responsibility as soon as the game started.

'As captain I'd go around and say good luck to everyone, say what might happen in the game. But, I would have done the same thing if I hadn't been captain. Kenny could have given the honour to Steve Nicol, it wouldn't have changed the person I was. Kenny was the same. He was offered the captaincy, but preferred to let Thommo or Souey have it. He took on just as much responsibility even without the armband. And he didn't want the hassle of all the other captain's tasks, off the pitch.'

He believes it was the same with all the Liverpool captains he played with. And each one would shout and be unmistakably clear about their feelings when something went wrong.

'I never went on the pitch thinking, oh, there's Kenny Dalglish or John Barnes. If any players made a mistake, they would get it, I'd have a go at them. And they would shout and swear back at me, but we'd have a laugh about it after the game.'

Whether he was captain or not, Whelan felt he was free to make changes on the pitch. At Liverpool, the captain had licence from the boss to alter plans during matches. His great ability to read the game came in handy, as well as his skills at registering where his team-mates and opponents were at any point in time, and the ability to see openings as the game developed. Ian Rush once said, 'If you freeze the game at any given moment, and ask all players to stand still, Ronnie could tell you exactly where everyone is, without looking.'

'I think this was my strongest asset as a player, I had a sound knowledge of what happened all over the pitch,' Ronnie agrees.

When Whelan signed for Liverpool in the late 1970s, he joined a very strong squad that was full of leader figures and captain material.

'Thommo was captain, Nealy was captain, Kenny could have been captain, Souey was captain and Jockey (Alan Hansen) was captain. With five or six captains on the team you learn a lot about how to train and what is expected of you.'

The team of the era was a well-oiled winning machine. Some years Bob Paisley would use only sixteen players throughout an entire season.

A small squad like that must have been an advantage when it comes to playing together, getting along – passion and togetherness?

'Yes, I'm sure it helped us, but I still think the difference from today is how international football has become. Now there's a Spanish clan, a French clan, an African clan, an English clan... In my time, the team-mates were Irish, English, Scottish and Welsh, and a couple of others – Craig [Johnston] from Australia and Bruce [Grobbelaar] from Zimbabwe.

'It made it much easier to form friendships and bond. If you told a joke, everybody would understand. We all spoke the same language. Now someone tells a joke in Spanish, and only two or three others will get it. The aspect of international players – so many different cultures and customs – I think that's why they don't go out together, or maybe they do sometimes, but we went out a lot in our spare time.'

Whelan believes this aspect will challenge modern football more than people realise. Subtle differences in commands on the pitch might get lost. Misunderstandings arise, and not least the intention behind those commands.

'I'm not shouting at you because I don't like you. I may not like you, but I would have said the same, in the same way, even if I did like you!' Whelan used to tell his team-mates.

Even though it is harder to communicate among the players now, he believes it is still easier for players to communicate on the pitch than to chat in the changing rooms. You can always point and gesture. He knows what he is talking about, from his experiences as a manager in Greece and Cyprus.

'I was really tested on how hard this can be. I tried to speak to my players, but I don't speak Greek, so I had an interpreter. And I think a lot of the time what I said was lost in translation. Things could go completely wrong.'

Ronnie Whelan grew up as a Manchester United supporter. In the 1960s, most of the kids in Dublin were United supporters because of Johnny Giles who debuted for United already as a teenager and George Best, the Northern Irish winger who became English football's very first true superstar.

Some experiences are so strong the impact stays with you forever. They make you see the world differently. For Ronnie's part, this happened when he was seven. Manchester United were visiting Dublin to play against the Irish national team. It was August 1968 – only ten weeks after the team had won the European Cup final at Wembley.

Whelan's father knew some of the Irish players on the Manchester United team – Shay Brennan, Tony Dunne – and he managed to sneak his boy into the changing room before one of the friendly matches. Here Ronnie junior stood in the corner, quiet as a mouse, admiring the stars. Not a word left his mouth (dressing room behaviour that would stay with him; always a man of few words).

Ronnie wanted to be George Best. So when he was invited to train with the club over the holidays a few years later, he felt like fortune was smiling at him. Manchester United had talent scouts in Ireland who visited school and club games. A scout called Joe Corcoran visited the thirteen-year-old Whelan and asked him if he would travel over to Manchester for a couple of weeks.

Meeting United's big stars on the training grounds inspired him. He met Gerry Daly, Sammy McIlroy and Dave McCreery; all of these were familiar names and of course he gave it his all in training. They must have spotted something early on, because the United coaches invited him back to train over the holidays for several years.

When he was fifteen, he was offered a trainee contract. But, just like Phil Neal's father had done, Ronnie's father said he was too young; he had to wait till he had finished school. Ronnie junior's disagreed – he feared that no other team in England would want him later, that this was his only chance.

Ronnie continued to train with United for periods until the year he turned eighteen, but there were no more offers of a contract from them. In the meantime, interest had started to trickle in from other clubs.

'There were several clubs in the running. I tried out for Coventry, they offered me an apprenticeship, and also for Everton and Celtic. Celtic wanted me to sign for them.'

But then Liverpool arrived, just in time. They offered him a two-week trial in pre-season, and managed to snatch Whelan from right under the nose of Celtic.

He signed for Paisley and Liverpool on 19 September 1979, just a week before his eighteenth birthday. He did not hesitate for a second. Now was his chance to find out if he was cut out for playing full time in England. He had signed with a top team, and he realised it would be hard, but was not prepared for just how hard.

He really struggled to settle in at the start. He was a home-loving, Irish teenager and missed his family tremendously. Homesickness was harsh.

'They don't prepare you for leaving home, you're only seventeen. They put you up in digs and pay for six months or so, the rest is up to you. It's pretty rough, it's up to you to grin and bear it, learn to be independent. That way the club finds out if you've got it in you to tackle the pressure.'

A lot of the other young players of about his age, with whom he competed for a place on the team, had spent a few years at the club already. After a while he found out that a lot of them were nice to him to his face, but slaughtered him behind his back.

'I just wanted to go home.'

But he was also aching to play top-class football in England. He was torn between the dream of a professional career and living closer to home. Liverpool gave him four flights home a year, and he also got to go home for Ireland Under-21 games. Every time he was over in Dublin he decided he did not want to return to Liverpool; he wanted to stay where it was safe, friendly and where his family was.

Ronnie Whelan offers a friendly thought to players who arrive in England nowadays from even further away. He can imagine how hard it must be, the pay they receive notwithstanding.

'You leave your home and your native country to go somewhere completely foreign, where you feel like an alien. You have no idea what goes on around you.'

Luckily for Ronnie, his father knew about homesickness from his time at Chelsea. He was very understanding, and would once again prove to be his most important supporter, this time in the battle to break free from his family, his home town and his country, where everything felt safe and familiar.

Eventually, his father made a suggestion: 'Don't come home for six months. Just try to stick it out.'

'I tried for six months, and the homesickness gradually weakened. At the same time I started playing better. I started playing for the reserves, I scored goals and did well. From then on, I stopped thinking about going home. I was offered a new contract and was in a good place.'

He decided to kick harder in training against those who had been on his back, competing for a future spot on the Liverpool team. His strongest supporter when he first arrived in Liverpool was Kevin Sheedy; they shared digs. Sheedy was supposed to take Ray Kennedy's position, but Ronnie Whelan got it. And Sheedy ended up signing for Everton. It's a life of battles…

His fight against homesickness paid off: eighteen months after arriving at the club, in April 1981, he was given the chance to play for the first team against Stoke at Anfield. There, he showed an ability that he shares with quite a few of the greatest Liverpool players in history: to play well, and more importantly score, on their debut.

It took him 27 minutes to demonstrate his abilities to the Anfield crowd by finding the net.

His apprenticeship with the reserves continued until the end of the season. Then he took over shirt number five from Ray Kennedy in midfield, and his time as an apprentice was well and truly over. He played brilliantly in his first proper season in the starting eleven, 1981/82. The team as a whole struggled throughout the first half of the campaign, but that all turned around, and they won the league title. It was the first of six he would win with Liverpool in the fifteen years he served the club.

Assists and scoring in finals became Ronnie's trademark. He started this fine tradition in his first full season in the side, when he scored twice in the League Cup final at Wembley against Tottenham, which Liverpool won 3–1.

'I scored out of desperation. We filled Tottenham's box with people and I equalised. They were getting tired and we were more and more on top of the game. With three minutes left, I did what I did for good parts of that season when the ball was played up on the right: I tried to get into the box and up to the far post and tried to score.'

It worked like a charm. There must have been some kind of positive conspiracy between Whelan and Wembley, because that is where he delivered the goods. The goal that the world remembers best from his long-lasting Wembley affair is the one against the team he had followed and supported in his childhood: Manchester United, in 1983. Another League Cup final, into extra time. It was 1–1 when Whelan got the ball 25 yards out, and the ball swerved past Gary Bailey.

'Thank God Gary Bailey had moved, leaving lots of room in the goal. It was a terrible distance to score from with my left foot. I'd come in on the left side, even though I was a natural right-footer. I did that a lot: stuck to the left side and bent it in. It's a matter of training right and then just do it in a match. Bang it in. I had practised it a lot in training. If you look back on my career, I scored a lot of goals that way.'

To this day, his goal against United is considered as one of the most elegant Wembley has ever seen.

Also on his conscience is one of English football's most bizarre own goals. Another game against Manchester United, this one in March 1990. Maybe this was Whelan's subconsciousness apologising, years later, with that long back pass towards Bruce Grobbelaar at Old Trafford, from about thirty yards out. The ball whizzed over the goalie and went straight in. Fortunately, Liverpool still won, 2–1.

The year Whelan signed for Liverpool, Kenny Dalglish captained Liverpool for a few matches. By that stage Dalglish had already managed the seemingly impossible task of filling the void after the departure of Kevin Keegan. Whelan cannot separate Dalglish the captain from Dalglish the player.

'No, he was always one to do everything he could to win matches, even if it meant screaming and shouting at everybody. Some may do that to work themselves up, but I think Kenny did it to give people a good kick in the behind; tell them what they had to do. But this was standard procedure whether he was captain or not.

Did he change when he became player-manager?

'No, he was the same fella. With the same will to win matches. Always a hundred per cent.'

I cannot free myself from thinking that it is some kind of mystery, that Dalglish enjoyed being both player-manager and manager, but not captain. I grab my chance to ask Whelan about this riddle.

'I think the responsibility of the captaincy was maybe too much for him. And that came into my way of thinking, when I became captain, I didn't want all the extra fuss off the pitch either, that you have to deal with. Things like asking on behalf of the team if you could go out for a drink, or talk to the manager if there was unrest in the team. I was happy enough with the responsibility on the football pitch, but not away from it.'

✦

In the 1988/89 season it was Whelan's turn to become captain. He could not know that during his first year wearing the famous armband two of his most challenging experiences as a captain would occur, as well as his proudest moment. Skipper Alan Hansen was injured and, ironically, he blamed Whelan for his injury.

Liverpool had a pre-season training session on a pitch with a running track around it. Whelan played left-back. The ball was played over his head, and Hansen came in sideways to catch the ball, but stumbled on the bar that ran alongside the track, twisting his knee.

'He lost most of the season to that injury, and he blamed me for pushing too far up.'

While Hansen was out with this severe knee injury, Dalglish, by now manager, decided to give Whelan the armband. The first few matches of the season went well, so Dalglish let Whelan keep the captaincy. The season went well until taking the darkest turn in the club's history.

On 15 April 1989, with Hansen still out injured, Whelan was captain for the FA Cup semi-final against Nottingham Forest at Hillsborough.

Nothing felt right when Whelan led his team out on the pitch a few minutes before three o'clock. There was complete chaos behind Bruce Grobbelaar's goal. The players witnessed how their fans were being crushed against the high steel fences that separated the supporters from the pitch. They saw desperate people being lifted from the throng of supporters to the stands above Leppings Lane.

It was a difficult moment to captain at Hillsborough. How was that day for you?

'I was the team captain, but Jockey was the club captain. I was captain on the pitch that day, but I don't think it was much different from any of the other players. We went through the same, we all had the same feelings. But whatever we went through was nothing compared to the people who were struck by the disaster. The Hillsborough families. Captain or not, we all did what we had to – or could do. We all went to different funerals. We... you know... we couldn't have every player at every funeral, so we went in twos, two to that one, two to another. It wasn't a nice time to be at the club.

It must have been so hard. So much grief...

'Yes, and... for so long... that was the hardest part. I don't think people realise how draining and tiring it was. And in that condition you had to go out and play games, that drained you even further. And we had to play seven games in eighteen or nineteen days because we hadn't played for the whole grieving period. In the end we had to play the last game of the season against Arsenal after everyone else had finished their season. And by that time we had no energy left. No matter how much I screamed and shouted commands, it was no good. Our energy had just run out. Such a long period of grief and strain.'

In the final league game of 1989, Liverpool would have won the league with a draw, or even a single-goal defeat, against Arsenal at Anfield. But with the score at 1–0 to the Gunners, Michael Thomas (who went on to become a Liverpool player later) managed to score in injury time to deprive Liverpool of the title.

'If things had been normal, we would have won that match without problem. To think we managed to win the FA Cup final during this time is an incredible feat. You really had to be there to realise just how exhausting and tiring that period of mourning was. And now I'm only talking about the football side of this, not about the families. It takes its toll at the end of the day. I really hope nobody else will ever have to go through anything similar.'

I just don't understand how you got through that season. I know playing football was your job, but still.

'Ronnie Moran was from Liverpool and it must have been extremely difficult for him. He talked to us in training, after quite a few had expressed a wish not to train and not to play matches. He said, "Listen, it's happened. It's horrible what's happened. But you're footballers! Professional football players. You've got to start playing football again. So let's start!" It woke us up a bit. We managed to get the intensity back in training, and we tried our best to get back into the game. I think we didn't really lose the league against Arsenal, but in our first league game after Hillsborough, against Everton at Goodison. It was like a testimonial to the city. We drew. I think it was 0–0. And we dropped two points that would have given us the league title. Nobody managed to get into the right mindset, how important this league match actually was. The fighting spirit just wasn't there.'

Football came second...

'Completely. Completely. And some suffered more than others. Aldo [John Aldridge] and Macca [Steve McMahon] were from Liverpool, and probably knew a lot more people than we did who were struck by this.'

I still think that, by playing matches, you did an important job. You gave the supporters something else to think about in their time of grief. That was probably the most important reason to carry on playing football.

'That was on our minds a lot. We couldn't let this season peter out because of the tragedy.'

Hansen had returned in the league match against Everton, and Whelan was prepared to return the captain's armband.

'I knew that as soon as Jockey was back, he'd want to captain again. I never expected, unless Jockey finished, that I would carry on as captain. Especially not since he blamed me for the injury.'

But Dalglish thought differently. He decided that Whelan was to continue his captaincy responsibilities for the remainder of the season.

What did Hansen think about this?

'I think he was OK with it. He never said anything to me about it. He may have even suggested it to Kenny himself, that I continued as captain until the end of the season, as I'd been for that long already.'

The most important match would turn out to be the FA Cup final against Everton. At Wembley, in warm summer weather, 20 May 1989, in front of 82,800 fans. A tragic, devastating semi-final in this cup would have to be turned into victory against their city rivals. Not much was said before the game. There was not much to say. Every single player had the same thought: this was a match they needed to win.

'This wasn't about winning the FA Cup, you see. It was about winning that match, regardless of what kind of game it had been. It was a cup final you couldn't lose.'

The match started with one minute's silence for the Hillsborough victims, and both teams played with black armbands (a tradition that has been kept up for the quarter of a century that has passed since then, in the match nearest to the 15 April). This one turned out to be unbearably exciting.

'And Everton pressed us so hard... how our lads almost had to drag themselves just to get over the line, and then went on to win the game. It was a huge job. It was our job. We owed it to the people, to those who'd gone to that semi-final, and for all those whose loved ones never made it back home. So, if we had lost that final... No, that would be unthinkable.'

Less than two years later the strain of Hillsborough brought an end to Kenny Dalglish's first spell as Liverpool manager. His successor, Graeme Souness, had once partnered Whelan in the Liverpool midfield.

'I'm telling you, he was the best player I've ever played with,' Whelan says. 'Huge influence. He made us listen. He was tough in training. He led by example. He did exactly in training as he would in a game. He was one of those characters who will go into battle, unafraid. He would stand up to anything that came at him, no matter what. He was the father figure that made sure we were all right. He kept an eye on the youngsters off the pitch too, just in case.'

Whelan was delighted at Souness's return to Anfield.

'Nobody was happier than I was when he came back as boss for Liverpool. I still don't know why it didn't work out with Souness as manager. Possibly because of some of his signings; they weren't the best. Just look at what the club's been going through over the past years: if you sign bad players, or a lot of bad players, you've no chance to do well. In Souness's time as a manager there wasn't enough top quality. He made too many bad signings.'

One of Souness's first acts as manager was to give the captaincy to the newly signed Mark Wright. To many this did not seem in keeping with tradition. Making Mark Wright captain was an exception to Liverpool's venerable captain factory: the best players, with the longest experience, would get the armband.

'I was very disappointed to lose the captaincy to Wright, nothing to do with Wrighty,' Whelan says. 'It was the way I lost the armband that was so disappointing. I'd worn number five for so many years, I felt it was my lucky number. Then I was given number twelve. I wasn't even in the eleven! I just wish Souey had come to me, said something like, "Listen, you're injured and been injured a lot. We need a captain who'll be on the pitch, so I'm gonna go with Wrighty. He's a centre-back, he wears number five, so…" I would've accepted that. But to see your own shirt on somebody else, without any warning, and then made to realise you're in the team as number twelve – you feel you deserve a little more than that.'

How did this influence your relationship with Souness?

'We got on great when we played, and we get on great now, but we didn't get on that well when he was manager. There were many small matters, and he could have been a little more diplomatic. Some of the stuff he asked me, he wouldn't even have asked a twenty-two-year-old. Things like telling me I'm not in the squad for Chelsea, then asking me to go home and pack my gear because I was going to London, and then not even putting me on the bench. Stupid little things like that. That was the type of thing Souey could have handled better as a manager.'

Whelan struggled with injury under Souness and, although he was offered a new contract by Roy Evans, he left in 1994 to become player-manager of Southend United.

When you have played more or less your whole career for one club, from your teens and for fifteen seasons on the trot, it must be difficult to leave life at Liverpool.

'Yeah, it's really bad, but that's football for you. I remember so well when Nealy quit, I remember thinking: It's so final. One moment you're here, winning medal after medal, and the next you're told, "That's it!" It really is a slap in the face. You're free to go play somewhere else, but you've got no idea what to do.'

Whelan finished playing at Roots Hall in 1996; he lost his job as manager a year later. Although there were managerial spells with Panionios, Olympiakos Nicosia and Apollon Limassol, by the age of 41 his career in professional football was over.

Whelan's managerial experiences made him realise how privileged he had been to have played his entire career in one city.

'I'd been lucky, I stayed in the same place for fifteen years. A lot of players move around non-stop, and move their kids in and out of schools. They constantly need to relocate.'

That must be tough on the families.

'It is. I first took my kids to Southend, then to Greece and finally Cyprus. It was a bit of an experience, looking back. The kids got to see different cultures. That side of it was all right.'

Through Whelan's entire adult life – both as a football player and as a football manager - up to that day, someone else had always arranged all practical matters: booked all his trips, looked after his passport, sought out any medical assistance he might need, provided the right diet. Told him how to train and how much. Given him a goal, week after week, matches to win, motivating him to take care of his body and his health. And now he would have to make do on his own.

'You're lucky if you have a wife who knows that you've got a doctor, the same the kids go to. Because right at that moment, you've no idea what to do with yourself. And then there's travelling. Who will book your flights? Who will take care of your passport? All these silly little things that you haven't had to think about throughout your entire career.

'You quit doing what you know best, the only thing you have nurtured and developed, while there are still many years left to fill after an active career. Do you stay in football and find other functions? Do you take a different education? Will you just live on the past and play golf? Maybe get a job as a football expert?

'Some people are stronger than others. Some people know that they will get past the big obstacle that leaving your playing career truly is. You know you've got kids and a family there, you don't have to drown your sorrows in drink. You've still got a few quid, you're not desolate and alone. You've still got a life to lead.'

7

GLENN HYSÉN
BE YOURSELF

'Someone you would happily go to war with.'
John Barnes

GLENN HYSÉN IS NINETEEN YEARS OLD WHEN AN INJURY GIVES him the opportunity to debut for IFK Göteborg in top-flight Swedish football. The year is 1978. In the dressing room before the match he sees the familiar faces he grew up with watching on television: his heroes. He is starstruck in the true sense of the word. The whistle blows, and he is off to a nightmare start: after 35 seconds he trips an opponent and concedes a penalty. It is 1–0 to Norrköping in front of 25,000 supporters. If only the ground would swallow him. But his captain comes over, his partner in central defence, Conny Carlsson. He pats him on the shoulder and says, 'It can't get any worse. Just get back into it!'

It is a story Hysén likes to recount.

'I've always had that little devil inside, saying, "Fight on, for fuck's sake!" I've done well in my career just by fighting. I haven't been quick or technical, I only have my willpower. A bloody strong will.'

Stig Inge Bjørnebye, he says the same thing about himself.

'Yes, but he was a better player than me. He was left-footed, a very good foot. I was never picked for the county team. From when we were thirteen, the best players were picked for these teams, but I wasn't in one until I was seventeen. By then, five or six of my mates had been on the county team all the time, because they had something. They were either quick, or technical, or both. But when you're picked at fifteen or sixteen, you have to come in fighting. Talent isn't enough. The training is harder, and more frequent.'

It takes more mentally?

'Yes! And if you've been sailing through training since the age of twelve to fourteen, and been the best without too much effort, it hits you hard at around sixteen-seventeen, when you have to start fighting. Not everybody has it in them. A lot of talents drop out. I'd had to fight hard to keep up with the others from when I was about twelve. That's why I tell all kids today, when I travel around and talk to different clubs, that even if you're not the best when you're twelve, you can be on the national team when you're nineteen.'

It's incredibly important they're told this, there is such a massive focus on talent these days. Look at Martin Ødegaard, who signed for Real Madrid at only fifteen. It's easy for youngsters to think: I'm sixteen, and I'm not even in Real Madrid! Better just quit!

'Let's hope it'll work out. That they're not squeezed out, that they're included and get to play, because you're not fully grown as a footballer before you're eighteen to twenty years old.'

Glenn Ingvar Hysén has made good use of his fighting spirit. He comes from a football family where talent runs through generations. His grandfather played top-level football, and was in the squad for two national games. His great-uncle also played in the top division, and won gold with IFK Göteborg in 1935. His paternal uncle and his father Kurt played for the IFK Göteborg reserves. His firstborn son, Tobias, played in the Swedish top flight ('Allsvenskan') for several years, and at the time of writing continues his football career in China, with his family. Glenn's oldest son from his second marriage, Alexander, has played football for many years as a goalkeeper. And his youngest son, Anton, has played professional football in the second tier. Incidentally, Anton was the first high-profile footballer in Sweden who came out as gay. Both Alexander and Anton have played for the national youth team, and their half-brother Tobias played several years as a striker for Sweden. Their father Glenn had nine years on the national team, four of them as captain.

'We had football knocked into us,' he says. 'My dad trained me when I was little. Some kids find it difficult to have a parent as coach but I didn't feel that way. He treated me like everybody else. I wasn't picked to play because I was his son, but because I was good enough.'

Football is full of stories of players who have had success and become big stars thanks to their parents, who were on the sidelines as coaches throughout their childhood. Children long to be seen and acknowledged by their parents, and they will often feel encouraged to continue a sport when one of their parents is giving their time and devotion.

'I've got three sons and two daughters. When Anton was around twelve or thirteen, he suddenly wanted to take dancing lessons. He played football too, and I was always at his training and matches if I had a chance. And then he wanted to dance. He's very good at it, he's so supple it's unbelievable. He wanted me to come and see him dance and I know nothing about dancing! But I was there, and he knew I cared. The only problem was, you weren't allowed in to watch them dance. You had to sit in a waiting room with a paper or something, you couldn't see anything. And I thought what's this? I sat there, two or three times, with my paper, waiting for him to finish. I guess he could tell that I couldn't take it any more, as long as we weren't allowed to watch them. Whether my kids collect stamps, dance or sail, I want to watch them. Not least to show them I care, even if I don't know the first thing about what they're doing.'

Anton's dancing career went well. He has won *Let's Dance* (the Swedish version of *Strictly Come Dancing*) and he has taken the hearts of the Swedish people with him.

Yet it is Glenn that attracts most attention on the street. Not only from those who were glued to the TV set for the weekly match in the 1980s. There are several other reasons why Glenn Hysén's face and voice are well known in his native Sweden.

'The older generation know their football. But sometimes a ten-year-old comes over to say hello. He doesn't know what I've done in football, but he recognises me from Swedish reality shows like Mästarnas Mästare ('Champion of Champions') or *Let's Dance*.'

You were in *Let's Dance* as well? How did it go?

'I said no for four years. I can't fucking dance, can I! I didn't want to make a fool of myself. But they pay you a bloody fortune, so eventually I said yes. I was on for four episodes. So for some people I'm known for other things than football...'

He possesses a football commentator's voice and for six years worked with EA Sports on their computer games. Sometimes kids yell at him because of something that happened on their PlayStation in the heat of a match. He smiles at me across the table: 'We read in a whole lot of sentences, and they're stored on a disk. Sometimes the wrong comments come out. "And there you are dissing me!"'

Once again, he offers a contagious laugh. Nobody can say Glenn takes himself very seriously. He is a master of self-depreciation.

✦

Glenn Hysén played for IF Warta for ten years as a child and into his teenage years, before earning the chance to 'fight on' in the Swedish top flight with IFK Göteborg from the age of nineteen. His contribution in central defence attracted attention both from other clubs and the Swedish national team. He was awarded Swedish Player of the Year in 1983, and bought by Dutch club PSV Eindhoven in February the following year.

'I came to PSV as a centre-back, and played ten matches as one,' he says. 'Then the coach, Jan Reker, came and told me to play midfield. We had two strikers, Hallvar Thoresen and Jurrie Koolhof, and they were quite short. They were scoring goals by the bucket-load, but no headers. So when a cross came, the manager wanted me to move in and head. It was a good thought, really was, and I scored twelve in two seasons, I think. It was insane, I usually never scored. But I knew it wouldn't work in the long run. And eventually I was put on the bench. I was a lousy midfielder, and I hadn't gone to the club to play midfield. I even got to play three or four matches with Hallvar Thoresen as striker! Him and me as strikers! He was so good, and me? I was crap. So I was benched again, and then I thought: I can't stay here! I can't sit on the bench because I'm a lousy striker!'

So Glenn went back to IFK Göteborg. He did not get straight back into the team and it took time to rebuild his mental strength.

'My confidence wasn't that good any more. I had to start from scratch. Fight. If I hadn't had the warrior instinct, I could have just hung up my boots. Actually, when I was about twenty-four, there was a journalist who wrote: "Hysén is done as a player." That's when I thought: Bloody journalist. I'll prove him fucking wrong! So it worked as a kick in the behind, made me soldier on.'

The fight brought results. IFK Göteborg won the UEFA Cup against Dundee United, Ron Yeats' old team, in 1987. That year he joined Italian giants Fiorentina, where Sven-Göran Eriksson, his old manager from IFK, was now boss. Glenn continued to develop, and put in his best performances when Sweden met England in two qualifying matches for the World Cup in 1990. By then he captained the national side. He was considered one of the top ten players in Europe according to a French list, and both Manchester United and Liverpool were after his signature.

'The success helped me grow as a person, and my confidence grew,' he says. 'But that's exactly when it's important to hold your horses. Not allow yourself to take off completely.'

✦

Hysén has looked up to several captains during his career, but he mentions two of them in an especially positive light.

'In IFK Göteborg, it was Björn Nordqvist, the centre-back, a generation above me. He was a bundle of energy. He would point, bark commands, talk to people – he was a giant. I saw how he was on the pitch, constantly working. I wanted to be like him.

'When I arrived at Liverpool, Alan Hansen was a huge role model. Both as a person and a player, he enjoyed enormous respect. But he didn't shout and scream. That was more Souness's style.'

But what was it about Hansen's leadership that was so inspiring?

'At that time, he was a centre-back, and he was a fantastic technical player. If you compare him to Tony Adams, Adams wasn't a great footballer. They were on completely different levels. Alan Hansen would go up in attack too, he even scored a few. He was an incredibly elegant player.'

Brave, too. It takes courage to dare play your way out of defence.

'Yes, I think it was him and Beckenbauer. But Beckenbauer was a deep libero, and would only rarely go up in attack.'

Glenn was appointed captain at the same time as he came into his prime as a footballer. He had been given the responsibility and honour already as a junior for Sweden. He thinks it is because he was extremely energetic and motivated, that he genuinely cared for people, and was good at reading them.

'As captain, you can't discriminate between your team-mates,' he says. 'But if you've got a starting eleven maybe only eight of them can take "Come on, for fuck's sake!" and can deal with it if you yell at them in the dressing room at half-time. Maybe two of the guys sitting there are nervous, then you'll have to talk to them in a different way. "Come on, we haven't been good enough. We need to up our game." You need a different tone, you know what I mean? You have to connect with people.'

Glenn thinks it is very important that the captain is outgoing.

'I've never been particularly shy. If we're out eating, or I'm out with my mates, I'm not the one in a corner sitting all quiet.'

You dare put yourself on the line. Be personal.

'Absolutely. Lots of people won't say anything at all on a night out on the town.

It's the way they are. You've got to respect that. But I'd rather have a captain who will show himself in matches, and give it to us plainly: "Come on, guys! This isn't working, we have to work harder!" I wouldn't want one who didn't speak.'

You're clearly good at getting information through, and you must have a sound football knowledge since you were given the captaincy?

'If you're not that fast, like me, you've got to read the game in a different way. You need to be a few seconds ahead of the game, know where to run, know if you need to hold back or if you should rush forward.'

Hysén thinks you have to be mad to choose a goalkeeper as skipper, and that the ideal position on the pitch for a captain is centre-back, because you see everything that is going on.

'Besides, the captain has to pass on messages from the bench. If the coach says something, the captain has to pass it on.'

Of all your managers, who used their captains most actively?

'Sven-Göran Eriksson, at IFK Göteborg and for two seasons at Fiorentina. Eriksson wasn't the shouting and screaming type. He was very calm. Eriksson was good at sharing with his captain the strategy and plans for the day both before the match and at half-time. In addition, he made sure to keep up a dialogue with the captain during match breaks, or if he was out with injury.'

Glenn was appointed captain for Sweden in 1986, when Olle Nordin took over as manager, and skippered IFK Göteborg from 1985 to 1987. In addition, he was given the responsibility as captain after only one year at Liverpool.

You had captain responsibility for a long time in different teams. Was it an extra burden?

'No, not at all. It was fun!'

✦

Liverpool were in luck. The Reds snatched Glenn Hysén from right under Manchester United's noses. And the Hysén family was happy about that; they all settled in well in the city.

'When we lived in Liverpool, both me and my second wife, Helena, thought about settling down in the city after my career, as we were so happy in Southport. But I hardly ever saw Tobias and Charlotte – the children from my first marriage – while we lived there. Three times a year, maybe, and that's too rare to see your kids. So if it wasn't for the children from my first marriage, I'd have lived there still. What an amazing city!'

The Liverpool players who lived in the same area were practically like family. They were very sociable outside matches and training, and their girlfriends, partners and wives became friends. That was very important when it came to the wellbeing of the players and even the performances on the pitch.

'When you're away from your loved ones that much, it's important that they don't feel lonely or ignored. Our partners would meet up for coffee in the mornings, and all the players' wives met up when we went to away matches. They would gather with the kids and have a few hours together in the afternoons. For Helena's part, there were four or five others in Southport that she met with every day, so she had her own circle of friends. It's absolutely vital, otherwise you feel guilty and get criticised for being away from your family too much. It wasn't on the club's initiative, the ladies started it themselves.

'When we were home, we'd all go out and have dinner together with our partners. Helena and I mostly went out with Steve McMahon, Ronnie Whelan and Gary Gillespie and their partners. Kenny Dalglish came along sometimes too, he also lived in Southport. Peter Beardsley, Barry Venison and Jimmy Carter did too. And sometimes only the lads would go out after training, to the pub for some stories, darts and pool.'

In Swedish football the tradition is that the players vote for who they want as captain. The Swedish national side does the same. That provides extra motivation as captain, Glenn says.

'It makes you even more motivated, because you know you've got the men behind you. They want you as captain. Not just the manager, but the squad. The most important thing is that you're close to the other players. What the coach thinks is one thing, what the rest of the team feel is something else. What would you do if they disagreed with the manager's choice of captain?'

At PSV Eindhoven and Liverpool, it was different, and the manager picked his captain.

'When such strong leaders as Kenny Dalglish or Svennis [Sven-Göran Eriksson] choose the captain, the players are prone to accept.'

But not always. Mark Wright got off to a rough start as captain, he was chosen by Graeme Souness. It wasn't the 'Liverpool Way', to go straight into the team as captain. Ian Rush, Ronnie Whelan and others on the team were fuming.

'I understood that when I was made captain. I'd only been there one season. One day I strolled into the dressing room, over to Ian Rush, Steve Nicol, John Barnes and Ray Houghton. The next thing I know, Kenny Dalglish comes in and hands me the armband! "Here, you'll be captain."

'What? Fuck it, there's all these other guys, Steve McMahon ahead of them all, he was expecting the honour. He was my best mate there, he and Barry Venison, so it felt a bit… wrong.'

Did they say anything?

'No. They lived next door to me in Southport. When we were out at the pub the same evening, I told him it didn't feel right to be captain. "Why not?" Steve McMahon asked. "There you all are, and I'm the captain. That's wrong. It's not like I need to be captain." "Fuck that," they said.

'The captaincy is huge in England. It's bigger than in Sweden. It's the biggest honour you can have. But I was worried they'd be pissed off with me. Although it wasn't as if I'd appointed myself as captain, was it? In the end I thought, If anyone has a problem with it, they'll have to take it up with Dalglish.'

Why did Dalglish want you as captain?

'He didn't say. He came in when Ronnie Whelan was out injured, and said, "You're the captain from now on." I didn't get an explanation.'

And he laughs again, that contagious laugh that characterises most conversations with Glenn Hysén.

The truth is that he had played extraordinarily well after joining the club in June 1989. Responsible and safe in defence, full of confidence and energy, he made a terrific debut and was voted man of the match in the Charity Shield between Liverpool and Arsenal, with Liverpool winning. But it had not been easy to come to Liverpool just a month and a half after the Hillsborough disaster. Both the team and the city were still strongly affected by it.

'It was like entering a hornet's nest,' he remembers. 'One of the first things I did was visiting a number of different people who had been affected by the tragedy. I went with other players on the team. It's unbelievably tough to see a poor soul dependent on a respirator. Severely injured people, and none of them older than twenty-five. They were all young people, their walls full of LFC shirts and pennants, and at their bedside, parents and siblings. It was unbelievably sad.'

It must have been a very special start in a new club. What did you think about it? You weren't there when it happened, but you'd probably seen it on TV?

'Oh God, yes. You can just imagine the people who were there. Everyone involved at the time. The fans, the players, the leaders. I know a lot of the people who were there. You never forget something like that. Going to as many as four funerals in a

In 1965 Ron Yeats became the first Liverpool captain in the club's history to lift the FA Cup. (PA)

Tommy Smith with the First Division championship trophy at Anfield in 1973 (PA)

Phil Thompson leads the Liverpool squad on their lap of honour around Anfield after securing the club's third league title in four seasons (PA)

Graeme Souness led Liverpool as captain for two and a half seasons and in that time, won the First Division title three times. (PA)

The all-Merseyside FA Cup final in 1989 saw Liverpool prevail over Everton with a 3-2 victory and Ronnie Whelan lift the trophy at Wembley. (PA)

Phil Neal's apprenticeship at Liverpool before he was named captain lasted a decade. He is pictured here with the manager that appointed him, Joe Fagan. (PA)

In Alan Hansen's absence, Glenn Hysen filled in as Liverpool captain – a role he had filled for the Swedish national team for nearly a decade before his arrival at Anfield in 1989. (PA)

After his appointment as manager, Graeme Souness took the unprecedented step of awarding the Liverpool captaincy to a new signing in Mark Wright. In 1992, Wright lifted the FA Cup. (PA)

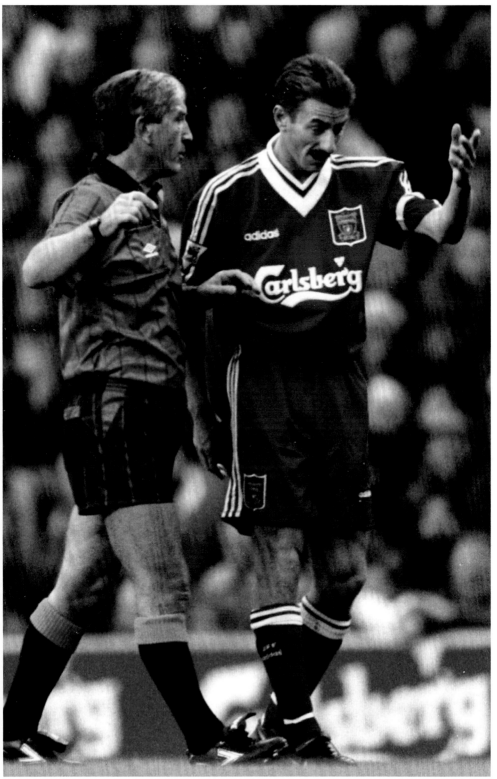

When Mark Wright was relieved of his responsibilities as Liverpool captain, Ian Rush was his replacement – the club's all-time leading goalscorer. (PA)

John Barnes led Liverpool as captain during the infamous Spice Boys era when he was the oldest player in the Premier League's youngest team. (PA)

Paul Ince remains the only player to have captained both Liverpool and Manchester United. He arrived at Anfield via Inter Milan in 1997. (PA)

Robbie Fowler was ultimately sold by manager that first appointed him captain, Gérard Houllier. The season where he is pictured here ended in a cup treble. (PA)

Injuries cruelly curtailed Jamie Redknapp's reign as Liverpool captain. In 2001, he lifted the FA Cup with deputy Robbie Fowler despite not being available to play. (PA)

Sometimes captains are strong but silent types. Sami Hyypiä, the Finnish defender, was in that category. Here he is scoring against Leeds United. (PA)

Jamie Carragher was Liverpool's vice captain for eight seasons. Steven Gerrard describes him as the eyes and voice behind him. (PA)

For more than a decade, Steven Gerrard was Liverpool's leader. During the period he won almost everything there was to win. The focus and pressure was always on him. (PA)

day, like Kenny Dalglish did… It's not hard to understand that it must have been extremely difficult.'

It's impossible to understand, the burden it must have been.

'I remember going to a ceremony in Liverpool Cathedral, on the anniversary of Hillsborough. Kenny was up there, giving a speech. All my time in Liverpool, we were reminded of the horrible disaster. It kept coming back. It's still like that.'

Because it had been a difficult year, in the aftermath and grief after Hillsborough, the league title victory twelve months later had a particularly sweet taste.

'We had the season finale of the previous year still fresh in our minds; we could have lost 0–1 against Arsenal and still won the league, but lost 0–2 in injury time. And that after the club and the city had been through the Hillsborough tragedy. The whole city wanted revenge: "We shall win back that league trophy!"'

Can you describe the day when you realised you'd won the league?

'It was Arsenal, Villa and us, fighting at the top. We were playing Queens Park Rangers. If we won, we'd be league champions with two games in hand. But at the same time, Aston Villa had to lose or draw against Norwich City at Villa Park. We won, and I remember we ran around in hats and scarves at Anfield afterwards, hoping we'd done it. When the results finally came through Villa-Norwich had ended 3–3, we broke into a wild celebration. It was a fantastic feeling.'

Hysén had won almost all trophies possible with IFK Göteborg, including two UEFA Cups, but the league championship with Liverpool in 1990 exceeded all else.

'When you win the league and go around town on an open-top double-decker bus, nothing can beat that. It just can't be surpassed. What an experience! Oh my God! And afterwards, people said: "You've won so much now. Isn't it enough?" No way! If you've won once, you want to keep doing it! There's no such thing as too many victories. You never tire of winning.'

When Hysén won the league with Liverpool in 1990, it would turn out to be the club's last league championship to date. The drought has lasted a quarter of a century.

'If someone back then had suggested it would take another twenty-five years or more before we won the league again, I'd ask if they'd hit their head or something. It's unbelievable. I can't understand it.'

What was the biggest differences between being captain for Liverpool FC, and IFK Göteborg or the national side?

'On the pitch there wasn't much of a difference. But in the stands it was different. There were 45,000 or more at Anfield, in Gothenburg we had maybe 15–20,000 for league games. At international games there could be almost 50,000. And the pressure off the pitch was a lot higher in Liverpool. We couldn't just go out to town. As soon as we stepped outside the door, someone would come over with something to say. You couldn't really move. So we mostly stayed in Southport. In Gothenburg, people were happy when things went well, but they didn't force their company on us. That being said, Italy was worse than England. Down there we could only go out if we'd won. If we'd lost, we'd better stay indoors…

Hysén was surprised at how little extra work there was, off the pitch, as captain for Liverpool. He had some extra responsibilities, but usually together with some of his team-mates. At that time social gatherings were arranged by the coaching staff. The language barrier was not too much trouble either. He had to adjust a little to understand the Scottish and Irish accents, but it was nothing compared to high-speed Italian conversations at Fiorentina.

'We met Fiorentina in Italy,' says Hysén of a 1990 pre-season friendly. 'This was before I was captain for Liverpool, but since it was my old club, they gave me the honour of the captaincy for that match especially. After the match I recognised a fella in the stands, a Fiorentina supporter. So I threw my shirt to him. It made Ronnie Moran mad! "Do you think you can throw away clothes just like that?" I thought it was a nice gesture. "Any idea what a shirt like that costs?" Sorry. I'm sorry! It ought to be OK to give your shirt away. They're at every match. Naturally you reward their loyalty with a shirt? No way, was Moran's opinion.'

Apart from being careful about giving shirts away; what did your years as captain teach you? Do you consider it an honour?

'Absolutely, my God, yes. Both at IFK Göteborg, for Sweden and Liverpool. But as I've said earlier, I don't put too much into it. It's usually other people who talk about what I've achieved. But yes, I'm damned proud to have been captain for Liverpool. How many people have had that honour? I'm very happy about it, but it's not something I go around talking to people about.'

Have you developed as a person through being a leader?

'Yes. I've developed my social and communicative skills. And I've learned a lot about respecting others. That's not only important as captain, or in big clubs, of course. It's a life skill. If you want to achieve something, you all have to pull in the same direction.'

As a top-class footballer you have to perform year in, year out. There is an incredible pressure to achieve good results. Where did Hysén, twice voted player of the year in Sweden, find his motivation?

'I'm not gonna lie,' he reflects. 'There's a completely different boost ahead of a Manchester United game than, say, Watford. You can tell there's something going on with the team, tension levels are at breaking point. It's easy to say it shouldn't be that way, but it just is. I miss that tension. The feeling before big games like that. Walking out in front of 40–80,000 and give it all you've got. You need days to recover after a match like that. Pre-season was dreadfully tough. But it was worth it, particularly on the big match days.'

How did you deal with the change from being right in the thick of things – the whole world paying attention – to life after your career?

'A lot of guys I knew got depressed. Some have died, too much drink. Or too much drugs. I had two mates from the "Blue and White" [IFK Göteborg] who collapsed completely when that attention was gone. It's not easy when you're in your mid-thirties. They had nothing. No education. I'm a certified electrician, but I could never have worked as one. The whole of Gothenburg would have been short-circuited!'

Hysén feels he has been extremely lucky. He commented on his first television match for Swedish channel TV3 while he was still a Liverpool player. Everton and Tottenham played the day after a Liverpool match, so Glenn accepted an offer to try his luck as commentator. He threw himself into it. And then Graeme Souness came in and made big changes to the squad. Glenn, who was over thirty by then, was one of those who had to go. But TV3 was waiting, and he stayed with them for eighteen years.

'So I never made it out of the limelight. It's still on me, but now in my commentator seat.'

✦

It is no secret that Glenn Hysén and his family have lived their lives in the Swedish limelight. Divorces and break-ups and a lot more have been fodder for the Swedish media.

'I never had any problem with that, because there hasn't been much shit, not really. They haven't printed lies. It's all been facts, and as long as that's the case, I don't give a toss. But if they'd written lies, I would have been livid.'

But one side of the Hysén family's private lives would see the media coverage blown out of all proportion – a topic that would also break some boundaries in macho team cults like football.

In 2001, Hysén was minding his own business at a public toilet in Frankfurt when a gay man approached him and groped his genitals. Hysén was furious and hit him. Afterwards, he was branded as a homophobe by parts of the media. Hysén felt it was unfair, because it had nothing to do with the sexuality of the man he hit, it was the fact that he'd laid his hands on him, a stranger.

'But I readily admit the climate in most dressing rooms is tough, whether it's football, hockey or handball. You joke about people of ethnicity, sexuality, people with disabilities and… yes, anyone. It doesn't mean you think they're inferior. It's just the tone in the dressing room, you know, they don't mean anything by it. But later, you might think about it, and if there was a gay person in the dressing room it wouldn't have been very nice for him. But I only thought about that much later, not during my career.'

In 2007, Glenn Hysén surprised a lot of people by giving a speech at Scandinavia's biggest LGBT event, Stockholm Pride. In his speech he said, 'How easy would it be for a sixteen-year-old footballer to come out as gay to his team-mates?' At the time, his youngest son Anton, born in Liverpool, was sixteen. Glenn had started to realise that Anton's sexuality may not be what he had expected. They had never discussed it. And Anton had never talked about it. But his wife, Helena, had long believed their son was gay.

'Female intuition, maybe?' he ponders. 'I guess your mum is always closest to you. But I did realise something was different. He still lived at home, and he'd bring home one girl after another, but send them all off again, one by one. It started dawning on me. This was the year I spoke at Stockholm Pride. I was so nervous. It could be taken the wrong way if I said "us" and "them" and "those over there". It's so sensitive.'

What did Anton say afterwards? Did it make it easier for him to open up?

'I think he felt very unsure about how I would deal with his sexuality. He didn't come out until much later, and that surely means I failed along the way. Or maybe it was because everything in football is so macho. Later I was told about his plan B: he'd been asking mates if he could live with them if I didn't accept him as gay. That made me cry. "Do you really believe that about me?" I asked. That means I've failed as a dad.'

In 2011, Anton came out in public. He was 21, and a professional footballer. He became the first Swedish professional to come out as gay. Indeed, he was one of the first professional footballers anywhere to take that step. Football remains an arena where the acceptance of gay players is very low.

Before Anton went public, he came to his dad for advice.

'I told him to do whatever he felt was right,' says Hysén. 'Nobody else should decide for him. "I support you whatever you do," I told him. Helena said the same thing. We love him regardless of his sexuality.'

The news got heavy media coverage, and the fact that former Liverpool player

Hysén had a gay footballer son made the headlines in many countries. The press was ruthless, and Glenn was on the barricades, speaking up for his son and for gay footballers in general.

'The best part of the support he received was a note from a hockey player in Canada, Sean Avery. He's a real bully and gets into fights a lot. He's a big star in the USA and Canada and in the NHL. He wrote to Anton and thanked him for his courage. He also wrote: "There's a lot of people over here too, who need to get stuff off their chests. But it's such a macho sports environment you're afraid of trouble if you dare stand out." His support meant a lot to our family.'

So Anton grew as a person after he dared come out?

'Oh, massively, yes! It's all been positive after that. The only negative thing that happened was when I was Anton's coach here in Gothenburg, in the second tier. We received a letter at the clubhouse, some guy wrote that he'd been a big fan all his life, but that he couldn't accept gays at the club. And then he added: "So now I'm handing in my membership card." What's with some people?! We couldn't get hold of the guy, there was no name or number, so we couldn't ask him what his problem was. He just wrote outright: "We don't want a faggot here." It's the only negative incident I know of, unless Anton is hiding others from me.'

Life is about being yourself. No holds barred. Glenn Hysén always supports all of his children, and teaches them to live their lives the way he has lived his: by being himself. It seems a good mantra to follow, because no matter who I talk to who knows Hysén, they always say: 'He's a good guy. Such a nice fella!'

'But the thing about being yourself, it's so simple,' he reflects. 'If I meet the King or a homeless person, I don't treat them any differently. I am who I am. Should I change into a different person, depending on who I meet? When I meet a celebrity, should I be somebody else? No! I'm the same, regardless of who I'm talking to.'

Do you swear as much when you see the King?

'I'm sure I did. I've only met him once. The King and Queen host four dinners a year where sports people, politicians and other cultural celebrities are invited. In 1988, Helena and I were invited, after we did so well in the UEFA Cup and all that. So we went to the palace. There were a lot of pompous, overdressed people there. There was a man in a coat with a huge cane that he knocked on the floor to tell us dinner was served. But after about four glasses of wine, we were all the same. People relaxed. Everybody was themselves.'

But you don't need those four glasses to go there. To be yourself?

'I already am. Always.'

8

MARK WRIGHT
THE OUTSIDER

'A hard person and a proper centre-half... and they make good captains.'
Ian Rush

I DRIVE THROUGH THE TUNNEL THAT CONNECTS LIVERPOOL TO the Wirral. On the other side of the River Mersey I stop by the big, white house where Mark and Sue Wright live. A smiling Mark Wright opens the door and welcomes me in, but he is not alone. At his feet are their two dogs: Ruby, a Rhodesian ridgeback, and Bohdi, a Border collie. Mark's wife Sue is dedicated to helping the less fortunate. She's involved with the RSPCA, and the Wright couple are strongly committed to helping foster children. Their daughter Sonia (10) is adopted, and they have opened their home for emergency placement of children several times. They also function as a visiting home for foster children when their families are unable to take care of them in difficult periods.

Right now Sonia is in town at a children's party, but four of her friends are here on a visit. That is what they usually do on days off and after school, because Sue and Mark work from home and – literally – keep the door open to the kids. While Sue, Mark and I sit and talk at the kitchen island, the girls come in. They greet us warmly, and obviously feel at home as they make their own lunch. Along one of the kitchen walls is a woodpile, floor to ceiling around the fireplace, giving it a log cabin look.

'I love Scandinavian design and elements of wood,' Sue explains. She is a lawyer and a die-hard Liverpool supporter who still blushes talking about how she celebrated the Champions League triumph in 2005. She and Mark had not yet met back then. She watched the match with friends and when victory was secured they drove around the city centre with hundreds of other cars. From Sue's convertible they waved their scarves over their heads like lassoes, blowing the horn of her Porsche, until the horn died. Sue describes it as a fairy-tale night. Everybody hugged everybody. A day when any boundaries in the town were erased, and everything was allowed. The whole city was turned upside down like in a riotous film scene.

Ten years later, Sue is married to a former captain of the team she has followed since a child. And not only a prominent captain of Liverpool, but of all the teams he played for: Southampton, Derby, Liverpool and, not least, England.

With Mark Wright's arrival at Liverpool, an old tradition was broken: he did not rise through the club system before being appointed captain. He started out as captain. Manager Graeme Souness wanted a change in the ranks, and that caused trouble. Mark remembers very well what Souness said when he asked him to be captain as soon as arrived at Anfield.

'We're making big changes here, and you're gonna be captain,' Souness said.

Short, and straight to the point. He smiles when he thinks back to that day.

'It didn't matter if it was gonna be for long or short,' says Wright now. 'The fact someone values you so highly, and has such confidence in you, that they want you to lead the team the minute you arrive at the club – that's an offer you can't refuse. It's the biggest honour you could get.'

Did it surprise you a little, that you were appointed right away, considering the club tradition was to honour the best and most faithful players in the club with the captaincy?

'You know, when you're asked something like that… If a Liverpool supporter had been asked if he'd consider being captain, what do you think he'd say? What would anyone have said?'

'Yes,' of course.

'Yes. Thank you very much! I was strong enough as a person to accept the challenge. I didn't know how they'd appointed captains before me in the club history, so the job started out pretty heavy.'

Mark looks up into the ceiling and pauses to think; he's searching for words.

'A lot of people were saying that I shouldn't have been appointed.'

That's not how we do it here?

'That's not how we do it here… I heard that from people in the club. It was incredibly disappointing to me, even though I could understand the team-mates who were unhappy about my captaincy. But I didn't choose! I never asked to be captain. I was given the honour. But it created so many problems in the squad that I had to go round to the most experienced players, like Jan Mølby, Steve Nicol, Bruce Grobbelaar, Ronnie Whelan and Ian Rush. Some said, "Wrighty, you're not the problem, the problem is that the captaincy was always given to the one who'd been here the longest." I replied that was obviously not my problem. They had to take it up with the manager. He made the decision and I wanted to be here at Liverpool Football Club.'

Mark talked to each and every senior player in turn.

'I said, "I've come to this club to do a job. And my job is to play with you. Don't give me trouble because the boss made me captain. Whatever it is, I'll try to help you, but first I need you to help me, because I'm the new kid here. I'm here now, and I've got a strong personality. I like winning, and I like leaving a mark."

'Some appreciated me making this round, some didn't. *Que sera sera*, I say. I'll always be who I am. We're good friends now, but it was a really difficult time.'

Did the conflict influence your game?

'No. I am who I am. I'm mentally tough, a balanced fella, I've never moved beyond my station. And I never will. But I think the situation sometimes influenced people around us, because there was a bad atmosphere. I was there to do a job and to enjoy myself. To me personally, it was an immense joy being able to lead the team out in front of the Kop.'

Can you describe your first match as a captain?

'You know, this probably sounds weird, but – as soon as you're appointed captain, it's important not to let it go to your head. And I never did. It was never about "Look at me! Look! Look how big I am!" No, no, no. I considered myself a team player, one who makes sure everybody does a good job. Someone who shouts and orders people about. That's who I am. That being said, when you play your first home game as a captain, walk down those steps, touch the sign, touch the club badge and come out into that atmosphere: it's impossible to describe. A full house chanting and singing, and Gerry Marsden, one of my neighbours, singing "You'll Never Walk Alone".'

Mark laughs heartily when he tells me this.

'He used to visit us at Christmas, and sing it to the kids too, as Father Christmas! Yes, he used to sit down by the piano and sing at the top of his voice. What a Father Christmas. I swear, it's true!'

✦

Mark Wright is not a man who gives up easily. He is driven by pride, by being able to show his worth, and that he is indeed worthy of trust. He always had the same attitude: you do not give up until you have succeeded where you are. You fight until you have proven your worth. And he says it is because of his upbringing, and the baggage he brought with him from home, that he became a fighter.

Like so many Liverpool captains before him, Mark grew up in a very rough neighbourhood. His was Berinsfield, in South Oxfordshire. It was an area of council estates. He says it was a neighbourhood where you learned survival skills. And that education is also good qualification for a captain.

'When we were in school we had to fight for survival. We'd often fight more than we'd learn. So it was a rough childhood. Add to that, my dad was a strong and very strict person. I inherited all my good sides from my mum, and all my toughness from my dad.'

The family of five – just three years separate him, his older brother Kyle and younger sister Dawn. On a wall in the three-bedroom council house was a coin-operated electric meter. When the box was empty, the home stayed cold.

His father was a Scouser, and had met Mark's mother when he was in the army. Later he had all kinds of jobs to provide for the family, including painting and decorating. He was away most of the time to make enough money, coming home at the weekends before going off again to make sure his wife had money for food.

'My mum did an incredible job looking after us. If it wasn't for my mum, I'd have… I'd probably have been in a worse place than I am today. I remember one morning I lay in bed, and Mum told me to get up, because we had to be in time for the match I had to play. I'd been out late with a girlfriend, and told her I didn't want to play that day.'

Next thing he knew was the novel sensation of a glass of orange juice tossed straight in his face while he was still in bed. His mother was furious. 'You're not about to let anybody down!' she yelled.

'I'm telling you, I jumped out of bed and got dressed in a hurry. I never objected to playing, ever again. That's how it was, my mother gave me everything. It was to her credit that I became a footballer later. She's the one who pushed me. She was the one who got up every Sunday morning to take me to matches, because I was too young to drive. She went everywhere with me. Even to my very first contract talk.'

To help make ends meet, Mark took on odd jobs from the age of eight. He did paper rounds and milk rounds, and as a bonus got a free pint of milk every morning. He laughs, thinking back. It taught him responsibility, and gave him ambition. An interest in football was also helpful.

'I had my football, that was important. Football can save people from landing in trouble. I decided early on that I wanted to play football, even though I was teased about it a lot growing up.'

On council estates, gangs rule. And on Mark's estate a group consisted of a band of brothers: his older brother and himself, and seven other sets of brothers. A gang of sixteen boys who did everything together and went everywhere together.

'We got into a few fights – it was stupid looking back now – not worth it. But that was a way of life for me then. My dad had always taught me to fend for myself, never back off but stand tall. I learned to be first in line to help, never back down, never walk away and never fear.'

This too was golden experience for a future leader.

'I think this came in very useful as a captain too. To stand tall no matter what people say. My upbringing gave me a solid foundation, and I went on to captain Southampton, Derby, Liverpool and England. Throughout my childhood and my career, my toughness always got me people's respect.

'I learned to give my seat up for women on the bus. Never to walk first through a door – if I did, my father would slap me. Because no matter how tough we were, we learned that manners and respect for others meant everything.'

The group of lads also played football matches against other bands of brothers in the neighbourhood. There were twenty streets within the council estate, and spots of green in the middle. They often played matches where half the neighbourhood was up against the other half. This was team-building in practice.

'We had so little – friendship literally meant everything. The strength and loyalty within our group was the most important thing. It's the same in football. You have to be able to create team spirit and strength in a squad. That's the only way to succeed even if you don't play well.'

But his friends were not happy about Mark passing on a fight or a party because he had a game to play. And they told him so in no uncertain terms. The lads had first priority, they said, before everything else. But today none of them criticises the choice he made, choosing football over getting into trouble with his mates.

Mark Wright had never been asked to try out for any clubs, but at seventeen, he got lucky. He was about to finish school and was in the middle of his exams when he had a phone call from Oxford United. Both their centre-backs were out injured, and they wondered if Mark could play a game for them? Of course he could! He went off and played, the team won and Mark signed with them on the following Monday. That was how he came into football without an apprenticeship and without a single try-out.

It is important to grab your chance when it is offered. You have to prove that you are worthy of people's trust. And you need good helpers and role models who believe in you. In addition to his mother – his greatest supporter – he can thank Coventry's retired giant defender, Roy Barry, caretaker manager for Oxford United. He trained with Wright every day, working on his touch and headers.

Mark Wright headed so many balls training on his own in his youth that he has a dent in his forehead to prove it. Sometimes they went to Southampton to play tireless sessions of football tennis with his friends Danny Wallace and Reuben Agboola, playing over a badminton net.

'It was great, I didn't want to stop,' he says. 'I was a sponge for knowledge. And there hasn't been a lack of role models along the way.'

He believes Ron Yeats is Liverpool's greatest captain – someone he took inspiration from.

'…A true colossus of a man in every sense. Fearless, a warrior. His words and actions as big, strong and tall as the man himself. He breathed leadership and that's the true quality of a captain. He was before my time but he is the true meaning of a legend. He led by example on and off the pitch, he directed and managed his team members with authority and respect. Even now I always feel I want to call him "Mr Yeats" when I meet him. I have the hugest place in my heart for him.'

Is he the best role model as captain you ever had?

'Yes, I believe he is. He was a defender that you didn't want to have to play against! He could head, attack, and he created lots of chances. And he had such energy! He'd run up and down the pitch non-stop for 90 minutes.'

There are so many different types of captains, according to Mark.

'You've got the likes of Gary Lineker, who doesn't say much, but who scores goals and leads by example. He was never yellow-carded, and he didn't pick fights. Then there's the type of captain who plays with his heart on his sleeve, and gives you loud and clear orders. When I started playing for England, I played with people like Terry Butcher, who'd always hit the wall and bang his head against the door and shout, "Come on! Let's get 'em!"

'I was that kind of captain too. I'm built the same way as Butcher. I have enormous respect for Terry. I met him only the other day, actually. I really rate him. You roll up your sleeves, you never stop talking, you never stop demanding the best from your team-mates. If someone needs a slap, you slap them. If someone needs a push, you push. If someone steps on your team-mate, you push back, you settle it. Looking back, I may have been a bit too keen on getting my own back, a bit too rough. I probably wouldn't have gotten away with it today, with all the cameras on the ground! But you're on the pitch because you want to look after your team-mates. You're a voice, both on and off the pitch. You're opinionated and you speak your mind because you want to succeed, you want to win! You've got the passion and the drive. That's what I had. When I stepped onto a football pitch I wasn't going to disappoint anyone. Even today I'd rather interfere with someone, or crash into them, than let them pass me. That's what it's all about.'

You were obviously both physical and vociferous on the pitch. How were you off the pitch, in the dressing room, away from training and matches?

'I would always be talking. In training I'd bark out commands, I'm a voice. I couldn't stop talking if I tried. If I disagree with something, I want to argue about it, discuss it. It didn't mean I was always right, of course not, nobody's right all the time. But I had my opinion and my view on how we could improve, and I believe that as captain, you have to speak your mind. I don't know how players feel about this today, but I sometimes wish they'd just roll up their sleeves and get in there. Go into the match, full body contact, show the opponents you mean business. I learned that from Jimmy Case, Alan Ball, Terry Butcher, Tony Adams, Des Walker and Bryan Robson. I played with them all.'

The hardmen.

'Hardmen! Really, really hard. They played with broken noses and open wounds. "Stitch me up and let me carry on playing," they'd say. That's how we were raised to play football.'

What would you do as captain if your team was trailing? Were you aggressive or encouraging?

'Both. You can have aggressive encouragement, right? I don't know quite how to explain it, though, not without swearing.'

Mark provides me with a few examples of how he'd 'aggressively encourage' and shout commands to his team-mates. He says he demanded from his team that they were tough, but not all his team-mates could take that kind of aggression.

'Some players just need a hug. Especially forwards. You can't yell at forwards much, it's just the way they are. You've got to learn which of your team-mates can stand the yelling and aggressiveness. But defenders have to toughen up anyway. We used to stand on the goal-line in pairs, and let the rest of the team shoot at us, they'd hit us everywhere, and we weren't allowed to turn away! They hit us in our heads and everywhere imaginable.

'Do they still do that? I'm not sure. Probably not. But we wouldn't turn away if a ball came straight at us. I'm pretty sure you've never seen me turn my back on a ball. If you have, I'd like to see the clip!'

As a captain, you are the go-between between the manager and the team, you have to be the glue in the squad, you are the strongest link between the fans and the club. You represent the team in the media and at major events. Where does a captain's strongest loyalty lie? Most captains I have spoken to say that their strongest loyalty was always with their team-mates. But how was it for Mark Wright, who had such a rough start to his captaincy at Liverpool? In a team where a lot of people outright disagreed with the selection of him as a captain?

'It's a difficult job, because as a captain you're trying to please everybody,' he says. 'But if you ask me where my loyalty is, it's with my team-mates. No doubt. You have to be loyal to your team-mates. They're the ones you go to war with. We're the ones crossing the white chalk line to play, and to be able to play well together, the squad must have a good team spirit and respect each other.

'Listen, you love the football club, you respect the football club. You've got to re-spect the manager, he picks the team. You love the supporters: they pay your wages, they create the atmosphere that you go out and play in – they're the ones you need to please. But still, to get everything right, the players have to play well. If that's not right, everything falls apart. The management wants to kick you out, the supporters might start booing you, and the club may say they want to get rid of you. That's why you, as a captain, have to make sure everything's all right within the squad, among the players. That's where your loyalty is. And I can't imagine any captain would say anything else… I'm a good team player at least. For me it's all about what we can do as a team. And if we play well and work hard together, we can achieve good results. That's how we get our reward. That's how we earn the fans' appreciation.'

His consistent performances resulted in career progress. He moved from Oxford, to Southampton and on to Derby County, playing for England at the 1990 World Cup in Italy. His proudest moment, though, came as captain of Liverpool. The year was 1992, and the Reds were in the FA Cup final, facing Sunderland at Wembley.

'When we arrived at Wembley, a few of us were particularly excited. Michael Thomas, Dean Saunders and I had never won the FA Cup, so we were all fired up. The others – Bruce Grobbelaar, Stevie Nicol, Ronnie Whelan and the rest – they told us to calm down. They'd all won it before, hadn't they! They'd won everything, achieved everything, so to them it was just another match. But for us who hadn't won the FA Cup before, it was a WOW moment. We enjoyed every second. In the dressing room, I caught myself thinking: Wow, Wembley stadium! Getting to lead the team out was amazing.

'And poor Sunderland, they ran so much during the first half, chasing after us, that they were exhausted. At half-time, the Sunderland team looked like death warmed up. We stepped it up an extra gear, it was all about passing the ball. Their match was all about running in between. Their entire squad looked knackered. They were marked by the big occasion, we could tell. We'd decided to be careful in the first half, and go get them in the second half. Second half became a hold-the-ball-in-play-within-the-team session, and we won by a pretty convincing 2–0. I was so grateful we did!'

When Mark Wright, team captain, walked up those famous Wembley steps to receive the FA Cup on behalf of his team, it was a dream come true.

'You wait your whole life to win something. I'd come so close to winning big with Southampton – lost two or three semi-finals. We played in Europe, and came so close to winning, many times. And I dreamed of winning the World Cup in 1990, we came really close there too. But we lost the semi-final against Germany, even though we were the better team. There had been so many almost experiences. And then we won the FA Cup. Getting to walk up those steps as captain, to lift that cup. There's only one word for it: fantastic. Fantastic.' He let out a 'You fucking beauty!' as he lifted the trophy.

' And you know, if I'd walked up those steps as number two, three or four, or last, not as a captain, it wouldn't have mattered to me. But of course, going up first, as captain, was very special. Still, the most important thing was winning something for the supporters, and be accepted by them and considered a good Liverpool player. That's what it's all about.'

But the happiness did not last for long. The Liverpool team with manager Souness and captain Wright struggled to live up to the results the club had been spoiling their fans and owners with for two decades.

At that time, the team were going through a generational change. And the more experienced players found that the younger players were not as receptive to corrections or orders as in previous times.

'This was soon to be the "Spice Boys" era, and I remember playing a match where – apart from John Barnes – I was ten years older than the next in line on the team. I looked around thinking, What's happening! They're just kids! And that was the Spice Boys. Once upon a time Liverpool dominated and the Manchester United boys were the ones who went out to nightclubs, who showed up everywhere. All of a sudden we found ourselves in a situation where all of our talented youngsters loved partying and took on modelling jobs. They were here, there and everywhere, showed up on all these events just to be noticed.

'Both me, John Barnes and a few other of the older players were frustrated by the nightclub habits that a lot of the youngsters had. We were frustrated because football isn't about being seen with celebrities. It's about the here and now. John would never have won so much with this club if he'd been busy mingling with celebs. And I think it was difficult for John and myself to accept the way it had become. Because as soon as training finished, it was all about what they were going to do after training or matches. It was like a culture shock to John, myself and the other more senior players. It wasn't that we couldn't handle it, we could, and we did have some fantastic players on the team back then too. But to Barnes, so dedicated and goal-oriented, it was difficult to accept the dramatic change in focus and attitude. And I don't blame him.'

When results did not go Liverpool's way, Graeme Souness tried a new approach, and that was to change captains, just as he had done after returning to the club. Ian Rush was appointed the new leader in 1993, and it was a huge disappointment to Mark.

'Was it a tough time for me personally?' he ponders. 'I think many players would have broken down, because it was a very, very unworthy treatment. But that's the only bad thing I'll say about the club: the way they handled this was wrong. Losing the captain's armband at Liverpool was probably the low point of my life as a footballer; that, and losing my chance to play in the World Cup when I was a Southampton player, and suffered a broken leg.'

You lost the captaincy at the same time as the club went through a huge reorganisation and sold off a lot of their most experienced players. Do you think the captain was sacrificed to try and make a difference?

'It had nothing to do with the captain. It was to do with how many experienced players we had sold. And I wholeheartedly believe that if Graeme had been allowed to stay as the club manager a while longer, he would have managed to set us straight. He would have succeeded. Changes needed to be done. A lot of older players were nearing the end of their careers and needed to move on, just like Steven Gerrard has moved on now. It happens to us all one day. Some said the changes happened too quickly, and I think Graeme would agree. But, you make decisions your whole life.

Sometimes they're the right ones, sometimes they're not.'

Players Wright had been looking forward to playing with were sold, and new ones brought in.

'Sometimes during that period, I heard things like: "Listen, we've bought Ruddock, Scales, Babb – your chances on the team will be limited from now on." I just said: "Oh, really? OK by me!" I could have gone to a different club at the time. I had several offers from clubs that offered me more money, a lot of clubs were in touch. But no way I'd leave Liverpool before I was a success at the club. If you go through difficult times, or really good times, the most important thing is that the supporters remember you as someone who always gave his best.'

Wright was told new players had been bought to fill his spot, but he felt he had not yet achieved that goal.

'I just said I wasn't interested in leaving the club. That I wanted to stay. Give Liverpool my all. And you know, I loved every second of it, even though it was so rough, a lot of players didn't make it. My friend Dean Saunders was one of those who disappeared quickly, and I felt really sorry for him. Not everyone is cut out for work in such a tough environment. But I was raised to be a fighter. I knew that a lot of stuff went on in the background, but I didn't let it bother me. As I said, I could have joined a number of other clubs, but I refused. Just ask Roy Evans. I downright refused to leave. I didn't want to transfer to another club before I'd left a positive mark at the football club where I really wanted to make a lasting impression. Not one they could sweep aside and say didn't work. I've never worked like that. I've never run away from a challenge, not once in my life, I still never would.'

It sounds like pride is also something that spurs you on.

'Absolutely. Pride is the result of hard labour, and giving it a hundred per cent the whole time is the most important thing to me. As captain you have to give it your everything. Nobody can play well in every match. Everybody has bad games. But there's always a way to make sure your team-mates work hard and get on with their jobs. For my part, it was a matter of getting more involved in the game if I felt I didn't play well. I'd wait for a high ball, jump up a little late and hit someone. That would usually get me going! Maybe that's old school? I'm not sure you can do that any more, going head first into a challenge, but it creates a spark and gets you back into the game.'

During the 1995/96 season, Mark fought his way back into the team and managed to earn a new contract from Evans. Yet in 1998 at the age of 35 he retired because of a back injury.

'If it wasn't for that injury, I'd have still been in top shape. I could run just as fast as the next man, but I couldn't carry on.'

In all he spent seven years at Anfield, but there was only one major trophy to show for it. He could not have been more unlucky with his timing to start playing for the club: in the decade before he arrived, Liverpool had finished in the top two in every year, and six of those seasons ended with league titles. Liverpool also won two FA Cups, three League Cups and a European Cup in this period. So, unlike the captains before him, Mark Wright did not have a CV packed with great results and trophies. He missed it by the smallest margin. The winning streak had ended. Liverpool never made it higher than third place, and were as low as eighth in his worst season at the club. The club only managed to win two trophies while he was there, but when Liverpool won the League Cup in 1995, Wright was injured.

And still, the boy from the rough neighbourhood with the coin-operated electric meter on the wall had picked the winning lottery ticket by signing for Liverpool. He captained both the club – one of the biggest in the world – and his country. It has earned him respect and recognition for the rest of his life. Nobody can take that away from Mark Wright.

In Mark's home gym, memorabilia still hang on the wall behind his exercise bike, the free weights and the gym mat. Pennants from when he led England signed by all of his team-mates; a framed photo of himself, as a joyful reminder to kids, foster kids and not least himself. There are a few art prints of the England squad, drawn in a colourful pen and signed. A few signed photos of world-famous boxers have been assigned a spot too. On the windowsill a very young Mark Wright smiles at you in black-and-white, together with his school team. In the room next door, a collection of memorabilia from his time at Liverpool is on display. Right now, three little girls sit huddled up on the sofa in there, enjoying a film on the big screen. They feel completely at home in the house of the man who still sees it as his joy and duty to take care of his team. These days, his team is the extended family.

Sue and Mark Wright both own and work for Premier Legends, where they offer team and network building to companies in various countries by arranging five-a-side cups. The winners get to play against a team of former footballers. Whenever they organise an event like this, they make sure they promote the needs of foster children too. They will happily gather foster children to play their own match against the football legends if that will help to get more people involved. Their hope is that people will open their homes to children who need new care providers and a safe home.

They have taken in several children in need themselves: short-term stays, emergency stops along the way, weekend stays, relief visits and as a temporary foster home. During this time they ended up with a daughter, after they adopted Sonia.

'My wife got me involved in the care for foster children,' he says. 'As a footballer you live your life in a bubble. Either you're not listening to anyone, or you're ignoring a lot of things that happen in the world around you because you're so dedicated to your profession. It was only when I married Sue that I found out about all the kids who need help. She made it crystal clear that she wanted to help them, and wanted to adopt someone who needed our help. I'd just have to accept that if I wanted to marry her. God knows where I'd be today if I hadn't accepted. She's got a big heart. She wants to save the world. Not only kids, but dogs too. And if she sees a little old lady trying to cross the road, she'll hurry over to help her!'

These days, Mark and Sue work together to spread information about the need for foster parents. They also try to inspire people to consider adoption. And to Mark it is a matter of reaching men with an important message.

'We organise a lot of events to try and inform about foster children,' he says. 'If more people opened their homes, there wouldn't be children waiting in line who need safe and stable homes. We target men in particular because we believe they often need more convincing. Women are easier to convince – they often want more children to care for in the house. But we talk to the men about foster homes and adoption, because they're usually the ones to say "yes" or "no", so we try to persuade them.'

Being a former Liverpool and England captain is a good help when trying to reach the men. As a footballer you are a role model that men of all ages look up to and will listen to. The message hits home.

'Football is the world's biggest sport, there's someone watching in every home. That's why I try to reach everyone. I use my network to increase understanding for the need for foster homes in England.'

They have already had amazing experiences as foster parents. They have seen frightened children entering their home, torn away from parents or other family, carrying everything they own in a black bin bag. They have taken kids to the cinema who have never been before, who think they will all share a soft drink and a box of popcorn, and who stare wide-eyed at the giant screen and the box of popcorn they were given all to themselves. For the very first time. Mark tells me there are so many kids out there who will never know the things that many people take for granted that all children have.

'The most important thing for me is to be able to help these kids get a childhood,' he says, 'even if they haven't really had one up to now. They've lost their childhood through being ignored, abused or mistreated – it's not their fault. So being able to give these kids a little normalcy, that's the most important thing foster parents can do. The biggest sense of pride imaginable is when someone, who isn't your family, comes to your home and slowly starts to come into their own. That's the biggest thing foster parents can experience – anyone can experience. That's when you know it's a success.'

And they were in luck with Sonia, who is now adopted and a full member of the Wright family; their daughter.

'We opened our family, and our reward is that we've got a daughter who is the life and soul of the house. The kids from my first marriage love her, and she loves them.'

Mark says his four children are the most important things in his life. And he is forever grateful that his four eldest, Lauren, Hollie, Tom and George helped him become a good footballer by keeping him grounded.

'There's no better feeling than making your kids laugh. All kids have a right to laugh. And those who've been disappointed in life deserve a new chance.'

9

IAN RUSH
THE ICON WHO LEFT THE CLUB A BOY
AND RETURNED A MAN

'My first hero was Ian Rush'
Sami Hyypiä

TWO THINGS YOU PROBABLY DID NOT KNOW ABOUT IAN RUSH: he always played with soaking wet boots, and he always keeps a fake moustache in his car now that he is clean-shaven.

First of all, though, some magic. Ian Rush is out on the pitch, listening to the noise and the chanting from the stands. But then the whistle blows, the game is under way and the noise, the chanting, the songs, it all disappears. Full concentration. Try to anticipate the next three moves. Guess how far to run. Know when to sprint home to help in defence. And – most importantly – know where to run when partner Kenny Dalglish has the ball and makes a cross pass. Dalglish, Liverpool's number seven, always knows where Liverpool's number nine will be running. Intuition. Telepathy. Magic. Whatever you choose to call it, it gives them a head start on the opposition defence. The cross has been made, and the man with the moustache has sprinted into the box behind the defence, fired, and done what he does best: he's scored yet another goal for LFC.

In total Ian James Rush did that 346 times: a magical record, still standing.

That is how we know Ian Rush. The duo Rush and Dalglish. But it was not a given that it would turn out like that. In the beginning of his Liverpool career, Rush had only one wish: to leave. Squeezed in between superstars in the dressing room, he struggled to fit in.

'I hated my first year at the club,' he admits. 'I was so shy, and had to get changed with all these superstars. Ray Clemence was to one side of me, Alan Hansen to the other. It was really, really difficult to make myself at home. The environment was completely new. There was constant banter in the dressing room and I had no idea how to respond. Were they just having fun? Were they taking the mick? And I didn't play well for the reserves. Everything just felt awkward and I desperately needed help to get into the team spirit. There was no one to protect me. Everybody was having a go, even the supporters. I hated it. In the dressing room they were teasing all the new ones on the team. They played sink or swim with us. I took everything to heart, but I didn't say anything because I was so shy. It gnawed at me and affected my performance.'

When I meet Rush now – well over thirty years after that awkward start at Liverpool – he is wearing the official charcoal-grey club suit, a freshly ironed white shirt and a red and white striped tie. On his chest there is an embroidered liver bird and the letters 'LFC'. We are looking over the Legends Lounge at Anfield, just inside the executive box; there are round tables with white tablecloths. The tables are set for a multi-course meal, and the lounge's own bartender is smiling at us from the bar. On the walls around us are photos and facts about the biggest club legends, Liverpool icons: Kenny Dalglish, Robbie Fowler, John Barnes, Billy Liddell, Bruce Grobbelaar, Steven Gerrard, and – not least – the man by my side, now white-haired and without the moustache, but still athletic and with icy, blue eyes.

I have been asked by the club to stand in for one of theirs, and interview Ian Rush in front of the VIP guests in the Legends Lounge before kick-off. At the tables there are suited-up men and a few women who have dressed up more than is usual for a match at Anfield. The assembly looks at us expectantly, admiringly. I have asked him all the obvious questions about what it is like to be the most-scoring player in the club. I've asked him about his special partnership with Kenny Dalglish, and he insists it was mostly built on intuition and telepathy. We have talked about his thoughts on this year's team and today's match. And I have decided it is time for a small revelation.

What was it you always had to do to your boots before a game? Even on those cold winter days? Your mother can't have been very pleased with you.

Ian Rush laughs at me and a question he is never asked in these standard sessions. Usually he knows all the questions by heart, because he has answered them hundreds of times before.

'Well, it's like this. The leather in the football boots was so stiff before a game against Luton Town, so I put them in water to soften them before we played, and ended up scoring five that day. That's why I always played in wet boots later, regardless of wind and weather.'

The people in the Legends Lounge chuckle.

✦

Doris May Rush must have been quite a lady. Giving birth to ten children in fifteen years. Imagine – a flock the size of a football team to provide for…

Always, she put her family first in everything she did. They lived in St Asaph, a tiny North Wales city of barely 3,000, only an hour's drive from Liverpool. Four girls and six boys needed attention, care, and being woken up at all hours (the eldest worked shifts). There were clothes to be mended, until the youngest looked like walking patchworks. Children needing comfort and, not least, food. Her husband was away most of the time. Like most men in the neighbourhood he was either at work or at the pub.

'She looked after us all her life,' Ian Rush says. 'She lived a hard and industrious life, my mum.'

Ian was the second youngest in the family, and shared a bedroom with his five brothers. Six boys in bunk beds in a small bedroom. But that is one way to learn how to function in a team. Find your place in the group.

'As you can probably imagine, it was easier for me to find an opening in the penalty box than it was to find space in the small bedroom with five brothers,' he chortles.

So now we know why he was such a natural, both at finding and making good use of room in front of the opponents' goal. His whole childhood consisted of broken sleep. He was woken up by brothers who worked shifts and started at the crack of dawn, and in the middle of the night by those returning from work, from parties, or from being with friends and girlfriends. But he is eternally grateful he shared his childhood and youth with a team of big brothers.

Ian was a football talent from when he was very little. But he gives his older brothers credit for becoming that good. They let him play with them. Not all big brothers would be keen to let their younger sibling tag along to the playground, the park or in the garden. But if you do, your little brother could end up playing 660 matches for the Reds and scoring a staggering 346 goals. Nobody has managed to find the back of the net more times for Liverpool. That is how you become a club icon. That is how you end up on the wall of distinction in the Legends Lounge, have books written about you, get a place in a football museum, and become full-time club ambassador – travelling across the world representing the club simply by being yourself.

We have moved from the Legends Lounge at Anfield to the distinguished Racquets Club in Liverpool city centre. Rush stirs sugar into his cappuccino and tells me about the time he arrived at Liverpool in 1980, eighteen years of age. Somewhere deep inside he knew he was good enough. That was the thought that kept him going. But he often toyed with the tempting thought of going back to Chester City. He had been happy there.

After three months' training with the first team, he knew he was good enough. But he kept it to himself. Carried it with him for strength. He believes the first six months at the club were the most important of his entire career. It seemed impossible to play his way into a team that kept on winning. Never change a winning team. Unless someone was ill or injured, but hardly even then.

Rush trained with the first team Thursdays and Fridays, even though the reserve team and first team usually trained apart. During this period, Bob Paisley made a very useful observation: Rush played better against better opposition. That was why he got a few games for the first team. After seven games he thought he was becoming part of the team, but Paisley kept his feet on the ground by saying, 'You're not part of this team. You're not good enough. You haven't scored any goals yet! You have to become more selfish on the pitch!'

It ended in a row, Rush demanded to be put on the transfer list, and Paisley agreed. After, the only thing on the young striker's mind was to play for himself. Be selfish. It brought results. In the next two games for the reserves he scored five goals. And then came the European Cup tie against the Finnish team Oulu Palloseura. Rush started on the bench for the first team and did not think he would play; after all, he was on his way out. But he still got a chance to play. And he thought to himself: I'll show them selfish!

The goal against Oulu Palloseura would be the start of the longest series of goals scored by the same player in the club's history. The great goal-fest had started.

From that day, Rush focused on being selfish on the pitch. And because of that he never had a strong desire to become captain. He believes strikers in general are, and should be, too selfish to be considered for captaincy. So when Glenn Hysén and Mark Wright were appointed captains, passing both him and John Barnes in the line, he did not mind.

'I wasn't interested in being captain and just wanted to concentrate on playing and scoring goals,' he says. 'And I don't think a forward has the ideal position for a captain. You're too far away and have your team behind you. As captain communication is key. I would always give my team-mates in the attack plain feedback. But as a striker, if you see someone in defence make a mistake, it's difficult to get a message across to them. It's the same with goalkeepers, that's not an ideal position for a captain either. They'll have trouble communicating with the whole team, even if they see them well enough from their position. I definitely think the ideal positions for a captain is in midfield or central defence.'

It also gave him room to develop a magical partnership with Kenny Dalglish. Their very different personalities and entirely different interests off the pitch meant that when they were team-mates they rarely talked to each other.

'We didn't need to talk on the pitch. Some say you have to talk to one another on the pitch, and usually that's the case. But we didn't have to. We were on the same wavelength out there and had a very special understanding of each other's game. It was telepathic. That's how I could score so many goals.'

In addition, it was about trust. Early in his career, Dalglish told Rush that his job was 'to score, not assist'. As Dalglish got older, Rush did part of his running for him, because he knew that Dalglish would be the perfect assist partner. From having the Scot run a lot and work for him earlier on in their careers, it was Rush's turn to work extra hard for Dalglish, so he would last as long as possible on the team and could keep serving the striker.

'I just couldn't understand how a person was able to place the ball exactly in that opening where I wanted him to. I was very fast at the time, so I would just start running, and Kenny would pass the ball in the exact space I was just moving into. Eventually I realised that Kenny could place the ball almost exactly where he desired.'

When Kenny became player-manager, he knew what to do if Rush had a bad game. The two of them would go out on the training ground and go back to the basics: shooting drills for as long as it took to shoot the striker's confidence back in place.

'The problem with a lot of young striker talents these days is that they're afraid to miss. So they don't shoot, or their performance drops because they missed their first attempt. But when I played, nobody remembered if we missed the first five, as long as we scored on the sixth.'

Rush believes the massive media coverage and TV broadcasting of even under-21 games today makes playing too serious too soon.

The 1985 European Cup final between Juventus and Liverpool was supposed to be a celebration. It was supposed to be the day when Liverpool showed their class, and brought home old 'Big Ears' to have and to keep, from Heysel Stadium in Belgium. Instead, Ian Rush and his team-mates, along with the Juventus team and a whole football world, became witnesses to one of the darkest days in modern European football history. It was a day when the worst of supporter culture was on display, a day when hatred, anger, hooliganism and rivalry led to complete chaos in a ramshackle stadium.

Thirty-nine lives were lost that day, most of them Juventus supporters. Liverpool and all English teams were banned from European tournaments for five years. That day both captain Phil Neal and Joe Fagan lost interest in carrying on their careers.

For the first time in our chat, Ian Rush slows down his speech: 'Phil Neal was a magnificent captain. He wasn't very vocal in the dressing room. But on the pitch he was outstanding. Even though he's not a Scouser, he loves the club with a passion. And having learned from earlier captains, he knew what it took. He did a great job after he took over from Souness. He was also great at helping the younger players.'

But he lost all joy of the captaincy that day at the Heysel Stadium. Can you understand that?

'I fully understand that. Both he and Joe Fagan were marked by it. We all suffered after Heysel. While it was happening, none of us really knew what was going on. As a player you keep your emotions to yourself. But as captain you have to tackle everyone's feelings. It must have been hard on Phil Neal, who needed to deal with his own feelings too in all of this. It must have been heavy.'

Yes, he wishes that he'd managed to stop the match.

'Yes, he went out and tried… It must have influenced him a lot as a person.'

But you signed for Juventus only a year after the tragedy. Was there much talk about Heysel when you arrived at the club?

'No, not really. I think the Juventus fans liked me because I always gave a hundred per cent. So not much was said about the tragedy, really, and I was just happy to have the Juventus supporters on my side.'

You were Liverpool's crown jewel, so to speak. Do you think you were sold to Juventus to build bridges between the clubs?

'I don't really know. That's for the clubs to answer.'

But have you thought about it?

'I've thought about it, but I keep those thoughts to myself.'

The Liverpool striker had scored shedloads of goals at Liverpool and was feared by every opponent. In the Juventus attack he was not quite as lethal. In his one season he scored 14 goals in 39 games for the Italians. It was not that easy adapting to the new culture and language.

'The defensive style of football in Italy didn't suit me all that well. But I still think going to Juventus was the best decision I ever made. It meant a lot to me financially, and I got a much better deal with Liverpool when I returned [in 1988],' he admits. 'Besides, I went there as a boy and returned as a man.'

There are a lot of Liverpool legends, but not all have become club icons. There are players or managers who are put on a pedestal, and decorate the Legends Lounge. Representatives for the club who have done exceptional things: players who make fans' hearts swell with pride. Icons, on the other hand, make supporters smile just by talking about them.

When you're a living icon for a football club that is considered one of the biggest in the world, how on earth do you motivate yourself to play for another club?

'There and then you don't realise the position you're in because you're focusing on the challenge, the next game. When your career is over you realise that you didn't give your all for the next club, after having played for the club in your heart. Because at the time you really think you're doing your best. But you get a hint every time the new team loses, it's not as painful as a Liverpool loss.

'But at the end of the day it's mostly about the supporters. The Liverpool fans were absolutely fantastic to me. It was wonderful to feel their support and how they looked after me when I returned to Liverpool. Not just once, but twice – when I became club ambassador. So thanks to them I feel very lucky, and it's great to be still involved in the club.'

Before he re-signed for Liverpool, he was at Anfield playing in the testimonial for his friend Alan Hansen. The fans chanted to Kenny that he should re-sign Rush from Italy. The shouts of joy were even louder when he pulled on the Liverpool shirt again, and was back at Anfield to play for the Reds. His welcome was heartfelt and overwhelming. 'Rushie is back! Rushie is back!' the Liverpool fans chanted again and again.

He came back in time to be part of the 1989 FA Cup triumph against Everton, where he scored two of the three goals in the thriller final that Liverpool won 3–2. It was one of Rush's best memories from a football pitch.

A couple of years later, when Graeme Souness had taken over as manager of the club, he changed captains from Ronnie Whelan and substitute captain Glenn Hysén to the newcomer, Mark Wright. But results did not go their way, and in 1993 Souness decided to change captains once again, hoping to lift results. This time he chose one of the most experienced on the team, Ian Rush.

Do you remember the day you were appointed captain?

'Yes. Mark Wright was captain, and things weren't going well. We were a mix of old and young players. Mark was England captain, and had done a good job there. But he hadn't had the effect as Liverpool captain that Graeme had hoped. And Mark had just arrived at the club, so perhaps he felt differently to Ronnie Whelan and myself? I remember clearly when Phil Thompson was captain – a very good captain – how Bob Paisley appointed a new captain just for the sake of change, as we weren't playing as well as we should. Which was obviously a massive disappointment to Phil Thompson. I think maybe Graeme thought back to when he was appointed captain after Phil Thompson: Maybe I should appoint a new captain and see if it will lead to any changes? I think that's why Graeme Souness asked me to be captain.'

Rush still did not see himself as an obvious captain. Most of all he wanted to ask if he could just continue as a selfish striker. But he had been at the club for a long time. 'Who else could I ask?' Graeme said. Whelan was not playing regularly, Jan Mølby was on his way out. Bruce Grobbelaar?

The old Liverpool striker from the 1970s, Phil Boersma, was back at Anfield as club coach for Souness. He had not featured much in his heyday as a player, the super duo Keegan and Toshack saw to that. In addition there was supersub David Fairclough.

'Phil Boersma asked all the lads who they wanted as new captain. Everybody said me.'

That's nice.

'Yes, and that was when Graeme came and asked if I would consider the captaincy.'

But, it's not common in England that the manager asks the players who they want as captain?

'No, and perhaps things would have looked different if Whelan had been captain another year before Wright became captain? I'm not sure. And then Graeme made changes too quickly again. I don't think Graeme quite knew how to go about a change of captains. So it suited him well that Boersma asked the players who they wanted as new captain.'

But Rush was not at all convinced he wanted to be captain. He considered the team situation very carefully.

'I looked around the dressing room and felt that it was my turn to do something,' he says. 'So I accepted. I wanted to give it a go and see what happened.'

It was on the pitch and in games that Rush changed after he became captain.

'The team was well aware that I was there for them off the pitch and in the dressing room, but it was first and foremost on the pitch that I did the talking as captain. My job was to make everyone run a little harder, increase intensity. If I could set the standard by my effort and dedication on the pitch, so could all the younger players. Besides, my job was to bring passion to the club. In the dressing room after a match I wasn't like Graeme Souness, or anywhere near him, but come match day, I was more passionate than anyone.'

So you were leading by example, by giving that little extra?

'Yes, to me that's what the captaincy is about, especially on match day. The other days of the week I didn't take any extra responsibility, I didn't want it. I just wanted to concentrate on my playing. So I actually only took over on match days, to motivate in the best possible way. I talked to people one on one, not all together. Someone who hadn't been picked I would tell to keep going. Not lose hope. And those who had been picked I tried to motivate to do their best.'

In matches, if the team was struggling, what kind of instructions would you give: were you aggressive or encouraging?

'Both! But I think the one that learned most from me was Robbie Fowler. He was closest to me and the one it was easiest to instruct and give feedback to. Attackers were easiest to talk to, as the defence was too far off.'

Did you have any allies in defence who could help you?

'No, not really. I captained a young side. If I'd had Jan Mølby or Ronnie Whelan in the team permanently, one of them could have taken responsibility at the back. But I had young players, and newcomers like Mark Wright, and their job was to concentrate on playing. Leading such a young team was very different to what Souness had as captain. It was another world. He had led a different generation and a team full of experienced players. As captain, Souness would hammer us to make us perform better. That didn't work with the team I led. Nineties players were different. They would have taken a hammering to heart. So we had to change the way we communicated. As captain for the Nineties Liverpool you had to focus more on positive feedback and not criticism. It's the same today.'

In what ways did your game change when you became captain?

'I wanted so badly for us to do well, I would run back more than I should have as a striker. The young and inexperienced players at the back made me feel I had to contribute in defence as well. With a more experienced team I could have focused on doing my job: scoring goals. I remember distinctly Souness's repeated instructions when he was captain: "Stay up there." But all the extra running I did when I was captain affected my job as a striker.'

You had a very strong will to win, amazing football skills, and great respect from the players after scoring so many for the club. But what else are you made of? Are you temperamental? Are you aggressive if needs be? What else have you got in you?

'I can put up with a lot. I'm the type who – if backed into a corner – will come out fighting. I didn't say a lot, but people had to listen when I spoke. They listened when I put my foot down or made clear that something wasn't up to standard. I can be easy-going, but if people aren't playing by the rules, I will let them know. And everybody on the team knew that.'

It's about a sense of justice. If someone isn't giving you respect or justice, you will let them hear it?

'You have to. And it reminded me of Joe Fagan. He didn't say a lot, but if Joe was mad, you stopped and listened. Coach Ronnie Moran let us have it every day, but the few times Fagan got mad, everybody stopped and listened. I was a little like that. When I opened my mouth and told people to listen, they did.'

When does an icon retire? There is the balance between quitting while at the top of one's game, and staying in the hope you will have even more triumphs and achievements. When do you know your own limits and retire from something that has afforded you legendary status? When you have been given leadership responsibility as well, maybe you would want to stretch your career a little longer?

On 5 May 1996 Ian Rush scored his last goal for the club, against Manchester City at Maine Road, in the last Premier League game of the season. He led the team out on the pitch as captain for the last time, and played up front with his striking partner Robbie Fowler, the boy from Toxteth who had learned so much from the veteran goal-scorer. In the 41st minute he netted, and made 346 the historic number of goals to beat. Nobody has yet.

The following week, 11 May 1996, dressed in a white Armani suit, striped tie and white Gucci shoes, he arrived in London with the rest of the team. The last match of the season would be played at Wembley, against Manchester United, league champions for the third time in four years. They had really found the winning formula, while Liverpool were thirsting for new triumphs and wanted to bring the FA Cup back home. The two teams who would contest the final had played the most attacking football and been the highest-scoring teams in the league that season.

Rush knew that this was his last game for Liverpool – he had come to an agreement with Leeds United about a transfer. He was desperate to play, but started on the bench. That was why John Barnes, the next in line for the captaincy, led the team out wearing the captain's armband. He was the one who marched out behind Roy Evans, shoulder to shoulder with Eric Cantona. For Rush, starting the FA Cup final on the bench reminded him of the final against Everton in 1989, when he came on in the 73rd minute as substitute for John Aldridge.

'I knew I wasn't starting, because Roy had rested a couple of players for the final. It was built up to be a great final. But 1989 had been different. I started on the bench then too, but at the time I had been fighting for a permanent place in the starting eleven and was absolutely desperate to play. I could have died for a place in the team. But not in 1996. I wasn't fighting for anything, because I knew I was leaving. But I still – obviously – really wanted to get out and play.'

'I might put you on,' Roy Evans had said on the morning before the game.

The 79,000 supporters at Wembley got to see a high-speed game with few chances. Both teams looked nervous. In the 74th minute Roy Evans gave striker hero Ian Rush his last official minutes playing for Liverpool, replacing Stan Collymore.

'It ended up as one of the worst finals,' says Rush. 'Nothing happened in front of United's goal, and Collymore didn't get anything done. Then I came on for him, and I couldn't do much either. It was one of those matches where it just doesn't happen.'

Cantona scored the game's only goal in the 85th minute; Manchester United would go home with the trophy while Rush had to end his career empty-handed.

'We tried as hard as we could, but we lost. It was an incredibly disappointing way to leave the club,' Rush says.

When I meet Ian Rush in May 2015, it is only days since he was in the front row of the executive box in his official Liverpool FC suit, next to Kenny Dalglish. They had seen Steven Gerrard take his leave, after playing his last official game at Anfield. History repeats itself: a club icon has departed.

'It was a very emotional day. Steven has done a fantastic job for the club,' he says. 'The way he was applauded and sung to coming off the pitch showed just how much the supporters respect him. He got an incredible send-off, which he fully deserved. But nobody's bigger than the club. We've got to move on.'

Players come and go. A lot of good players are loved by the fans while playing for the club. But not many are still loved after their time is up. There are not that many icons, who turn into superheroes for the club. But the day will come when even they have to leave the club.

What's the biggest challenge for a club icon the day he's no longer a part of the club's daily life?

'The biggest challenge is to succeed at your next club. It's only when you go to a new club you realise just how big Liverpool Football Club is. You have to leave to be able to see how big the club is. At least that's how it was for me. Maybe it will be different for Steven, but in my eyes, there is no better club. Steven has left, and maybe he'll enjoy his life in the US. Maybe it'll be easier for him? But if it doesn't [work out], there's always a chance he can come back to Liverpool and hopefully have a role here. We just have to wait and see what happens.'

Two captains, two club icons. Rush and Gerrard. You need quality in a lot of areas to take over the captaincy after such players and personalities.

What type of qualities do you have to possess – in your opinion – to be able to captain Liverpool?

'You need a lot of different qualities both on and off the field. And your connection with and feelings for the club are important. You have to know the club well. You must have a lot of experience to play in and lead a top team. And you need the ability to pass on your experience to the other players. Experience is a huge part of it. And you can't play as an individual. As captain you must be strong enough to tell the other players they need to step up their game, even if you're not playing too well yourself. You need that mental toughness. But most important of all is your connection with the club. You're not fit to be captain if you only go out to play for yourself.'

The players said they wanted you as their captain. Why do you think that was?

'I think it was because of my love for the club, and because I had the supporters' backing, for always giving them a hundred per cent. We may not win all our matches, but what the supporters want is for us to give them a hundred per cent.'

For someone who has won the league five times, the FA Cup three times, the League Cup five times, the FA Charity Shield three times and the European Cup twice, there are many proud moments to choose from in an active career. Rush has been voted PFA Young Player of the Year and Player of the Year. He has won the Golden Boot and he was top scorer for Liverpool for a staggering nine seasons. But what was his proudest moment as captain, captain of the team that gave him so many triumphs and that eventually led to his incorporation in the Most Excellent Order of the British Empire, when he received his MBE?

It's none of these things. Instead we have to go back to 2 April 1995 when Liverpool were facing Bolton Wanderers in the League Cup final.

'We played our way to the final, and it was great to be able to put on the white captain's armband and lead the team out at Wembley,' says Rush. 'I knew what it was like to go out there and play finals, but walking out as captain is something else. Especially when you know you may only have one year left, and that this may be your last chance. So I felt privileged to lead the team out, especially for Roy Evans. The supporters were outstanding. It was emotional to lead out a team full of youngsters.'

A 23-year-old Steve McManaman scored the goals in a match Liverpool won 2–1.

'Steve McManaman had a fantastic game, and was awarded man of the match. That's when we realised he could become a player out of the ordinary.'

Roy Evans was overjoyed at his performance, even Bolton's manager was impressed and the Liverpool supporters were ecstatic to have such a jewel with them into the next season.

'It made a strong impression on me, walking up those steps while people shook our hands and congratulated us on the way up. Then to accept the cup from Stanley Matthews and get to lift it up, while the Liverpool fans went wild. Being lucky to win the cup as captain, and get to lift the trophy on behalf of the young team and supporters... I was thinking, Wait a second, hopefully we'll go from here to win bigger things. Taking a lap of honour around the pitch with the team, just like I used to in the old days. This time I'd won as captain with a bunch of youngsters. And I thought: These young kids can achieve so much. Potentially they could win anything after this.'

10

JOHN BARNES
STAR IN TWO ERAS

'John Barnes was my favourite player in the whole world'
Jamie Redknapp

JOHN BARNES IS RELAXED ON A BAR STOOL ON STAGE, somewhere outside Reykjavik. He is wearing a charcoal suit, freshly ironed shirt, no tie and black pointed patent leather shoes. It is March 2014 and the Iceland Liverpool supporters' annual dinner. Earlier that day, he and his wife Andrea went swimming in the Blue Lagoon, as the worst storm in decades was ravaging the picturesque landscape: ripping the roofs off big sports halls, tearing up trees and throwing huge containers into ditches.

Nothing seems to faze Barnes, however, who has an easy manner as he talks from the stage about his life and times.

'When people come up to me and say, "I love you," I stop them and say, "No, you don't love me. You love John Barnes the player, who played ten years for Liverpool."'

John strokes his chin before he continues. He speaks with thoughtfulness and enthusiasm, all delivered at high speed. This is a side of football he loves talking about, and he talks a lot. There are a few hundred festively dressed Icelanders in the room, watching intently.

'Listen to me, people. Fall in love with the football team,' he says. 'Don't fall in love with players. They come and go, but the club will last.'

John Charles Bryan Barnes knows the subject well. He was a top player in two different eras. He played at a crossover time in football, that saw two different generations of players: he was among the last of a generation that stayed loyal to the same club for a number of years, in a club culture where the hierarchy of senior players set the standard for the youngsters on the team. He also got to see up close how football changed radically with the money that followed from the inception of the Premier League circus.

Barnes was born and grew up in Jamaica, where his father was an inspiration in leadership. Roderick Kenrick Barnes, or just Ken, was captain of the Jamaica football team, and later became manager, then president of the Jamaica Football Federation. He was also a military officer and diplomat. He went to watch the Olympics in West Germany in 1972, a trip given as a gift from his wife, and came back with what was to be eight-year-old John Barnes's first pair of football boots: 'Adidas, Gerd Müller', after the national player Gerhard Müller. The legend.

John played football all the time from the age of four. He both admired and tried to copy West German football. Only when he moved to London with his diplomat family at thirteen was he taught that you should not cheer for Germany. Because of the war.

'They hadn't bombed my country!' he reasons. 'Although I still loved the West German side, and still knew the whole Germany squad by heart, I realised I couldn't say out loud that I loved Germany. I had to say that my favourites were Pelé and Brazil. But deep down in my heart, West Germany lurked.'

John Barnes was always full of confidence. That helped him score some true wonder goals. He would just make a decision and go for a shot, unafraid. He puts it down to his background and upbringing, his strong belief in himself. He grew up upper middle class, unlike most former Liverpool captains, who came from working-class backgrounds. His mother, Frances Jeanette, was a lawyer. Very efficiently, she gave birth to three children in only three years. His father was sports mad, a high-ranking military leader, and a very important person in several top-level sports in Jamaica outside football: president of the swimming association, and later one of the founders of Jamaica's first bobsleigh team – later immortalised in the John Candy movie Cool Runnings. Ken Barnes was passionate about anything from squash to football, and his son was named after the Welsh footballer John Charles.

When John was thirteen, Ken Barnes was appointed Jamaica's military attaché to its London embassy. The whole Barnes family moved to London, and it was here where the son would get his introduction to English professional football. John was discovered playing football for the non league team Sudbury Court, and only a handful of people where watching the game when a taxi driver drove by. He stopped and watched and was so impressed with young Barnes, he told a scout he knew from Watford about the abilities of the 16-year-old. A few weeks later the scout came to see John play, and recruited him to the club. When Watford's interest was first registered he joked that he would sign for the club in exchange for training gear.

As a teenager he invested his heart and soul into making it as a professional, and stayed behind in London when the rest of the family moved back to the Caribbean. It was a decision that changed the course of his whole life. He made his debut for Watford aged seventeen, and while at Vicarage Road he played in 296 matches and scored 85 goals.

All these years later, he has done a good deal of thinking about how football has evolved since he first made his way in the early 1980s. He is in high demand as a speaker, talking about football, motivation, team building and racism. He gives speeches to trade and industry, supporters, sports clubs and at universities and schools. In addition, he is a football pundit on television, and appears regularly on screen in various parts of the world, commenting on English and European football.

He came into the Liverpool team in the glory days, and in disbelief he saw how the league winners' medals were just handed over in a plastic bag in the dressing room by Ronnie Moran, with the simple message: 'Meet up for pre-season training, first of July'. Walking over to the physio bench and digging out his medal of that bag was how he marked his first league championship success in 1988. No ceremonial festive speech. No resting on one's laurels. The focus was already on next season.

I have met a lot of football fans who claim that Barnes, at his best, was the world's finest footballer. He won the Football Writers' Player of the Year award twice, was named as the PFA Player of the Year once and finished in the PFA team of the year on three occasions. Before all of that he scored what is arguably the England national team's most beautiful goal, when he dribbled past six Brazilian players and finished by putting the ball in the back of the net at the Maracana in 1984.

On the flight back to England, he was told by representatives of the right-wing extremist party the National Front that his spectacular goal did not count, as England was not a team for black players. He was met with monkey sounds playing at Anfield. As one of England's first internationals of colour, and as Liverpool's first high-profile black player, he heard it all.

His way of dealing with the abuse, his mental strength and his ability to perform so incredibly well under such depressing, racist working conditions, is nothing short of impressive.

'At the time I played, racism was an accepted part of football,' he says. 'It was rife in the stands, and nobody said anything, not even the press.'

It was worse before he came to Liverpool. Following his success at Watford, there were nasty, racist slurs and chants from opposing fans, especially supporters from teams like Millwall and West Ham United. The songs were horrible, and fans threw bananas at him from the stands. When he came to a bigger club, Liverpool, the racism became more visible. But only when Everton fans threw bananas at him in one of his first home games at Anfield did it reach the front pages. The photo of Barnes giving a banana a heel-kick made its way around the world.

'Meeting racism is like everything else in life, really. It's all about how you look at something,' he says. 'Nothing can belittle me or make me feel less because of my skin colour. It's like water off a duck's back. Nobody could make me feel any less worth, or make me angry, if they didn't like me as a black person. I was completely comfortable with who I was – so all the nasty chants didn't get to me at all.'

He says it is solely thanks to his parents and his upbringing, first in Jamaica, and later in the capital of England, that he has such high self-confidence. Growing up in a beautiful and resourceful home in Jamaica made him reflective, strong and unassailable. He believes that if he had grown up in London at the same time, many things would have been different.

'In such an environment you feel like a second-class citizen. If you see that your parents can't get a job because they're black, or if you as a child don't get the same opportunities as white English kids, it will affect your confidence. For me it was different. My mum was a lawyer, my dad was high-and-mighty in the army, and my sisters are both doctors. So I didn't feel inferior. And then I came to London as a teenager. And I experienced that all these white, working-class supporters, with no jobs, sang ugly songs about me. I thought: What are these people on about? Are they trying to make me feel less? I could have dealt with it differently. I could have been a young man who went out there to fight racism. I didn't.'

His mental toughness is impressive; so are his reflections on racism, and his ability to rise above what went on for many, many years. It could have eaten him up and ruined both his career and his life. Mental strength can be a lot of things. It can be the ability to reflect on life and can enable you to reach incredible goals, even under immense pressure.

Barnes says there is a big difference to experiencing racism on the pitch, and if it had been in private.

'If I'm walking down the street, and someone comes up to me and abuses me for my colour, that's a completely different matter – that would be personal. In football it was different, I felt: I got racially abused by the West Ham fans. But the same people would have cheered for me if I played for them. When I played for Watford, I got racist abuse thrown at me from Liverpool fans, but when I played for Liverpool, it was players and fans from Everton who harassed me. My point is, the attacks weren't personal. So I didn't take it personally.'

John Barnes remembers the story about two Kop season-ticket holders. In January 1987 there was a lot of talk about his ability and potential; he was playing incredibly well for Watford and rumour had it he would be signing for Liverpool. But Watford, a club of limited financial means, were always looking over their shoulder and fearful of relegation. Liverpool, therefore, agreed with them to wait until the summer to complete the transfer. The Liverpool rule was never to mention transfers until they were happening. It is said that when Watford then visited Anfield in between Barnes's move, there were two fans on the Kop and one said to the other, 'Just as well we didn't sign him. We don't want black players on our team anyway.'

In June 1987, Barnes was signed for Liverpool by Kenny Dalglish for £900,000. Work was going on to repair the pitch drainage at Anfield, so the first matches Barnes played for the team were away from home. Liverpool's new number ten was impressive. By the time he finally got to play his first match at his new home ground, the fans had already been won over and the Kop sang his name.

Barnes responded to the tremendous welcome in the match against Oxford, scoring with his left foot in spectacular manner. He was fouled and won a free kick; Peter Beardsley took it, rolled the ball to Barnes, and his shot went straight into the top corner.

At that moment, the guy on the Kop, who six months previously had said he did not want black players at Liverpool, looked at his mate and said, 'He's not as black as I thought…'

John loves to recount this story in his speeches. And he smiles telling it.

'I've got to be who I am, not the one you want me to be,' he says. 'I can stay in control of what I do, and my perspective of life. Whether you like me or not.'

May 21. 2015. We are back in Liverpool to talk about the captaincy, the city he chose to settle down in after his playing and managerial careers drew to their conclusions. Yet again, he is immaculately dressed in a suit and newly ironed shirt. No tie. Top button undone. At other times he is often seen in a pair of jeans and a cool T-shirt. He lives with Andrea on the Wirral and they have three children

together. Barnes also has four grown-up children from his first marriage, and with a flock of seven children, and a grandchild on its way (at the time of writing), he has good experience being boss at home.

If you had to try and describe the perfect, ideal captain for a football team, what qualities would this captain need?

'First of all: There is no such thing as a perfect captain! There are so many different types of captains, and they're good for different reasons. There are so many ways to lead and to inspire. But the most important thing for leaders, and anyone else – captains or not – is to be true to your own character. That you're honest enough to be yourself.'

He stirs his latte energetically, and clinks the long teaspoon against the glass.

'Some captains lead by example, like Steven Gerrard. Even though he's become more vociferous over the years, he was a captain who led by example. Other captains lead by talking a lot, shouting, controlling, like Jamie Carragher. My captain at Watford, Pat Rice, had won the double with Arsenal in 1971, and came to Watford late in his career. He would shout and scream and lead that way. We came second in the league under him. There are captains who don't speak at all, but who are simply inspiring through what they do, and how they are as a person. Portugal's Luís Figo was that kind of captain, and he was magnificent. Then there are captains who aren't necessarily the best players on a team, but who lead by having such a strong integrity they control and organise how the players live their lives even outside football.'

Who stands out as a particularly inspiring captain from Liverpool's history?

'Graeme Souness was one of the most inspiring captains Liverpool ever had. He was an aggressive type of player. The same with Tommy Smith, in the early 1970s. Inspiring and aggressive.'

A lot of the captains you mention were aggressive players. Is aggressiveness an important element for a captain?

'No, not necessarily. Alan Hansen wasn't aggressive at all. And Phil Thompson was aggressive vocally, but not in playing. The most important thing for a captain is to be true to your own personality. That you remain true to the type of person and the type of player you are. If you're not an aggressive player or aggressive in communication to begin with, but you adopt the style because you believe the captaincy requires it, you will get found out. The players will see that you're trying to be something you're not. That you're just pretending because of the armband.'

He believes a lot of clubs have a tradition of choosing their captain based on player ability.

'Cristiano Ronaldo is an example of someone who is appointed captain because he's the best player, but who mostly cares about his own game. He's captain for inspiration, and he enjoys great respect on the team and in the club. Captains like that are appointed more out of love than for being great leaders.'

Now that you mention Ronaldo, it makes me think about Ian Rush being appointed captain, before you. Being a good player, a good role model, scoring lots of goals...

'Yes, exactly! Same mechanism. I didn't consider myself a typical captain either. Both Rush and I were among the most experienced players when we were appointed captains. But I'd learned a lot about team ethics through my time at Liverpool, and my time under Graham Taylor at Watford. Both Rush and I understood what it took to make the team work together, and the type of instructions we had to give the players in the various positions.'

In addition, you need the ability to lead the team regardless of whether your own game goes well or not, don't you?

'Phil Thompson was like that. He was strong and influential even when he didn't play well. Even if the captain is struggling in a game, he's got to be powerful and strong enough to continue to discipline the rest of the team. A good captain has to see beyond his own performance. Those are the best captains.'

Barnes played under a lot of captains through his twenty-year playing career. One he characterises as a very good role model is Bryan Robson, who was his England captain through the 1980s. Robson, says Barnes, had the most complete set of captain qualities.

'Robson was a huge role model because of his abilities as a player, but he was also a wonderful captain when matches didn't go that well, he lifted the team with his support and encouragement. We called him "Captain Marvel", and he was an absolutely fantastic captain. But there's still no such thing as a perfect captain.'

How big an influence and how much power does the captain actually have on the pitch?

'That depends. Captains like Phil Thompson are organisers who know what it takes to make the team function at its best as a whole, rather than evaluating and adjusting their own individual skills and performance.'

But what type of influence did you have as captains back then, compared to now?

'No influence! None whatsoever! The managers were so powerful we had no influence, and we shouldn't have either. Or – what do you mean by influence? Team selection? Influence on the pitch, how we played, that kind of thing?'

Being able to change a match if it didn't go according to plan.

'That's a Liverpool phenomenon. Ronnie Moran would always say that you as a player will have to make the changes you feel necessary, whether you're a right-back, goalkeeper, captain or not. In Liverpool we had lots of captains, even if only one wore the armband, because you need lots of leaders on the pitch. And this attitude helped us, but it caused trouble in other clubs. It would cause problems in teams that had a lot of individual players with strong egos. They might end up thinking: The manager has given me permission to change things on the pitch even though I'm not captain. And those players would often end up making changes that were for their own good and not the team's best.

'In Liverpool, on the other hand, everybody had it drilled into them what playing for a team meant, and what it took to make a team work together. Captain or not, if you wanted to change something, it wasn't based on egotistical thinking, but a wish to make a change for the best of the team. We were taught the Liverpool Way that has been the way to build teams since Bill Shankly's time. Whether you'd played under Shankly or not, as soon as you arrived at the club you learned that you did not make selfish decisions. That's not how Liverpool works. We want players on the pitch who understand what's best for the team. Being able to make changes on the pitch whether you're captain or not is a philosophy I believe in with all my heart.'

But still, with so many strong personalities and leader types on a team, and the right to make changes: there must have been some arguing over how to do things?

'Oh, absolutely. Graeme Souness and Kenny Dalglish were always at loggerheads. Even though Souness was captain, Dalglish wanted to tell the team of changes they needed to make. And he had that right, despite not being captain, because of who he was, to the club and to the other players. The two of them would shout at each other in the dressing room, and the manager would just sit there and listen, quite calmly. Usually it's the manager shouting and screaming in the dressing room if there's a problem. If Ronnie Moran came in when Dalglish and Souness were at it, he'd respond by saying, "Work it out for yourselves."'

And that was all he'd say to resolve the situation?

'Yes. Because the players were able to work things out among themselves, and by that he meant for the best of the team, not for their own best. Despite having big egos in the squad, like Thommo and Souness, we had one ego that was bigger than every other: the team ego. It was always that way at Liverpool.'

Barnes says Liverpool would have won the trophies in their heyday regardless of who had been captain, simply because the team had such good players – and they were all leaders. But modern football is something else entirely. He believes captains are more important today, because a lot of players are afraid to take responsibility. Very few players have the strength of character to go against the manager.

'Liverpool today is symptomatic of how modern football has changed. Because of textbook tactics, the game has changed enormously. You've had so many elements of statistics and technology added to football. When a game doesn't go well, the players look to the bench and the manager for advice. You've no longer got the players who can take charge and change things themselves, because that's not how they've been trained. [They're] shaped by statistics and analysing tools, and tactics adapted from analysis results. And because you've moved away from the independent ability to change, there aren't that many leaders on the pitch any more. The manager is the sole leader these days, hopefully helped by an inspiring captain.'

So today the captain is more important than he used to be. If you find the right captain, he'll function as the manager's extended arm on the pitch?

'Exactly. That's why captains today are much more important. Because very few players have the personality and courage to defy the manager if matches don't go well. The Istanbul final between AC Milan and Liverpool is an extraordinary example. It proves how the captain helped turn the match around. Of course, you could argue that Rafael Benítez changed the match at half-time by bringing on Didi Hamann, and you hear the commentators say, "Oh, the manager has really improved their play by these changes." But in that Champions League final, Gerrard was an incredibly important part of the turnaround. Not many captains could have done what Gerrard did.

'If you look at captains in top international football, the most inspiring and influential captains are players who rose in the ranks before the crossover time in football, that is when TV rights came in with the big money. Gerrard and John Terry are examples of that kind of captain. But remember, they grew up admiring the old-school players. If you look at the next generation of captains, twenty-five and twenty-six-year-olds, they haven't got the same personality. Players of Lionel Messi's generation aren't the same as the old-school captains. They lead the team because they're fantastic players, but if they meet heavy opposition, they can't change tactics for the best of the team.'

The strong captain with big influential power seems to be a dying breed, so to speak. Barnes also thinks that communication within the team is a huge challenge today, with all the different nationalities and languages.

'Just imagine Jamie Carragher, talking quickly in his strong Scouse to Jerzy Dudek before the penalty shoot-out in Istanbul, telling him about Grobbelaar's spaghetti legs in Rome. Dudek probably didn't understand a word of what Carra said. Not even I understand Carra!'

John smiles his biggest smile.

With all the nationalities and language barriers in top modern teams, you need to put together a team of similar-type players. Players who adapt well to a certain style of play, and who identify with the one of that club. A style chosen by the manager, Barnes says.

'Look at Diego Costa at Chelsea, for instance. He doesn't need to speak the same language as his team-mates, but they speak the same kind of football language. Chelsea pick aggressive players who can play their type of aggressive football. It can be a success if it works out.'

Is there an ideal position for a captain on the pitch?

'There isn't one ideal position, but there are ideal people for the captaincy. It will often be the most high-profile player of the team. And that's a wise move, because if you make unpopular choices, it's easier for the bigger stars to front them. Because of their star standing, they're already making both fans and owners happy.'

Do you think some clubs give their biggest star the captaincy in an attempt to keep him at the club? I mean, using the captaincy as bait?

'I hope not! I would have questioned the player's character if he needed a captaincy as motivation to stay at a club. If you're not motivated, you shouldn't be there. But unfortunately, I think it does happen.'

From 1993 to 1996, Ian Rush was Liverpool's captain. When he left the club for Leeds United, Barnes was appointed his successor by Roy Evans. But the appointment was so insignificant for his career that he cannot even remember how he came to succeed Rush.

'I never considered myself a proper captain,' he says. 'I wasn't a Souness or a Phil Thompson. Ian Rush and I were the most experienced players, and that earned us the captaincy in turn, but it didn't make us proper captains. Rush and I were the last of the old Boot Room culture, where the captaincy went to the one next in line. It wasn't meant as a reward.'

You didn't consider it a kind of reward, even so?

'Yes, I mean, it's nice. And I felt that my most important responsibility was to teach players about our club culture and club mentality. The Liverpool Way. But being appointed captain didn't make me more inspired or more responsible as a player. The captaincy didn't change me at all. I just tried to be the person that I am, and continued to help my team-mates, as I had done for years, leading them. Whether I had the armband or not. Because you're not supposed to work even harder when you're a captain. You're supposed to work as hard as you can anyway. So I didn't change. And I don't think Rush did when he was captain.'

But weren't you given more jobs to do, outside matches, when you were captain?

'Not at all. Football has changed a lot in that respect. In my time as a player, and until 1997, there wasn't much to do for a captain outside match days. Back then, the captain first and foremost had to help the nineteen/twenty-year-olds on the team in matches. Other than that, you were just a normal player.'

There are so many different types of captains. So many different types of leaders. What kind of leader is John Barnes?

'I'm a leader who thinks the team is the most important. It may sound extreme, but you must be willing to die for your team. Go into war with the team, and protect the players. An example of that protection part would be, if Gareth Bale of Real Madrid makes a mistake, Cristiano Ronaldo should applaud and encourage him, instead of pointing and criticising him. Modern players don't deal well with criticism.'

Barnes thinks that another sign of the gulf between 'old school' and 'new school' football is the will to pull in the same direction, and listen to team leaders.

'Take Raheem Sterling. He's an example of a modern-time player who didn't want to be led by Liverpool, he had his own agenda. And then there was Bryan Robson, a complete opposite from a time long gone. Even though he was the captain, he was willing to be led by Manchester United. Would he leave the club if they weren't winning? He was good enough to play anywhere. But he didn't, he still wanted to lead Manchester United. It's a big problem in football today, a lot of players don't want to be led by the team, they have other agendas.'

Barnes draws a deep breath and takes a rare and, for him, very long pause to think.

'I wasn't very happy towards the end of my career, because I was playing with people who weren't interested in being led,' he admits. 'I was unlucky enough to become captain at a time when the youngsters suddenly became more important than the older and more experienced players.'

The Bosman ruling, from the European Court of Justice in Luxembourg, made it possible for players to leave their club for free when their contract ran out. It made it more important than ever for clubs not to lose their best young players.

'Young players were given big contracts so the club could keep them. And all of a sudden these youngsters felt indispensable and important, with all their focus on contracts and agreements. Suddenly it was important not to provoke them, in case they demanded short contracts. That's why the captain doesn't have the same authority as in the old days; football changed completely.

'Back then, if Phil Thompson said jump, you jumped. Even at the end of his career, when he was no longer among the best players. But it was an authority the players just accepted that the captain had. Whereas I was captain at a time when the players who came in didn't have that discipline, so as a captain I no longer had that authority. The long-standing tradition of the club was that younger players listened to their seniors, but now all that had changed.'

Football has, indeed, changed forever. Old club traditions were abolished for new business practices. The huge influx of television-rights revenue has altered the focus of many clubs. Barnes, as a captain, admits he left the training field twice in frustration at the shift in attitudes and motivations.

'As a captain, I would try to make sure we had good training sessions. We lost matches, and I tried to work on the discipline and quality of training, but the players didn't want to do what I said. And when I ordered them to do something, they ignored me. So I left the training field out of frustration at the lack of discipline in the squad. I didn't leave training because I thought I was a superstar, an arrogant bloke who just ran off. It was unbelievably frustrating coming from the football tradition I did, where the captain and senior players had strong authority and influence. And then not to have the required authority as a captain. And I didn't get the necessary support from the club either, when I was trying to consolidate my authority as captain.

'So I ended up as captain in the transition period when it became hard for senior players to control younger players.

'Before Bosman, in the old time, the young players knew there would be consequences if they behaved badly towards the captain or the senior players, because the club would always side with the most experienced players. So it was extremely frustrating during my year as captain when people at the club asked me to do certain things, as a captain, and all I could say was, "I'll do my best." Because unless people are willing to be led...

'Shaping young players is a little like raising a child. If you eat chocolate every day, your teeth will eventually fall out. Someone has to teach you what to eat instead of chocolate, and explain why.'

And amid all this, there was a shift in power in English football: the unstoppable Reds of Merseyside were repeatedly beaten by the Red Devils from Manchester.

'There wasn't really that big a difference between players like Scholes and Beckham and our players. Ours were just as good. The difference was that Alex Ferguson kept his players under his thumb. He controlled their lives off the pitch as well as on it. He made sure they didn't go out partying at the wrong time, and that they kept focus. Ferguson was like a father to them. It's incredible how important such knowledge and routines are before the age of twenty-five. After that it's too late to teach players discipline.

'One important difference was how Manchester United's manager controlled his team, compared to our boss. While Ferguson controlled his team with an iron fist, Roy Evans came from a tradition and a time where there was no need for the manager to discipline the players; that was the job of the senior players. But the mid-1990s was the beginning of the end for a time when senior players set the standard.

'Roy Evans was torn between what he thought was the right way of doing things, and what was right in modern football. He had to fight during a crossroads in football.'

Did you sometimes make suggestions for Roy Evans on which team to pick?

'No! I'd never have picked Roy's team. That's not something you can do. But I told him how I felt about the training sessions.

'But as captain, coach or manager, you need to be clear about what you're trying to achieve, and I believe I'm very clear and distinct in my coaching ideas. The most difficult part of being a leader in football after the mid-90s is to have the players follow your thoughts and ideas. In the old days, it was all about doing what the boss told you to do, but now the manager has to massage the players' egos. I would have loved to be a manager in the old days.

'The reason I left Liverpool in the end, was that the club's hierarchy no longer supported me.'

After playing for Newcastle for a couple of seasons, first a year under Kenny Dalglish, and then half a season under Ruud Gullit, followed by a short stay at Charlton Athletic, Barnes retired as a player after an impressive eighteen years in football's service. Then he started his managerial career by becoming Celtic's head coach, working under Dalglish, who had been made director of football. The move was ill-fated and Barnes was sacked after a notorious Scottish Cup defeat to Inverness Caledonian Thistle.

'I think I'm a good communicator, but you do need a team that's willing to be led,' Barnes says. 'At Celtic, when I was assistant manager under Kenny Dalglish, the players wouldn't let me lead. Then the fans won't support you, they're on the players' side. And if the fans don't like you, the owners may fire you. Unfortunately, players aren't loyal, so it becomes a vicious circle for the club. That's why it's important that fans support the club, not the players. They come and go.'

John Barnes does not select a proudest moment as a Liverpool player. Instead he prefers to reflect on a collection of memories.

'I look back and take great pride in playing for Liverpool for a decade,' he says. 'I could have been selfish and said that one particular match was my proudest moment, for instance because I scored five. But what good is that, if we lost 5–6? I don't separate one individual moment from the rest and say that is my proudest moment, because the life experience I got at Liverpool is from both the good and the bad experiences. It's made up of the first time I won the league with Liverpool, the next year when we lost so narrowly to Arsenal, that I've been through the Hillsborough tragedy with the team, the city and the families. I've been through tragedies, and I've been through triumphs. And I look back and can tell myself that I'm happy about how my career has gone.'

John Barnes is one of Liverpool's greatest legends. The boy from Jamaica who, in 1974, in his first pair of football boots and a West Germany supporter cap, saw his heroes play the World Cup final against the Netherlands, and win. Watching it all on a big screen in the Caribbean heat. The country, the culture and, more than anything, his parents and his upbringing shaped him into one of England's wisest football heads, and a leader.

'The most important thing I learned was humility,' he concludes. 'We're all just people. If you've got a talent, respect that talent more than you respect what you achieve. I'm just so grateful for the opportunities I got. I'm very grateful I had a chance to play for Liverpool. I'm more grateful for that than for what I've achieved.'

11

PAUL INCE
FROM ABANDONED CHILD TO ENGLAND CAPTAIN

'He was a typical captain in the way you think a captain is:
a big personality with a strong presence. Big mouth.'
Jamie Carragher

PAUL INCE IS THE LONDON CHILD WHO WAS ABANDONED BY his parents, but went on to achieve what no one else has: to captain two of the biggest clubs, and rivals, in England. He also lived the ultimate boyhood dream of millions: he became captain of the England national team. He then made history as the first Premier League manager with black skin. If you listen to Paul Ince, you realise anything is possible: that you can reach as far as you want, even without the support, love and security that every child should really grow up with. When he talks about his childhood, the light in his eyes goes out.

When Paul Ince was two years old, his dad took off and his mother was left alone with three children in Ilford, a tough neighbourhood in north-east of London. When he was ten years old, his mother left as well. She took her daughter with her as she moved to Germany to work. Paul's eldest brother was placed with an aunt in Ipswich; Paul, the youngest, ended up with another aunt, in Ilford – where gang mentality was prevalent and crime was flourishing. Until the age of fifteen – the years where many feel at their most vulnerable, and your body and mind go through enormous changes on the road to becoming who you are – Paul had to find his own way. His aunt was almost never home.

'I had to fight for my life,' he says starkly. 'I had no support around me, and had to take care of myself. I was always on the streets fighting. It was an incredibly rough time in Ilford.'

His mother never returned to England. Being abandoned by both his parents as a young child left its marks.

How could she leave such young children? Did you become bitter towards your mother?

'No, I didn't, life's too short,' he says when I meet him in Liverpool the first week of June 2015, to what will be Ince's first in-depth interview about his whole life. No documentary has been filmed, and no autobiography has been published that tells his powerful story.

'I have asked myself many times how she could just leave us,' he continues. 'But it is what it is. And as I grew older I understood a little better: she had to leave us to make money. If she hadn't, she couldn't have sent money home. And if she hadn't sent money, I couldn't have bought football boots. And I wouldn't have become a footballer.'

His mother did send money home from time to time, but nowhere near as much as he needed for equipment. He played till his boots were full of holes, and eventually the temptation to find gear in other ways became too much.

'I had holes in my shoes, holes in my football boots, and I didn't get money every month. I had to take the bus everywhere because I had no one to drive me, and it was freezing. I remember very well this one match we played, I was about twelve. We were up 4–0 and I got myself sent off on purpose, because my shoes were so full of holes. I'd been playing with the same pair for two years. The temptation was just too big: I went into the opposing team's changing room and stole a pair of football boots.'

A gang of twenty boys who met regularly on the street corner became his family. That was where he found belonging and comfort. That was also where he learned to fight – because this was a notorious gang that was often visited by other gangs from other neighbourhoods, that wanted someone to measure their strength with.

Paul defines these weekly fights as 'good punch-ups'. It is difficult to fathom how anyone can define hitting and kicking each other as hard as they could as in any way 'good'. But perhaps some are born warriors and some are not. And for some, the path life gives you is what makes you a warrior. And maybe even a leader. Because when you are alone in the world as a child, you have to take charge of yourself.

'When you're little and you haven't got a family, but you'd love to have one, and there's this group of boys around you, all willing to die for each other, they become incredibly important,' he reflects. 'They become your family.'

School was defined as not cool. For most of the boys in his gang, there were few or no responsible adults around who could or even wanted to convince the kids that school was a sound investment if you wanted a future that was something else other than street trouble.

'I was never really in school,' he says. 'I wasn't thick, I was streetwise, but I just didn't like school. We'd rather meet up in the park, play football and fight with the other gangs.'

But the gang was divided between those who sometimes went to school and those who almost never did. You had to make sure there was enough muscle from your gang in school to help your mates in fights there.

'I remember one day in secondary school, we were fighting against this other gang. A teacher came out and told us to quit. But we ended up attacking him too, which led to more teachers coming out and trying to stop us. It was complete chaos.'

Paul was suspended and when he returned, they took away from him all the subjects he enjoyed, like PE. He was made to choose between needlework, metalwork or typing. Just the thought of all the teasing if he did needlework made him cringe. And he hated the metalwork teacher. Out of the question. The typing class had a lot of cute girls, though, he could always brag about that. That was how he ended up the only boy in an all-girl typewriting class. He got excellent grades too, proving to himself and others that he – despite bad grades in most subjects – was not stupid. The biggest problem was that his school was not interested in him.

And when it came to football, despite being a troublemaker, he was lucky enough to have a huge talent. And he had cause to be very grateful to West Ham's manager John Lyall.

'Not a lot of people know this, but to begin with I trained with both Fulham and West Ham. But I chose to sign for West Ham because they had indoor training facilities where I could keep warm in the winter.'

When he was fifteen years old, West Ham put him up in digs in Dagenham, with a woman called Barbara. By then his mother had moved from Germany back to Barbados, where the family came from, again taking only Paul's sister with her.

Barbara, a widow in her sixties, living on her own, had room both in her house and her heart for a troublemaker from Ilford. The boy finally had a safe place to live: a house where genuine, dedicated care was included; a refuge where he did not have to watch his back, but finally – finally – got some parental concern after so many years without a mother. Paul describes her as being 'like Mrs Doubtfire' due to her 'loveable face and caring eyes'.

Barbara would have dinner prepared after training. She would be ready with food and questions about how training had gone. The two of them would sit and drink tea and chat all evening. She bought him a record player and he used to listen to Thelma Houston, Luther Vandross, Keni Burke and many more in his room.

'I could lie and listen to music. In the evenings Barbara would come up to my room with dinner on a tray. After an hour she'd come back up and get the tray again. Later in the evening I'd go down to check on her, sometimes she'd fallen asleep in a chair. I would make sure she made it upstairs to sleep in her bedroom.'

Bennett's Castle Lane, where Ince used to hang around with the gang, was just up the road. Despite the improved living arrangements and care, he continued to fight with his gang every weekend, even after he started training and playing for West Ham.

'It must sound weird, but it's a nice time to think back on, all the fights with the gang. None of us had knives or anything like that. It was good fights. Solid rounds of beating. We went to King's nightclub on Friday nights to fight. Other groups showed up to fight us. There were a few broken noses and slashed faces and black eyes...'

I don't see any scars on your face.

'That's because I was such a good fighter. But look at my nose! I've no idea how many times it's been broken.'

The fights where regular and a behaviour just as normal to him as playing football. It was a part of him growing up, and he is certain it helped shape him into the player and leader he would later become. The group fights were something his friends looked forward to.

'That's just how it was. This was my way of looking after my team-mates. My family. This was my way of being a leader of my men.'

What did this upbringing do for your development as a leader?

'My background and growing up in the gang was no doubt the most important factor of my life to make me a leader. I've had to take charge my whole life, even as an irresponsible kid. But I was responsible in my own way, as no one else was responsible for me.'

Ince's double life of nightclubs, drinking and fighting every Friday as 'preparation' for matches had to go wrong eventually. He had signed a trainee contract with West Ham, and as part of this programme he had to return to his old school to do sixth form part-time. During his first year, the school arranged a party for the second year sixth form students. His gang decided to gate-crash the party, which was not popular. And unfortunately it ended as it often did: in a huge brawl.

About four weeks later, Mick McGiven, who was John Lyall's assistant, came over to Ince with a face that told him he was in big trouble. He was told to go and see the boss in his office.

'It was like walking the long, green mile. The feeling you've got when you're going to see your parents and you know you're in trouble.'

In the office, he found West Ham's manager with two policemen. Lyall asked Ince if he knew why the police was there. Ince said that he had no idea.

It turned out a boy had a broken jaw and a pierced eardrum after the fracas in school a few weeks before, and Ince had been reported as the perpetrator.

'There were ten or twelve of us showing up at that party, but of course the boy had said it was me – Paul Ince, the footballer.'

Lyall explained that he had spent the last hour persuading the police not to arrest him. Instead he was punished with a six-week training ban, the worst punishment thinkable for a kid who loved his football. In addition, he had to paint the Upton Park gates, ten layers at least, and the whole stadium entrance. Every day he felt the humiliation of standing there painting while his team-mates walked past him. Coat after coat.

'That was the turning point for me,' he admits. 'When something goes wrong, you want someone to support you. Lyall could have given up on me and listened to his staff who said I was just trouble and extra work. But he gave me a second chance, because he knew there was something in me. It was my salvation. He made me believe in myself. John Lyall was like a father figure to me, and I wanted to give something back by showing him I could play football. It's quite simply thanks to John that I've had a successful career. Without him, it could have all ended very abruptly. '

What did Lyall see in you that made him not give up on you, even though you did cause him trouble and extra work?

'I've asked myself that many times… it's a good question. I was a nuisance, but he knew I could play. So if he managed to teach me some manners and respect, he knew I'd make a good footballer.'

What were the most important things you learned from John Lyall's leadership?

'He was a hard, hard man. It was always scary to go into his office, but nine times out of ten he was fair. Besides, he had an aura about him, a massive presence. His management style made everyone stop and listen when he talked. That inspired me.'

West Ham had finished inside the top ten positions for three seasons in succession in the mid 1980s. During the 1988/89 campaign, Ince scored twice in a stunning 4-1 victory over Liverpool in the League Cup. Though West Ham would reach the semi finals of that competition, they would never recover from the disappointment of defeat to Luton Town and relegation was soon confirmed.

Ince was twenty two and the club was struggling financially. It was time to move for the young talent. But he had no idea who had been watching him in match after match for several weeks. One day when he was at a hotel he was told to go upstairs and then instructed to enter a door. Alex Ferguson was waiting on the inside. No prior hint or warning.

'Would you consider playing for Manchester United?' Ferguson asked.

'Are you kidding?'

Paul Ince is remembered now as a supremely confident sportsman but it has not always been that way. His first thought was that someone was having him on, pulling his leg. When he sat down with the Manchester United manager, he realised the Scot was serious.

Ince had admired United from afar – and modelled his game on the England captain, Bryan Robson. He wanted to play like him. Tackle like him.

'Bryan Robson was all I wanted to be. Because of him I'd followed Manchester United closely growing up, without being able to afford as much as a Man United scarf. So it was a bigger dream for me to go to Man United to play with Robson than it was to play for Manchester United.'

Ince wanted to shout it from the rooftops, but had to wait. He underwent the medical test, and took the famous photo with the Manchester United kit – the one that leaked out before the shock: he had failed the medical. The doctor had discovered a problem with his groin when Ince was doing some stretches. He was rejected.

With his tail between his legs he returned to West Ham, where half the supporters were happy to have their big talent back, while the other half was furious for the disloyalty of this kid, who had been in the West Ham system since the age of twelve. They let him – and his girlfriend – have it. They booed both of them.

Two weeks later, the phone rang. Alex Ferguson called to confirm that Manchester United wanted to sign him despite the failed medical. Ferguson knew that Ince had not missed a game in three years, and had a lot of faith in him. If his groin troubled him in the future, the club would do whatever it took. Ferguson vouched for Ince. £1 million was transferred to West Ham – and Ince made sure to ask for a percentage of the transfer. That made for a nice sum on his way up north.

'Again there was one man who believed in me, despite the medical warning. One man who allowed me to develop as a player. My career could have taken a completely different turning if I'd stayed at West Ham.'

What sort of manager was Alex Ferguson?

'He was tough, had a massive presence. He scared us, we were actually frightened of him, but he cared too. He saw us boys as family. He had a great knack of bringing fifteen or sixteen egos together every weekend to win matches. It took a strong personality to lead us. Once again I was in an environment where you had to fight for your spot, but I've been fighting my whole life, and I'm good at it.'

But what was it like, playing your way into a team of so many egos?

'I decided to be quiet for a week, and observe how they did things there. It was really hard. But I quickly realised I just had to be myself. Be true to my character – and the lads knew what I was like anyway. We won my first match 5–1, but we lost the second 5–1 to Manchester City, and couldn't get out of the hotel afterwards. The fans were fuming, results really mattered to them. We were getting criticised by the press afterwards, but it didn't affect me as much as some of the others. I'd dealt with stuff like that my whole life. But Man United are a big club. You've got to train well and perform well in every game. You can't have an off-day.'

In the 1989/90 season, Liverpool won the league title, finishing 31 points ahead of Manchester United. After the 5–1 blunder, Ince did not play for four games. Robson was back in midfield. Later he got a chance, but as a right-back, a position he kept for ten games.

'It was amazing to play alongside Bryan Robson. I was like a kid again.'

His voice thickens.

'Robson took me under his wing. For the next two to three years he instructed me and taught me. He showed me what it takes to play for Manchester United – when it comes to team-mates, fans, coaches and other employees of the club. Steve Bruce was a massive help as well. I was still cocky, but I quickly learned to be a bit more respectful thanks to Mr Robson and Bruce.'

He got on well with Ryan Giggs and Lee Sharpe, and found himself in a new little gang in the northwest of England.

Life as a right-back came to a sudden stop when Manchester United met Liverpool, and he was up against left-winger John Barnes, who was unstoppable. Ince stood no chance, and was written off as a defender immediately. Liverpool won 2–1, and Barnes scored both.

This was March 1990, just before the shift in which northwest red team would dominate English top-flight football. Ince was one of the important reasons why the devils of Manchester won the league again in 1993, after a 26-year drought.

'Beating Barcelona in the Cup Winners' Cup in 1991 was the turning point for the club, it changed our mentality. That's when we knew we were ready to win things. Not just that year, but for several years to come.'

They certainly did. And it was huge for Liverpool's arch-rivals to finally win the league again.

'It was quite a pressure from Aston Villa, Norwich and Blackburn. But as weeks went by towards the end of the 1992/93 season, the fans sensed that we might just be able to pull it off. The most important thing about winning that year was that we managed to win the league before Sir Matt Busby died.'

Bryan Robson was at the end of his career, and Steve Bruce had taken over as captain. But Ferguson had not appointed a vice-captain. Bruce had to miss a match, and Ince had been wondering about his chances of being appointed. And sure enough, inside the changing room, the captain's armband was on his hook, over shirt number eight... but not a single word had been spoken about it.

'When I walked out of the players' tunnel with the armband, I suddenly thought: What if the armband had been put on the wrong peg, what if it was actually meant for someone else? That would have been so embarrassing!'

They won the match, and afterwards Ferguson said that he ought to appoint Ince captain more often.

'"No, Bruce is our captain," I said. A few years earlier I'd probably have agreed with him, but now I had matured both as a person and a player. It earned me respect from the other lads.'

He eventually succeeded Bruce as United captain, and later made history when he became the first black person to captain England.

'It was the most nervous time as captain in my career, leading England out against Italy at Stadio Olimpico in Rome [in 1997 for an important World Cup qualifier]. I wasn't doubting my own game, because by then I'd probably been captain at least two hundred times. But I was nervous because I knew how important it was for the team to qualify for the World Cup. There was a lot of pressure because we hadn't qualified in 1994. Now I'd taken on responsibility after the legend Tony Adams, and if we didn't qualify, it'd be my mistake. I think sometimes that's a good sign of a captain, to be willing to take responsibility and blame for the other players. I think I didn't fall asleep until three in the morning the night before the game. The atmosphere in the changing room was tense. And I felt I had to say something. Ten minutes before walking onto the pitch, I got up and stood in the middle of the room. I stood still, no need to shout, it was so quiet. I said: "Listen guys. This is the lions' den, and we need to remember that we've got the lions on our shirt. Listen to the crowd, let's go out and show them why we're wearing three lions on our badge!"'

His pep talk lasted maybe fifteen seconds. But he thinks this short speech made a big difference. Something happened in there. Ince could sense optimism and self-confidence spreading across the changing room. England played beyond expectation, and the goalless draw secured them a spot at the World Cup.

'I've thought about it later, why did I say just that? And why do the things we say make a difference, why does it affect people? Maybe I'm able to say some of the right things because of all the crap I've been through in life?'

It is not every day that inspirational words come to you and give you the knock-out effect you want them to. Or rather: words do not always have the power you want them to. When Ince was about to give his very first pep talk as manager for Macclesfield Town in 2006, he wanted to motivate and inspire the team before the match. But who was Paul Ince, the manager? He knew well the player Paul Ince, and the captain Paul Ince, who had done this hundreds of times before. But the manager Ince?

'We were in a small changing room, about to play Boston United. All the players were staring at me. I felt nervous, my hands were sweating, my mouth was dry. And then I just started talking. They seemed to be listening, but I felt like it had no effect. I was out of my comfort zone. As captain of a team I know well, and that knows me, it's a different matter.'

You lacked self-confidence, so you lost the power?

'Exactly! Spot on. They respected me because I was Paul Ince, but I still didn't have the same influence. We lost 3–2, Boston scored in the last minute. It was devastating because the team had played their best football in a long time. And you'd like a good start. The lads all left the pitch with their heads down. By then I'd had ninety-five minutes to evaluate them and to plan what I was going to say, it was easier to talk after the game, because I had something to grab hold of. Afterwards I talked as if I were the captain of the ship. And that's exactly what I am: the captain of the ship. The team ship. And from then on we started winning matches.'

In 1995 Manchester United missed out at the death on a league and FA Cup double, losing the title on the last day of the season to Blackburn Rovers and then losing the FA Cup final to Everton. Alex Ferguson sought to rebuild his team around youth and instigated a cull. Steve Bruce joined Birmingham City; Andrei Kanchelskis left for Everton; Ince was a £7.5 million departure to Inter Milan. Serie A was the biggest league in the world and Inter were desperate to step out of the shadow of their dominant Milanese neighbours. In two years at the club Ince was a qualified success, Inter losing the UEFA Cup final on penalties in his second year but failing to overcome the stranglehold of AC Milan in the league.

Ince rates some of his football friendships highly, like the ones that developed on the England team with Robbie Fowler, Jamie Redknapp, Steve McManaman and David James. These friendships made it clear for him that Liverpool were the only club he really wanted to play for when returning to England. In 1997 his wife wanted to return from Italy. Their oldest son Tom was five and about to start school. When Liverpool came calling, the lure was strong thanks to his England team-mates.

'Everything was so serious on the England team when I got there. It was a little intimidating. Luckily, there were a few with a mad streak about them: Robbie Fowler, Macca [Steve McManaman], Ian Wright, Les Ferdinand and Paul Gascoigne. We'd mess about and fight and try to get that club kind of feeling to the team.'

Roy Evans told me that he brought you to Liverpool because the team needed change and he felt that called for your leadership experience. What was it like to come straight from enemy territory and be selected captain?

'I didn't look at it like that. I went from Manchester United to Inter Milan, and then my wife wanted to return to England. I knew that Liverpool needed a player like me in midfield. I knew about the Spice Boys term, from the year before, and sensed that the player mentality wasn't quite right in the squad. They suffered under the Spice Boys stigma, the will to win and the focus just wasn't quite right with everyone. They needed someone to take them by the scruff of the neck and make them do everything right: train enough, stretch, not go partying.'

Ince knew that John Barnes, who was captain at the time, was nearing the end of his career.

'I didn't have to come in as captain. I was a leader type anyway. But I was confident Liverpool needed someone like me. There weren't enough winning types on the team. And there's a saying: Surround yourself by winners – and you'll be winners. Winning motivated me, but I realised that for some, winning wasn't important enough.'

He got off to a good start, scoring on his home debut against Leicester City, and then later that season in the Merseyside derby, which always helps to win the supporters' hearts.

'Luckily, the Liverpool fans accepted me. Otherwise it would have been tough. I think it would have been different if I'd come directly from Manchester United. But even the fans felt they needed a player like me. And the players accepted me as their captain, they realised they needed an Incey! Unfortunately it didn't work out quite as I had imagined.'

What was the biggest difference between leading Manchester United and Liverpool?

'The biggest difference is, I was younger at United. I thought a lot more about whether I had the knowledge and respect to be a captain. When I was Liverpool captain, I knew I had the knowledge and respect straight away when I arrived at the club. And this isn't me being clever, the Liverpool players also knew right away that I could lead them, and they wanted me to do it. It gave me more responsibility and more excitement. In United the players were drilled and disciplined into doing the right thing every week, but in Liverpool it was more on and off.'

Ince remains convinced they would have succeeded at Liverpool if he and Roy Evans had been allowed more time together.

'I think we would have got there under Roy. Because I'd have known who was interested in doing things the right way, and who wasn't. And those who weren't, we would have gotten rid of. And remember, a young Michael Owen was coming in, a young Stevie G, Steve McManaman, Robbie Fowler, Jamie Redknapp. They were all young, and all top, top players. But there were some players I just couldn't influence. That wasn't open to change. In other words – some wanted change and some didn't. And we didn't have time to get rid of the latter.

'At Manchester United this wouldn't have been a problem, because everyone was taught how to respond. You entered a cycle as soon as you came into the club – you learned how everything was supposed to go from the top of the club downwards. How you were meant to behave. But when you came to Liverpool and other clubs it wasn't like that. How do I behave here? How do people do it here? What's the club philosophy? It was difficult, because without clear lines, a club philosophy and discipline, it was almost impossible to make the players understand what they needed to do to succeed.'

John Barnes said that the most frustrating part of being a captain was that a lot of players didn't want to be led.

'Barnes probably had the worst of it. Because when I came in after him, half the group had realised that change was necessary. But then there was still a group that didn't want change. That makes the team-leader job very difficult. Do you concentrate on the ones who want change or those who don't?'

Paul Ince thinks the collaboration between the captain and the manager is very important.

'I worked well with Ferguson, and I worked well with Roy Evans, but I couldn't make it work with Gérard Houllier. I saw Evans as my manager, not Houllier. He wasn't my manager; Evans was the boss when I came in from Inter. It just doesn't work with two managers, so I was sad Roy couldn't continue. We came third and fourth, which qualifies for Champions League today – and he was fired for it. It really disappointed me.'

Paul Ince is the only modern player who has captained both Manchester United and Liverpool – two clubs with extremely proud and rich histories, several steps ahead of any other English club in terms of triumphs and the number of trophies in their cabinets. He has several hundred matches altogether as a captain. Between 1997 and 1999, he was the leader on the pitch for Liverpool.

What was your proudest moment as captain of Liverpool?

'The match against Manchester United at Anfield was one of the absolute highlights. I'm not a goal scorer, but I always wanted to score in front of the Kop. So doing that against Man United was fantastic. We were 2–1 down, when Denis Irwin was sent off for United. There were only a few minutes left. McManaman went down on the left side, someone tackled him, but as he fell the ball went through the player's legs. I slid underneath Schmeichel and scored. I just had to celebrate the goal. Because this was a memory that I wanted to last.

'We could have been such a good team. Unfortunately, we weren't that good defensively, but the midfield and attack was definitely the best in the league. So it frustrates me that we didn't get more time together.'

Having been a Manchester United player for six years, several of them as team captain, celebrating the Liverpool goal in front of the Kop left the away fans fuming. He certainly had his share of abuse from previous fans.

What was that like? First being worshipped and loved, and then being at the end of abuse from the same supporters?

'With a childhood like mine, stuff like that doesn't bother me. It would have been different had I been born with a silver spoon in my mouth, and never heard anything like that before. When you've been through the stuff that my siblings and I've been through, nothing really fazes me.

'In a way I like that the fans sing ugly chants about me, it means they actually respect me, and want to stop me from playing well. It must mean they think I'm really good. It's a sign of respect from the fans. That's how I look at it.'

That sounds the best way to look at it. Just think of all the abuse that was thrown at Steven Gerrard. It has to mean that they are trying to tear down the best man.

'Yeah, and it doesn't affect Stevie G at all. He's mentally tough. It can really spur you on to play better, behaviour like that. And if that's the effect, it's a sign of a good player, a good captain, and a good leader.'

✦

Ince has chosen to stay in Liverpool. He is happy there. It has been a good place for his three kids – two boys and a girl – to grow up in; his oldest son, Tom, began his own professional career at Liverpool's academy. Paul retains a lot of good friends in the city. Robbie Fowler lives just up the street, and they maintained their friendship after hanging up their boots. And not only in Liverpool – they have also been holiday neighbours in Portugal for ten years.

A few years ago Ince was back on his old street corner in London. A friend still lives there, in the same run-down house, with his mother and brother. He told him that twenty of their old friends were dead through sickness or drugs.

'Half of my gang could have been professional footballers. Some of them were better than me. Football is a way out. But if you don't understand that, and don't grab your chance by both hands, it can end really badly. My life could as easily have gone to pot. I've said to myself many times: "Why did I get lucky?" Was it because I was tougher in myself than a lot of others?'

Some people simply seem to have it in them. A natural-born leader and inspired footballer who – against all odds – goes on to captain the two most successful clubs in English top-flight football, and becomes the captain of the English national team, the very first black England captain. And again he made history in 2008, when he became the first black Premier League manager, at Blackburn Rovers.

You were a ground-breaker…

'I never thought of it that way. I never thought about me being the first black England captain. That I should be a flagship, a pioneer, for black people. And for them only? I see myself as a flagship for all kinds of people. Whether they be black, pink, white or yellow. Yes, I was the first black Premiership manager. But if that works as an inspiration for others, regardless of colour, to become managers? I don't know… So far there hasn't been a lot of other black managers in the Premier League.'

Nevertheless, the appointment of Paul Ince as England captain created an avalanche of responses.

'I've never told anyone this before. But when I was appointed England captain, I must have had mail from at least six hundred people. Some from black, others from white and some Asians. Their involvement was as much about my background as the colour of my skin. There was mail from kids in ghettoes; young Asians dreaming about playing football, others from white kids with divorced parents. They saw me as an inspiration. I think it was most of all my background that inspired people. But maybe it was the fact that I was the first black captain that made them notice my story, where I came from. And it inspired teachers, kids and parents to write to me.'

Tears well up in his eyes.

'People realised that you could come from a tough background and still be rewarded in the end. The most important thing for me wasn't that I was the first black England captain or manager in the Premier League. The most important part was to affect other people. That's what I always try to do: influence people in a positive way. If I can do that, whether it's in football or somewhere else, I feel like I'm doing my job. That's my outlook on life.'

12

JAMIE REDKNAPP
FOOTBALL AS AN ESCAPE

*'Jamie Redknapp was a good captain. He was just really unlucky to be in a
suit and tie when we were winning trophies.'*
Jamie Carragher

A TWELVE-YEAR-OLD RUNS AROUND BOURNEMOUTH FOOTBALL
Club's training ground, trying to keep up with fully grown professionals. If he misses
a pass he's told off, like anyone else would be.

The twelve-year-old is meant to be studying. His mother thinks he is in school.
But he does not like school. Kids are picking on him; the older ones threaten to beat
him up. His escape is football. Training with his dad gives him peace, and it lets him
work towards his only goal in life: he wants to become a professional footballer.

He does not have to fear mean words from other kids here, he can be himself.
This is the secret escape that will never get him through his A levels, but will give
him a chance to fulfil his dream of lifting a trophy as captain for one of the greatest
football teams in the world.

Jamie Redknapp's life has been marinated in football since his earliest days. He is
the son of a high-profile manager, Harry; the nephew of Frank Lampard senior and
cousin to his son, the legendary Chelsea midfielder, also named Frank.

'Football has always played such a big part of my life, ever since I was born,' he
says on a large, stored away TV studio sofa in a small back room at *Sky Sports* on May

9 2015. 'My dad was coaching, and I followed everything he did. I started tagging along to training at the age of five, interacting with the senior players. Sometimes I'd talk myself into trouble, mentioning a bad game the day before. Football was all I ever knew.'

He believes his emergence is both a consequence of the environment he grew up in and his own ability.

'Lots of other dads have been good football players or coaches, and have introduced their kids to football early, and it hasn't necessarily made them professionals. So I must have had something extra, something that made me good,' he reasons. 'But being able to train with first-team players every day from that young, getting told off if I lost the ball, it was quite a bit of pressure, but very useful. There were days I should have been at school, but Dad would say: "Come to training with me, why don't you, you're a little late anyway." I told Mum I went to school, but spent the whole day on the training field with my dad. It didn't help me academically, but from a footballing perspective it helped a lot.'

Your mother, Sandra, was she upset that you were skipping school?

'No, she's a very relaxed, very calm person. She's a generous and lovely lady. She used to say, "Whatever your dad wants, it's OK by me." She wouldn't pressure us to do anything. She wasn't even particularly interested in football, she didn't go to see my dad play. And only occasionally would she watch me when I was playing. But she's been a pillar of support. It wasn't always easy for her to live in such a football-mad family. You can imagine meal-time, we were always talking football. And then there's the stress that football has brought to the family. When Dad won, he was on top of the world, when he lost, he was on the floor. So she's had to put up with a lot in her life. But I've always said that football has been so good to us, any negative sides have been more than made up for.'

Don't you think it might be healthy in a football-mad family that someone creates a bit of balance by not being so consumed by football? Your wife isn't all that interested either, is she?

'Yes, I think you may be right. I want our boys (aged eleven and seven when this interview took place) to be as interested in football and as absorbed in it as I've always been. So every now and then she runs me through a little reality check, and reminds me that the boys aren't me. That we just have to let them be themselves. And it's a good thing she isn't football mad, I can't imagine coming home after a bad game and being told off for not having done well on the pitch? Losing is hard enough as it is.'

When Redknapp's father's teams were playing, he would observe all he could about the game. He was like a sponge, absorbing knowledge.

'I watched all the matches of the teams my dad was coaching, and could hardly wait till the matches finished, because my brother and I were allowed to run out on the pitch and kick a ball against one of the goals. We could do that since our dad was the manager. As a kid who was obsessed with football it was all I dreamed of.'

And yet, his close relationship to football would bring its own punishment.

'I've never really talked about this before, but the reason I didn't like school was that I was bullied. It started a few years in and went on till I quit school. It wasn't constantly, and I could look after myself. It wasn't my peers; it was some of the older lads. Especially two made my life pretty miserable for years. These kids didn't like me because of who I was, because I was good at football, because my dad was a well-known former footballer and manager in Bournemouth. They called me names and threatened to beat me up.'

Envy that turned into bullying, perhaps?

'Probably. But it was tough. All I wanted was for people to like me.'

The solution was to immerse himself on the training pitch with his father. When he was eleven and the bullying peaked, the older boys in training – the apprentices at seventeen and eighteen – became his friends and extended family.

'There was this guy called Paul Jones, he ended up living with us for a while because he had some trouble at home. He was always so kind and looked after me. When he heard that especially this one boy, four years older than me, was bullying me, he took action. Paul waited for this kid outside school, and told him in no un-certain terms that if he ever laid hands on me, or threatened to, he would personally come back and beat him up. He never bothered me again after that.'

Unfortunately, this is not a one-off story. Bullying and harassment of kids or siblings of high-profile football stars and other celebrities happens frequently, but is not talked about much. Many children and teenagers suffer in the shadow of their parents' success.

'My boys have seen some of that too, unfortunately, because their dad is a well-known former footballer and TV presenter. It's the seamy side of success, I'm afraid. When I grew up, we weren't rich. My dad had a regular salary at Bournemouth, so we had no more than others. I didn't go to a private school, I went to a regular school, and I never spoke highly of myself or my family. But as my dad's managerial career got better, so did the house.'

I find it weird how some people think it's OK to troll well-known or famous people. It's almost as if they'd think you wouldn't care; that it's allowed…

'Yes! That's why I haven't got a Twitter account or anything of the sort. I see no value in it, because it gives people the chance to be really horrible. I don't handle it well when people attack me.'

He returns to the issue of bullying: 'Unfortunately, the bullying made me hate school, which is a shame, because I did have some great teachers. A couple of them, Mr Jackson and Mr Broadwell, were important when it came to [me] developing as a footballer. They were always encouraging me and let me train extra. You need those kind of teachers.

'The worst part is, if I'd been able to focus, I would have done well. I wasn't stupid. But when I was sixteen, I made it into Bournemouth's first team. Quickly, my homework became football training. It's not the right thing to do, and I wouldn't recommend anyone else to do the same. It leaves you with no options if your dreams of a football career fail. But I was lucky, it worked for me.'

Jamie Redknapp has invited me to join him on a Saturday night at Sky Studios in the far west of London. He is working as a pundit with Thierry Henry, who sits with him in the Green Room beside sandwiches, salad, fruit and soft drinks that wait to be devoured. We rewind to his childhood and his close relationship with his father, Harry, a man who was also the manager of two of his clubs.

'We've got a special bond between us, my dad and me,' he says. 'In over forty years we've never argued, barely exchanged the odd, harsh word. We get on amazingly. He's my idol and we've been through so much together. He's been an important counsellor for me, always there for me, and hopefully he feels the same way about me. We're extremely close and talk about everything. I've been with him through his entire manager career, every step he's taken, and he's followed me through my entire playing career.'

Harry Redknapp would always come to Anfield to see the matches his son played, unless his managerial obligations kept him away. So did his grandfather. And so did Jamie's big brother Mark, three years his senior.

'I could never have been as good a brother to Mark as he's been for me, if it was him who had succeeded at football and not me,' Jamie admits. 'He'd been a player himself, until a fractured ankle ruined his career, and suddenly his kid brother was playing for England and for Liverpool. It can't have been easy to tackle, but he's been tremendous support. He came to every match and loved the nights out in Liverpool. I used to tease him that he enjoyed the nightlife and the girls more than my matches. But he's a great guy. We're a close-knit family, and you need that playing for a club like Liverpool. If my family on rare occasions couldn't make it – this was before I met Louise – I felt pretty lonely.'

We all need attention and recognition. And the recognition from one's father somehow counts a little extra for many, regardless of how old you are.

'Absolutely! Even as a Liverpool captain I used to look up to my dad for recognition, feedback and advice. No disrespect to my managers, but I wanted Dad to see me and respond to how I did. A thumbs up, or gritted teeth in a "Come on, son, you can do better!" If I saw him clench his teeth in the directors' box, I knew I hadn't done a good enough job. If I got a thumbs up, I felt super. I knew, of course, if I'd played a good game or not, but he would give me little signs, instructions, like pointing if I was too deep and needed to advance. And afterwards we'd always discuss the match, of course. It meant a lot, because he knew the game so well. I've overheard parents advise their kids and I've thought: They've got no idea what they're saying. What you're telling your son is wrong. But having a dad who used to play, and knows football so well, was a great help to me.'

What was he like on the sideline when you were younger and played matches? Did he shout and scream commands, or was he quieter?

'He was very quiet. Once in a while, if I wasn't playing well, he would correct me, saying things like "Too many touches, work on your touch, work on your shots. Now you're not doing your best, focus." But he was calm on the sideline. He never shouted at me, and it was probably because everybody knew who he was. Even when I played for Bournemouth as a kid, everyone knew who Harry Redknapp was. He was like the King of Bournemouth. So he didn't want to correct me in public. He'd rather go through the matches in quiet with me afterwards. My uncle on the other hand – Frank Lampard senior – was very verbose on the sideline with my cousin Frank. He'd shout so much people would react. But there's no right and wrong in this. It worked for them, and the opposite worked for us.'

You obviously learned a lot about football from your dad. But what did he teach you as a human, and a leader, that came into good use as a Liverpool captain?

'I was raised by Mum and Dad to always watch my manners. Always say thank you and please. The rule was that you should treat people the same way you wanted them to treat you. Be nice to people. I think it meant a lot to my relationship with the fans too. When I came to Liverpool, I always tried to sign as many autographs and pose for as many photos as possible. It was the set of values my mum and dad had taught me: be nice and respect others.

'But I've also inherited my dad's sharp edges. If someone provokes or try to hurt him, he'll let them have it, and I'm the same way. You can just ask my wife: if anyone is unfair, or if I disagree, I'll let them know. I can imagine these were the qualities that made them see me as a leader. You can't always be nice. Certain situations require you to say something. I dare – and I can take it when others confront me. It works both ways.'

Aged fourteen, the Bournemouth prodigy joined Tottenham's youth training programme. But when he was offered a seven-year contract, highly unusual for a player that young, he decided to back out.

'I was a teenager with great self-confidence. When I was fourteen I signed a contract for Tottenham that was supposed to see me through to twenty-one. But when I started at Tottenham I didn't enjoy it as much as I had Bournemouth. At home I could play my way into the first eleven quickly, and prove my worth, instead of playing for the Tottenham reserves. At this time, Paul Gascoigne played for Tottenham, so I figured it might be ages before I could play my way into their first team. I said to myself I'd be as good as the other Bournemouth players in a couple of years, and play for their first team instead.'

Father and son had a meeting with Terry Venables, Tottenham's manager. He was not impressed by the U-turn.

'Tottenham loved me as a player, but I was homesick. We worked out a deal where Tottenham would get twenty-five per cent of the income if another club bought me.'

Harry Redknapp was well known as a footballer with West Ham United in the 1960s and 1970s and by the late 1980s was acquiring a reputation as an up-and-coming football manager too. Not long after deciding not to send his son to Tottenham, Redknapp senior attended a football writers' dinner.

'My parents were dancing and Kenny Dalglish was following them around the dance floor. Dad thought it was a little odd, until Kenny suddenly said, "I want to sign your son. We've seen him play and we like him." "Brilliant," Dad said.

'That night he woke me up, and enthusiastically told me that Kenny Dalglish wanted to sign me. It was massive. I supported Bournemouth – or any other team my dad managed for that matter. But at that time, I thought Liverpool was the best team, and John Barnes was my favourite player in the entire world. So this was incredible news.'

He went up to Liverpool to have a look around the club and see what it was like.

'I did very well in training. I couldn't have done better. I was on fire, and I could see that Kenny liked what he saw. I loved being at the club and the club loved me.'

Kenny and his wife Marina invited Jamie home for dinner, and talked about the opportunity for a bright future with Liverpool. Despite this, the young footballer wanted to stay longer at Bournemouth. He was still only sixteen, and his dad had recently been in a horrible car accident in Italy.

'I wanted to be close to my mum and support her, because Dad had fractured his skull, it was very dramatic. Besides, I wanted more playing time, and I'd get that at Bournemouth. But Kenny promised me I'd have a chance with the Liverpool first team soon.'

The dialogue with Liverpool continued. Every weekend Jamie played for Bournemouth, and every Sunday Kenny Dalglish called him to ask how the game went.

'It's really unbelievable that he did that, now that I think back on it.'

And eventually Dalglish got what he wanted. Jamie Redknapp signed for Liverpool in January 1991 and became Dalglish's last signing before he resigned dramatically in the aftermath of a 4–4 draw in the FA Cup with Everton.

What did Tottenham think about your decision to join Liverpool so soon after you rejected them?

'They weren't exactly happy, but they got a good deal of money for me. And I'll grant Terry Venables that – he never used it against me later. When he became England manager in 1994, he called me into his squad right away.'

The first weekend after Redknapp's arrival in Liverpool, the team were playing Wimbledon. After training on Friday, Kenny Dalglish invited Redknapp to dinner at his home where he told him that he would be in the squad for the following day's game.

When Dalglish then read out his squad in front of all the other players in the dressing room, Redknapp still could not believe that he'd been selected.

'It was like I was in a fog. Surrounded by all these players I looked up to and admired. My team-mates came over, shook my hand and congratulated me. Well done! I was still in a world where I sat thinking how unbelievable it was that I was going to play for the same team as John Barnes.'

Liverpool drew 1–1 against Wimbledon.

'It was a bit of a shame, really, because if we'd been winning, I'm sure I'd have played. But they had a few big fellas on the pitch, so I think Kenny was a little nervous on my behalf. It was still a great experience for me to be on the bench.'

A month later, though, Dalglish announced he was leaving Liverpool.

'It was incredibly sad. But the most incredible thing with this, and I'll never forget, happened the same night that the shock message of his resignation was announced. In the evening I came home to my digs not far from Anfield, where I was staying with a woman and her son. I was so sad. I was inconsolable and called Dad to tell him the sad news. But then, just afterwards, when I was watching TV, the phone rang again. It was Kenny Dalglish who called, and he said to me, "You're going to do well at Liverpool. I'll always make sure you're OK. Don't worry. I'll call you tomorrow and we can play a bit of golf. Then I'll explain to you why I've come to this decision."

'This speaks volumes of him as a man. It meant the world to me. It showed me that he liked me as a person, and to this day I sometimes pop over for dinner with him and Marina. Kenny was my hero then, and he still is.'

Dalglish later explained that he felt he needed to have the answer to every question as a manager. But does a leader have to know everything? Can he not delegate the search for some of the answers?

'Remember, Kenny was only in his late thirties at the time. There's an enormous pressure being manager of a club like Liverpool. Look at Pep Guardiola, for instance. When he was in Barcelona he said he could stay maximum four years, then he had to move on because of the pressure. Liverpool are something of the same. I was surprised that Dalglish backed down that time, but at the same time I respected his decision, and realised he had to do what was best for him and his family. Football is important, but so is your health.'

After Dalglish left, Ronnie Moran was appointed caretaker manager.

'It was a difficult time for me after Kenny retired, because I wasn't part of Liverpool's plans for a good while after changing managers. I wasn't in Moran's squad, and I felt my fitness level dropped. Phil Thompson was manager for the reserves, and at the time I didn't get on too well with him. Then Souness came. And it was a bit odd, because I played well for the reserves, but nobody noticed me. I was unsure if Graeme even knew my name, and that's pretty rough for a young player.'

But then, in October 1991, Redknapp was called in to train with the first team and told that he would be in the squad travelling to France to play Auxerre in the UEFA Cup. He then created history: as an eighteen-year-old he was the youngest Liverpool player to play a European match. He was in the starting eleven and didn't play too badly. Liverpool lost 2–0, but won on aggregate in the return match at Anfield.

'That's when I realised I could do it. My self-confidence grew. Early in December, a few weeks later, we played Southampton away, and I scored my first top-flight goal. Punted it in. After that, my self-confidence got a boost. Sometimes you need a little break, a pause, to be able to improve.'

Despite the increased self-confidence, pre-game nerves continued to be an issue.

They were strong before every game.

'I think I was too nervous at times. I shouldn't have been, but I couldn't keep my nerves in check. I wanted so much to do well in every match; it's probably the same way with a lot of players. Ronnie Whelan often became physically ill; he'd throw up before matches because he was so nervous. I often felt so nauseous I almost threw up too. I wanted so badly to play well, because I knew how much it meant to people in Liverpool. I couldn't let them down.'

Redknapp remembers looking at Robbie Fowler, who would sit unfazed in the dressing room, reading the match programme before the game. Fowler was two years his junior.

'I wish I could have been like him before a match, because I almost lost it to nerves. And it affected my performance. During my England career my ankle was broken twice, and my hamstring was injured. It isn't normal. It must have happened because I was so tense, eager to prove myself. Or hyper-motivated.'

Were you superstitious? Did you have rituals hoping the games would go better?

'Oh yes! I tried everything. I would vary which shoe I took off first, I tried to always eat the same before matches, I even took it to the level that I'd say the Lord's Prayer before every match, hoping it would help. I tried so many silly things. But then again, what's the worst that can happen? If I'd played again, I'd rather have been thinking like that. It's football and it means so much. You definitely need a certain aggression, but the best games I played were when I managed to be a little more relaxed mentally.'

If he played badly, he was devastated afterwards.

'I couldn't think clearly, and it would be eating me up inside. It's not healthy. Passion is good, but I wish I'd managed more of a Fowler approach to the game.'

In a time of transition, and with more experienced players sold, Redknapp advanced in the first team and became a regular. By 1994, at the end of Souness's time as manager, he was twenty years old and had really begun to show a lot of promise. And he realised he could learn a lot from Souness. But in Souness' final match, an FA Cup defeat to Bristol City, Redknapp injured his knee badly, and was out for a long time. In the meantime, Roy Evans was appointed as manager.

'Roy was very good for me. If there's one manager I wish we could have won the league with, it's him. He's such a good man. In addition, John Barnes took good care of me, we set up a pretty good team. McManaman came up front, then Fowler, and that's when I thought: This is where I'll spend the rest of my career. And hopefully, one day, I'll get a chance to become Liverpool captain.'

It was not until Gérard Houllier came to the club that he was given that chance. Evans had bought and appointed Paul Ince as his new captain – a player Redknapp also enjoyed playing alongside.

'Incey was my favourite midfielder to play with. We were a great team and our statistics playing together were really good. We almost never lost a match playing together. And he got the best out of me – made me all set to attack. He was a pretty aggressive type and sometimes I needed the type of challenge he gave me. He would yell at you sometimes, but I enjoyed playing with him.'

What made you such a great match?

'We were so different. He'd pass me the ball and let me play. We complemented each other. I'd have loved to play with Incey when he was twenty-one years old. We'd have been brilliant together. He wasn't at the height of his career when I played with him, but I still learned a lot from him.'

Having been vice-captain, Redknapp was appointed new captain for the 1999/2000 season.

'I'll readily admit that I didn't get on great with Gérard Houllier, but I'll never forget the moment he appointed me captain. It was the proudest moment of my life,' he says. His first match as captain was against Sheffield Wednesday at Hillsborough on the opening day of the season.

'I remember I was even more nervous than usual. It was a new chapter of my life. Being appointed captain for Liverpool Football Club is like receiving an honorary title. The first thing I did after Gérard Houllier told me I was the new captain was to call my dad. Then I talked to the rest of the family, because it meant so much to me. It felt like a reward for all the hard work I'd laid down in my career. I felt unbelievably proud and honoured to be allowed to carry that armband. I had flashbacks to players who had carried it before me: Souness, Yeats, who still worked for the club as a talent scout. And I hoped that I would do them and the club proud.'

Liverpool won the match 2–1.

'I played really, really well, and so did my team-mates. And although I'm not the kind of man to collect physical memorabilia from my own career, I had the kit framed and kept the armband. Some decorate their houses like temples, full of memorabilia from their football careers. I've kept some of my kits, but only had my first England shirt, my first shirt as a Liverpool captain and one of Zinedine Zidane's shirts framed. Unfortunately, there was a break-in at my house, and someone stole the shirt from my first match as Liverpool captain, so now I've no idea where it is.

'For some reason they only stole my Liverpool shirt, and left Zidane's hanging. They must have been out of their minds!'

Redknapp was not too surprised he was asked to take over the captaincy once his predecessors John Barnes and Paul Ince had left the club. He knew he had it in him. But he also knew it would be a bit of a challenge, since the club was going through big changes.

'It ought to have been the best time of my life,' he says now. 'I was playing better than ever. I was living the dream as Liverpool captain, but I realised there would be highs and lows, because the nightmare of injuries had already started.'

He had worked hard to get to where he was after injuries sustained while on England duty in the summers of 1996 and 1997. Not just by intense training, but also mentally. Early in his captaincy he felt the pressure almost physically, but after a while he managed to relax more and played better and better.

'I evaluated what had happened so far in my life, and thought about how the captaincy really shouldn't be affecting my game in a negative way. I realised I had to use the honour as motivation. Imagine that – captain for Liverpool Football Club! Life doesn't get much better than that! That's why I always look back with a huge sense of pride. And I will always be grateful that Gérard Houllier saw me as a leader and made me captain.'

The team he led was made up of many young and inexperienced players. The old core Liverpool traditions were gradually being phased out and the team initially struggled to live up to fans' expectations.

'When you're captain, of course you want the team to do well. A minority of captains have the ability to drag their team through a match, even those days where they don't play well themselves. Steven Gerrard and John Terry are good examples. I, on the other hand, felt that the biggest challenge as captain was the extra responsibility on a bad day. The armband felt like a huge weight on my arm, something you practically had to drag along when your team lost. Because it just means so much more to win when you're captain. It's the greatest feeling in the world to play with the armband when you play well. You walk off Anfield with the fans singing "You'll Never Walk Alone". But if you walk down the tunnel and the fans are at you after a disappointing game, you take it even more personally as captain. Because you know that men like Ron Yeats, Phil Thompson and Graeme Souness had so much success as captains, and you'd love to be looked at with the same kind of admiration as them.'

What type of captain were you?

'If you ask some of the young players under me, players like Steven Gerrard,

I think they'll say that I always tried to help the youngsters. I talked to them and helped them with their performance. I took care of them all week, both on and off the pitch.'

The last vestiges of some traditions remained and young apprentices still cleaned and polished the boots of their seniors. Steven Gerrard was responsible for keeping captain Redknapp's boots spick-and-span before he made it into the first team.

'We had a great relationship, Steven and I. There are some elements of our game that are similar. How he passes, for instance, I like to think that I helped him develop some of his skills.

'From the first time I saw him kick a ball I realised he would become a world-class player. He was so good he could have been captain when he was eighteen. He's a rare breed. Maybe there's one every generation, maybe not quite that often. What a talent! And Steven really wanted to learn. As captain I felt a big part of my job was to help other players but if some of the young players weren't interested in learning, I didn't go out of my way to help them. Not all captains think that way. Some fear that the young players will one day come and take their place, but I've never thought like that. That's not how I was raised. I knew I was only there to be part of a short period of the club's history, and I wanted to make the most out of it. If that meant helping others, it was simply part of the job.'

Graeme Souness defines you as the obvious captain. What do you think he means by that?

'That was nice of him to say. I'm not stuck up, I don't look down on anyone. I was a good player, and I tried to help others. You've got to check off a number of items to be a good captain. People have to respect you and like you too. Or, they don't have to like you, but they've got to respect you. And the players respected me.'

Were you a very verbose captain, on the pitch too?

'Yes, I tried to be. But the game is so fast now, that often there's not enough time for more than a word, no time to juggle the players' positions. The tempo in football today is practically without breathing space. Often being a captain is first and foremost about doing your job as a player as well as possible. Then the players will follow. I've talked to a lot of other captains who agree. In addition, you try to slip in the odd word of advice where there's opportunity for it.'

Did Houllier give you extra instructions or brief you as captain?

'Yes and no. Often I'd only say what I felt I wanted to say to the players. And of course after the manager had had his say, out of respect for him.'

But could you change the formation, and intervene with the game that way?

'No, not really, but I could make sure that players who played well got the ball more frequently, and I wanted to help young players, like Jamie Carragher, to feel safe. I would talk to the least experienced before a match, tried to think about what it was like for me to be a young and inexperienced player. I'd pick out bits and pieces of my life experience in my captaincy.

'I was a responsible player. Of course, I'd go out at night too as a young man, but as I got older, and got married, I realised you've got to be more careful.'

Redknapp played at a time when footballers were no longer just hard-working, tough players – they were also branded goods, icons and practically pop stars. They were showered with offers of modelling and other red-carpet events. Everybody wanted a piece of the media favourites and superstars of the world's biggest sport. What was it like, combining all this with a football career?

'To me, football players were always superstars. But football started to generate much more interest and money. At the same time, we were an incredibly talented team, who didn't win as much as we should have, considering our talent. People began calling us the Spice Boys. But I can honestly say I never let the offers from outside of football get in the way of what I was meant to be doing, even if many started to think that was the case. But injuries appeared at the wrong times for my part. I was very disciplined in training: I trained hard, I loved the training, I would go the extra mile. But I did get a lot of stick at the time, and it didn't get any better when I married a pop star.'

No, that probably didn't help…

'And yes, I did take on a few modelling jobs, but so did others, from other clubs. Ryan Giggs and David Beckham, for instance. I used to see Beckham cruise around in his neat little convertible in Manchester; he was never told off to the same extent by the public as us because he was playing for a winning team. The big difference between them and us was simply that they won matches and trophies and we didn't. But it was a subtle difference.'

What became the archetypal symbol of the Spice Boys were the white Armani suits and white Gucci shoes that Liverpool wore before the 1996 FA Cup final defeat to Manchester United.

'That was a ridiculous idea – the white suits. What on earth were we thinking?! So many people have asked me whose mistake it was, and I don't actually know. Even though I was a young player in that team, I had influence. With me, John Barnes, Ian Rush, manager Roy Evans – one of us should have stood up and said no to those suits. A lot of people have tried to blame one or the other. But as a collective, we should have said: "No, we're not wearing those. We'll either wear our club suits or our training kit."

'We were so unbelievably confident as a team. We were convinced we would win that final. And the suits had nothing to do with our defeat that day. We just couldn't take our chances. We were actually the best team that day. But we were wrong to wear those suits, and we'll forever look back on the photos and think about how foolish they made us look.'

Robbie Fowler made a good point. If you'd won, they would have been the coolest suits ever!

'Yeah, definitely!'

Redknapp's biggest frustration as a player is that he didn't win more with Liverpool.

'I believe that, if you compare player to player, we were at least as good as Manchester United. But the key was, we didn't manage to win the big and important games – they did. It was about mentality. I'm sure Liverpool supporters will agree, though, that watching us was just as entertaining as watching other good Liverpool teams in the past twenty years. The Rafa Benítez years paid off more in terms of triumphs, but I don't think his teams were more entertaining to watch than our team. But fans want to win trophies, and unfortunately we didn't win nearly enough. I would like to think I was influential in building players for the team that came after us, and won trophies with Benítez.'

Each and every captain up until Redknapp has said that their loyalty as a captain first and foremost lay with the team. For Redknapp, however, it was different.

'I always felt my loyalty lay with the fans; I was always nervous I'd let them down. I had my ups and downs with the Liverpool fans. I would take to heart a lot of what they said. Sometimes they'd be mad at me because I hadn't played well. That's understandable, but I mostly played badly when I was injured, or coming back from injury. I remember when I was coming back from a fractured ankle, and was struggling because I couldn't play as well as I used to, and boy did I hear it from the fans. But when I played well they were unbelievable – they made me feel I could achieve anything on a football pitch, singing my name before the games. They were amazing then. Having played in front of the Liverpool fans is something I tell my kids about. The supporters are incredibly inspiring.'

At the end of the 1990s, not only were the team struggling to live up to the supporters' expectations, Redknapp was also struggling to make his body perform.

'I was so desperate for success, moving towards a peak in my career. There was a point in time I was sure I'd be appointed England captain too, because as Liverpool captain you were in with a good chance to captain the national side. I was in my life's best form. And in 2000, the season before we won the three cups, I was really beginning to enjoy being a captain. Responsibility felt good, quite simply. But then there was the knee injury that would eventually ruin my career.

'Unfortunately I ended up not being able to play for a year. And I never managed to get back to that level I had been playing, even though I did play for Liverpool after the injury too. But so much happened that year when I wasn't playing.'

Jamie Redknapp was plagued by an injury nightmare that seemed to have no end: two fractured ankles, several knee injuries; hamstring. Too many to mention. And most of them happened when on national duty.

'A lot of Liverpool fans asked me why on earth I kept playing for England. They asked me to stick to Liverpool, I was a Liverpool player. And they were probably right, I did pick up a lot of injuries with the England team. But it's difficult to turn your country down.'

Injuries robbed him of the opportunity to play in the 1998 World Cup and the 2000 European Championships. He also missed the entirety of Liverpool's treble season in 2000/01.

'I was unable to play when success arrived at my club, and it was extremely tough to tackle. I was there and I thought, I should have been part of this, but I couldn't.'

He was still the team captain in training, and off the pitch. He would encourage and advise players, and in particular he supported and helped the youngest players on the team, people like Steven Gerrard.

'Robbie, Sami Hyypiä and the other guys were great with me. They knew I was the real team captain, and involved me in their success, even though I wasn't actually part of it. That's how I am. If I haven't been involved fighting to win something, it doesn't feel like I'm part of the victory.'

Still, it was an incredibly moving moment when Robbie Fowler, captain in his absence – a job he shared with Sami Hyypiä that year – brought the real captain up with him to accept the FA Cup trophy. Before the presentation, though, in the midst of celebration, Redknapp noticed that Houllier was talking to Hyypiä.

'I knew what Houllier was up to. He asked Hyypiä to accept the trophy. And that's when I thought to myself: I'm not having this. I'll go and pick up the trophy, damn right I will! Because the players wanted me to do it, but Houllier wanted Sami to do it. As the cunning fox I am, I decided to go with Robbie's plan and accept the trophy on behalf of the club. It was a fantastic moment, together with Robbie and Sami.'

With the high tempo in top football today, a lot of players are hit hard by injuries. There are large sums of money at stake, humongous transfer fees and sky-high weekly wages, and the fans expect value for the club's – and their – money. As a player you really get to test your mental strength if you're hit by long-term injuries.

From the sidelines, Redknapp saw his team-mates thrive, and it was even more frustrating because he knew that if he hadn't been injured, he would have been able to contribute to the team. How did Redknapp handle the injury nightmare mentally? What did he do to not lose courage and motivation?

'Looking back, it surprises me how mentally strong I actually was. That I managed to play my way back into the team after injuries. Again and again. It's a bummer seeing your team go out to the field to train, while you've got to go alone to the gym. Especially when you're the captain, and feel you should have been on the pitch, helping the others. It broke my heart so many times. But every time I thought: It'll be all right. I'll come back even stronger. It wasn't until the last knee injury, when I went to the US to consult Dr Steadman, that I realised it couldn't be fixed. I realised I'd never be the same player again. I could never train as much as the other players any more.'

What went through your mind?

'I didn't want to believe it was true. It just couldn't be. It wasn't part of my mentality. I'd always been a winner, I'd always reached my goals. So I started thinking: I'll be all right. I'll get through this too. It was only when I realised I couldn't train as much that I understood I was fighting a lost battle.'

The injury nightmare quickly became a source of conflict with the manager, whom he generally had gotten on well with before.

'Gérard Houllier knew that I couldn't train twice a day, but still tried to make me strain my knee too much by doing just that. And that's how we fell out, my knee just couldn't take it. It got worse.'

Redknapp felt that Houllier was less than helpful with his injuries and that he wanted to sell him.

'The players in the team that played in my position were outstanding players as well: Steven Gerrard, and Didi Hamann, a brilliant player. That's when I realised, with that type of knee injury – a severe wear-and-tear injury— that I'd never be good enough again to be able to compete with them.'

It was a tough time. But when he meets Houllier today, the man who chose him as his captain, they are on friendly terms. Life has moved on.

Liverpool offered their captain a new one-year contract.

'To be fair, the club did offer me a new deal. But it didn't feel right. That's when I decided it was time to move on. But I'd never have left Liverpool if it wasn't for all my injuries. I felt that the one year they offered me was more in the way of a thank you than anything else, and I didn't want charity. So we moved to London [to belatedly join Tottenham]. Louise would have loved to stay in Liverpool. If only my body had worked, I'd have stayed at least another five years.'

Jamie Redknapp, the kid who had gone all out, training so hard and determinedly his whole life, was, despite he didn't retire until he was 32, in reality finished as a football player at the age of 27 because of all his injuries. An age where he could have been at his best, with a better combination of experience, mental strength and football skills than ever. If only his physique had played along, he'd have had many good years ahead of him as a player.

'It annoys me that I didn't get to show Liverpool fans my best years. Everybody says twenty-seven to thirty are the best years for a footballer. A lot of people feel that's when they're at their very, very best, your optimal years. It's agonising in many ways, but what can you do? You can't jog backwards in life.

'I don't look back at what happened with bitterness or anger, but of course I think a lot about what would have happened if I hadn't been troubled with injury. I was just incredibly unlucky. There was nothing I could do. When I got that serious knee injury in Souness's last game, I was already on borrowed time, I had already had so many operations on my knee.'

He believes he probably played too much too soon, and that he paid for this through his many injuries.

'At seventeen I was already playing over forty games a year, without rest. It was too much for a teenager. Today I would have been rested every now and then. I was quite slender when I was a kid and wasn't physically prepared for such a strain to my body. But back then, playing as many games as possible was all that mattered. If you got benched, it felt like punishment. Maybe if I'd played fewer games as a teen I would have been able to play for the team a lot longer, but of course this is only speculation.'

Looking back at an era that is now behind him, I ask Redknapp how Liverpool shaped him as a person.

'I spent eleven years of my life at the club, it's a massive part of my life. The club saw me grow up. I came from Bournemouth, a quiet seaside town, to Liverpool. I went there as a boy and came back a man. While other eighteen-year-olds were at university, I was playing for Liverpool's first team.

'The club gave me great morals and values. They made me understand Scousers – that's an experience in itself! They're different, and they're fantastic people. I still keep in touch with a couple of families that I stayed with at the beginning. It's a close-knit society at Liverpool, and I'm from a close-knit family. That's why it was so good for me to play at Liverpool, because it's a family club.'

Now that he works in the media, it's safe to say it's not all friendly when he hears from his Liverpool family.

'Sometimes people think I'm negative towards Liverpool. Some fans think I criticise the club, when I'm only doing my job. And sometimes it's out of frustration because I'm so desperate for Liverpool to do well. But my love for the club has never changed. The club gave me a fantastic experience, I'm very proud of it. When people ask me if I've played for Liverpool, I can say yes. It makes me smile to think: I was even captain at the club.'

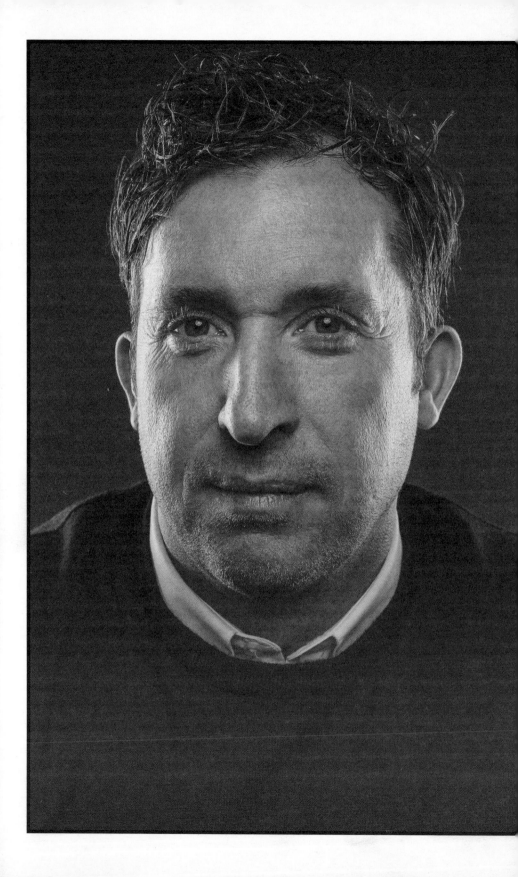

13

ROBBIE FOWLER
PLAYFUL MADNESS THE BEST FORM OF ATTACK

He didn't talk much, but when he did, we all listened.'
Steven Gerrard

ROBBIE FOWLER TAKES US BACK TO HIS TEENS, TO THE EARLY 1990s, and to the canteen at Melwood, Liverpool's training ground. More than twenty kids enrolled at the Youth Training Scheme are huddled over their Friday task: gathering up training gear for Monday's training. The necessary garments are packed and tied together with the socks, bundle after bundle. Boring routine work that could do with a little spicing up. And with so many teenage boys in one place, the inevitable happens.

'They were like kid's pillow fights, you know,' Fowler says.

Bundles of tightly stuffed training gear fly across the room. Throwing, hits, laughter, bouts of anger, and sounds of revenge. Fowler sees Phil Neal's son, Ashley, coming into the room to do his share of the work. Fowler aims, and throws as hard as he can. The bundle spins through the air. It is the perfect throw, practically a bullet. Bull's eye. The power it hits him with knocks Ashley off his feet and sends him straight into a door. There is blood everywhere. He needs immediate medical attention and four stitches over his eye.

'I was called into the boss's office, Graeme Souness, and we at the YTS were hardly ever there,' Fowler recalls. 'So it was incredibly frightening going in.'

Souness was at his desk. He gravely told Fowler to sit down, and spoke in a low voice.

'He let me understand that I had this one chance in the club, and that I had to make sure I didn't ruin it for myself. Luckily he understood that boys are boys, that things like that just happen, but he did give me a written warning. One more warning, and I'd be kicked out of the club. I left, tail between my legs, and had learned a lesson. Thanks to that written warning from Souness, I had to behave from then on.'

People who know Robbie Fowler understand he is quick with a joke. Anything from a witty comment to a prank. He loves fooling around and has never, even after earning the nickname 'God' from the Liverpool fans, taken himself very seriously. He needs fun and games in his life. He needs it as a counterweight to all that is serious and humdrum.

'I've always been described as a cheeky chappie. I don't really know what that means, it's just the way I am, it's my personality. I just can't be serious all the time. I've tried to be nothing but serious for periods at a time, because I've felt that it was expected of me, but that made life incredibly dull. I need a blend of fun and seriousness, and I'm grateful I was created this way.'

It is genuinely amusing hearing Fowler recount all the practical jokes he has contrived during his football career. The English club culture has been that way for generations: you break the ice and build a team culture with all the banter. In addition, they serve as a mental test to see if you can stay afloat in a squad environment, if you are tough enough and strong enough.

On a flight coming back from a match, Robbie woke up from a nap to see his trainers in pieces. He got up to get his spare shoes from his bag, but saw that the handles had been cut off. And in the bag he found his extra pair were in shreds too. He reasoned with himself and decided it had to have been Neil Ruddock. As soon as he fell asleep, Fowler started cutting Ruddock's new leather boots – a present from his wife – into pieces.

'When I'd finished with them, they looked like a pair of Jesus sandals,' Fowler grins.

After landing, there was trouble. Ruddock was livid, and hit Fowler as hard as he could.

'To this day, that's one of my proudest moments, that I managed to stand up straight after a blow like that.' He gives me a wry smile. Then turns serious. 'It's important to divert yourself with little stunts like that, but within certain limits, obviously. You can't be super-serious and train hard all the time. Hard training will make you physically strong, and able to handle several matches a week at a top level, but you need to recuperate mentally as well. There are many who don't play well even if they're super-fit, because they're worn out mentally. The mental strain will get to you if you can't sometimes relax and laugh a little. The art is to learn to relax.'

Fowler's popularity had exploded after his scoring five goals for Liverpool's first team in a League Cup tie against Fulham in October 1993, his second game at Anfield. At the age of 21 he scored his 100th goal for the club. Two years in a row, in 1995 and 1996, Robbie Fowler was awarded PFA Young Player of the Year.

Did you feel a pressure living up to the expectations so many had of you, because you were a role model to so many millions?

'Yes, it was a massive pressure. You don't exactly ask to become a role model when you're a footballer, but you do become one. I didn't start playing football to impress anyone, I just loved playing. And I didn't stop fooling about on or off the pitch just because I was a role model, because that was a part of me too. It did get me into a bit of trouble from time to time. I didn't quite realise the influence my actions could have on some.'

He believes his spontaneous, playful personality had a positive effect on his career.

'I think it was my personality that made me a good striker. A lot of what I do in life is spontaneous. It made it easier for me to read defenders, and to guess where the ball would end up. The playful part of me was always open to different kinds of attack, and that's how I managed to score from all angles and positions.'

So you're saying, as a striker, it's an advantage to have a streak of insanity? I'm think-ing Maradona, Suárez...

'Definitely! They were and are such good players because of that. Very creative.'

Maradona, Suárez and Fowler. All three of them have done controversial things on the pitch when that streak of madness has grown to a broad brush stroke in some situations. 'The hand of God', biting your opponents, or – as with Fowler – going down on all fours in front of the Everton fans and pretend to be snorting the chalk line.

Rumours were strong that Robbie Fowler was on cocaine. That he had taken the jet-set life to a new dimension. And the rumours were everywhere. In the end speculation about his drug abuse even made it to the front pages.

At the same time, the Everton fans sang in full voice about Robbie being a smackhead.

'I celebrated that way against Everton because it was my way of saying, "Do you really think I can train this hard, score goals and succeed like I do if I'm on drugs?" Come on! Anybody home? It's a matter of common sense, you ought to know nobody can be a top athlete over time and abuse cocaine at the same time.'

But you got a hefty fine, £60,000, and were banned for six matches. In retrospect, do you regret doing what you did?

'No. I'd planned my revenge. The only thing I regret, is the fine. I got so much stick from the Evertonians for years, they were at least as bad as the worst supporters from other clubs. The abuse I got from the Blues was both mean and vicious. A lot of them got the joke and understood what I wanted to say by doing what I did. A lot of them found it funny. But of course, it's not good if kids see things like that and don't know the background for the celebration. Luckily, after the introduction of social media, such misunderstandings have become fewer. Players have a chance to explain things directly to the fans without any media filtering.'

He still gets thrown at him accusations of being a smackhead. The moves and stunts he pulled after that episode are often blown up to a bigger scale than the original act of putting his nose on the illustrious chalk line.

'I got more grief for things I said and did after that episode. People hate you or love you, depending on what team they love. But as long as my family knows I've never taken drugs, that's good enough for me. You grow thick-skinned with time. Nothing really gets to me, as long as my closest family and I are doing fine.'

Fowler's football talent was obvious from a young age. The game was inherent in his upbringing. He used to play football all the time; he brought his ball everywhere, even to bed. He went to the local park in Toxteth every day to play, either with his mates, or training with his dad, Robbie Fowler senior. They practised hard with both feet, and shot balls against the wall, in endless sessions.

His dad and his mum – Marie Ryder had four children together. Robbie was number two, after his big sister Lisa – the two of them were very close growing up. Anthony is five years younger, and eventually the baby, Scott, was born when Robbie was fourteen.

It was a tough neighbourhood. When he was six, he witnessed the infamous

Toxteth riots, happening right outside their home. They could not leave the house, in fact, his mother only left to check on her own mum. But even though this part of town, just south of central Liverpool, has a negative reputation, Fowler only has good memories from growing up in a multicultural area that was anything but boring.

From a leadership perspective, he realises he has always had good role models in his life.

'I've always had someone who led me in the right direction. My gran was the "Queen Bee", the head of the family, and the whole family gathered at her place every weekend. She was strict when she needed to be, but within reason. My mother was very much like her as a leader: strict, but fair. The way they led was also influenced by the time we lived in. A time when kids were allowed to go out in the streets and play. Kids in England today are hardly let out.'

Freedom within boundaries?

'Exactly! It gives you the chance to develop independence. This also came in useful as a captain. The leader gives you advice, but you also have to be clever and solution-oriented, able to figure things out for yourself. It's the same way on the pitch.'

Your parents' generation was, in general, not the best at giving positive feedback, and a few from our generation suffer because of that. How were your parents?

'My mother was amazing, she comforted us and gave us positive acknowledgement. After a bad match she would reassure me that I needn't worry, that the next match would be a lot better. My dad was the complete opposite. In his eyes I never played a good match! They were like "good cop, bad cop".'

The Roy Evans and Ronnie Moran of the family?

'Definitely. It was the perfect mix. If you're praised too highly, it might make you pretentious. But then again, too much criticism can destroy your confidence. Of course, my father would give me some praise if I played well in finals and so on, but mostly he wanted to make sure he kept me on my toes and ready for the next match.'

Even though it was discovered early on that Fowler was a football talent out of the ordinary, he did not sign with any club until he was eleven, though not for lack of offers. Every time, his parents would say he was not old enough. But until he signed the school boys' forms he was allowed to train with both Liverpool and Everton, as Everton wanted to sign him too.

'At 14 I chose to sign my school boys' forms with Liverpool because I felt Liverpool had more to offer but also more importantly I chose Liverpool since I had been with them since I was 11 and wanted to stay loyal.

'If a player signs with a big club too early, he might end up taking some things for

granted, and not work hard enough,' Fowler says. 'It is, of course, purely hypotheti-
cal whether this affected my game, but maybe my dad was smart to choose this way.
At least he made sure that I worked hard during my growing years, to prove that I
was good enough. You could say it worked…'

It certainly made clubs very eager to sign you, and they made that extra effort
because they wanted you. Usually it is the young players knocking on the doors,
dreaming of a contract with a big club.

'True. I guess I was lucky. Mostly because I was a talented player. I was also very
conscious about what I wanted, and I wanted to play for a club where I had the best
chances to develop. That's what I learned while not committing to one club too
early. I don't know if kids today think like that. Now it's more about what club will
offer you most. Maybe I became the player I did because I had to work extra hard
to achieve what I wanted.'

*But didn't your father gamble with your future by turning down so many offers on
your behalf? Clubs could have lost interest. Or given up on you?*

'Yes and no. There's always a risk. It wasn't about greed. It was never about where I
could get paid most, but which club that would be the best place for me to develop.'

I admire your dad for that. Taking the chance to wait.

'Then you have to admire my mum as well, she and my dad agreed on this! It was
a good decision between them.'

Jim Aspinall was the Liverpool talent scout who recruited Fowler. He had seen
him play school matches, and was very impressed with what he saw. He was there
every week from when Fowler was ten to sixteen. He became an extended part of
the family. After every season for the first few years he brought home a contract
proposal from Liverpool, and every time the answer was no. Until finally the answer
was changed to a yes.

'Jim was a giant among the leaders I've had in my life. And he was vital for
bringing me to Liverpool. I'm incredibly grateful to him for that. I wouldn't have
played for the club if it hadn't been for him. To me this is about loyalty. And that's
why I wanted to give him something back, by signing for the club. I'm just one of a
lot of players who are grateful for what he did for us.'

This was how the boy, who used to be an altar boy in church, started his journey
with Liverpool. Later he ended up earning the heavenly nickname 'God'.

Aspinall became the first leadership example for Robbie. He had led Fowler into
the club, something that would change the lives of both him and his family. After
Aspinall, there were a number of leaders shaping him along the way, but they let him
keep his streak of madness, mischievousness and playfulness. The next influential

character was Steve Heighway, Liverpool's legendary winger – the club's centre of excellence manager. Heighway developed players like Fowler, Steve McManaman, Michael Owen, Jamie Carragher and Steven Gerrard.

'He was strict, but he led by being a good example. He might have been a little too loud for some of the kids, but only if they deserved it. As a child, being shouted at is horrible. It gives you the feeling you've done something wrong. But Heighway saw the bigger picture. He had the ability to know what you were capable of, and that's how he managed to pull it out of you, if you had more in you. It was incredibly self-developing, even if it could seem rough at the time.'

Another character who was infamous for his uncompromising style was the re-serve team manager, Phil Thompson. Fowler will never forget a morning when he was nearly sixteen. One of his responsibilities was to organise the first-team kits for the game the following day, hanging the shirts on the correct pegs inside the dressing room at Anfield. Looking up at the number nine shirt, he said out loud, 'That ought to be mine.'

He did not realise Thompson was standing behind him. What followed was the worst scolding of his entire life: a tirade about how he should not even begin to think he was worthy until he had proven it.

'At that time I was miles away from the first team, and well off the reserve team too. I was just daydreaming. I had no idea Phil Thompson was in the room, and I don't think I've ever been yelled at more. Now that I'm older, I understand why he did it. There are a lot of ways to lead. That was his way. And again, it's about wisdom, because the good leaders know what players can take a hiding and develop from it, and who needs consolation.'

Back when Fowler trained with the Liverpool youth programme, his family could not afford a car. So he and his dad had to take two different buses each way to get to training and back. On a cold winter's day, Fowler junior and senior were at the bus stop, freezing in the rain, Robbie with only his school uniform to protect him from the icy-cold downpour. A huge, white Mercedes drove towards them, slowed down and stopped in the bus lay-by. The window opened, Kenny Dalglish, club manager at the time, popped his head out, and asked if he could give them a lift home.

'His Mercedes was almost bigger than our house,' Fowler recalls. 'I couldn't believe he stopped to take us home. I'm in his car, a little embarrassed to be from Toxteth, since he lived in an enormous house in Southport. That's why I didn't want him to see our house, and I told him to drop us off about half a mile away from home. I'll never forget it: Liverpool's manager drove this little kid, me, home. He didn't have to do it, but that's how he was. He worked such long hours for the club his wife barely saw him. I appreciated both him and the club even more after that happened.'

Like so many others who have found success, and become legends at the club, Robbie Fowler had a magnificent debut. He scored in his first match, away against Fulham in the League Cup.

'I'd been in the first-team squad for a while, but I don't think I was even close to playing. But then Liverpool went through a patch when things went against them, and the team struggled to score. The previous weekend we were beaten by Everton. On the bus to the match I still didn't know I was playing. I only found out when we were in the dressing room, and Graeme Souness called out the starting eleven. 'Clough, Stewart, Redknapp, Rush, Fowler!' Getting to play in the Liverpool shirt with such good players, it was the ultimate dream. I'd watched these boys play for years. I'd trained with them, but never had a chance to play with them before.

'I really do believe that you don't just need talent to succeed as a footballer, you need a bit of luck too, and I had a lot of luck that night. I laid up to one and scored one. I never looked back after that. And I'm forever grateful to Graeme Souness for giving me the chance.'

The rest is history. In the return leg against Fulham two weeks later, he scored all of Liverpool's goals in the 5–0 rout, becoming only the fifth player in the history of the club to achieve the feat. The last person to do so was his mentor, Ian Rush, a decade earlier.

'My head was so big I barely made it into the dressing room after the game! I thought I had been absolutely fantastic. So I sit down and I'm ready to be told that I'm the best player Liverpool ever had! But no such thing. First thing Ronnie Moran says is, "You should have scored six, you spotty little bastard!"'

Robbie still lived at home, so he celebrated the wild scoring feast with a special fried rice from the corner shop, and talking through the match and the experience with his mum in front of the television. They watched the highlights of the match, and after a while Robbie's best mate, Steven Calvey, came over with a portion of chips in brown sauce.

'That night I was so happy on my mum's behalf. Without her I would have strayed off the path and a football career early on in life.'

With the change of millennium, Gérard Houllier appointed Robbie Fowler captain when team captain Jamie Redknapp was out injured. All in all, Robbie started 32 matches as captain, and in addition took over the armband in quite a few other matches.

Whereas Redknapp sometimes felt the captaincy weighed him down so heavily it influenced his game, Fowler did not feel the same way.

'Getting the armband doesn't change you as a player,' he insists. 'At least it didn't change me. It gives you a higher status, but it's not like a Superman cape. You won't run faster or longer. And you won't win every match. The armband is a massive honour, especially when it's Liverpool Football Club you're captaining, and it makes you feel more responsible. But it won't change your game, except that you'll focus even more on your fellow players and your surroundings. But first and foremost, it's a role that tells people you're in charge.'

Fowler feels the captain's power of influence on the team should not be exaggerated.

'If you, as a player, need a captain to perform at your best, then you've lost. Imagine athletes in individual sports. They've got no captain to whip them on. Both as an individual athlete and as a team player you need inner motivation. That's the most important part.'

Robbie Fowler led a number of games under Houllier. He took turns captaining with Sami Hyypiä in the most successful of his years with the club: the treble triumph in 2001. The reason the captains rotated that year was that Fowler did not always start games due to the strength and variation of Liverpool's attack. This made his role more difficult.

'In my opinion, the captain has to be one of the eleven who will most likely start every match, as long as he's injury-free. So I asked Houllier how I was supposed to lead from the front, and as a role model, if I didn't play. And I asked him to relieve me of the captaincy.'

But Fowler continued to captain matches when he did play. Two captains took the job in turns, whereas the third – the one they called the real club captain, Jamie Redknapp (who was injured) – contributed off the pitch by taking care of the young players, encouraging them and working to promote team spirit.

'Jamie played midfield, I captained from up front when Jamie didn't play, and Sami was responsible from defence when I didn't play. Three different positions. Thinking back, it's quite clever by the manager, splitting responsibility between three positions like that.'

Fowler does not consider it a problem to give an attacker the captaincy. The most important thing for a good captain, he feels, is to play football at a level that is inspirational to his team-mates.

'To be a good captain you need to be wise. You have to be football-smart, and read the game well. You also have to be a good listener, because your opinions or choices won't always function best, so you need to be open to good input. But all of my points here don't just describe the perfect captain – they describe the perfect footballer. Captains can be incredibly different as leaders, but still function very well.'

✦

Fowler has no trouble picking the proudest moment of his captaincy. From when he was a young boy and carried his football with him everywhere, he had always dreamed about playing and winning the FA Cup. So let us go back to the day of the 120th FA Cup final: Liverpool v. Arsenal at the Millennium Stadium in Cardiff, 12 May 2001.

The day began as one of the worst of his life, as he knew he had to start on the bench. After captaining the team that had played its way to the final, not starting was painful.

Sami Hyypiä led the team out to deafening noise from the stands. On the bench, Fowler looked down at his boots in despair when Arsenal's Fredrik Ljungberg scored the game's opening goal with eighteen minutes to go. In the final quarter of an hour, and with Liverpool losing, Fowler and Patrik Berger came on for Vladimir Smicer and Danny Murphy. What followed was two Michael Owen goals. Liverpool had won the cup.

Robbie went straight over to Jamie Redknapp, who had been out injured the entire season, and asked him to accept the trophy with him.

'I could have been all about me, and lifted it alone,' says Fowler. 'This was the trophy, the one I'd always wanted, but my first thought was that I wanted to lift it with Jamie. He deserved to accept it with me after all the injuries he had struggled with. He was embarrassed, and at first he refused, but I made him go with me. Accepting the trophy with Redknapp was a captain's decision that I made.

'I lifted the UEFA Cup with Sami Hyypiä, and I accepted the League Cup alone. So I shared the glory and honour with my fellow captains. I would like people to remember me as that kind of captain.'

Winning the FA Cup was Fowler's greatest moment as a captain. But being reunited with his beloved Liverpool after his time at Leeds and Manchester City was his most emotional experience.

In 2006 he was on the second hole at a golf course when his phone began to vibrate. While a City player, he'd travelled to Istanbul a few months before as a Liverpool supporter and had seen Steven Gerrard lift the Champions League trophy after the most remarkable of nights.

The voice on the phone asked if he'd like to sign for Liverpool again. Fowler thought the discussion was a wind-up. But when the caller insisted he drive to Anfield, he dropped his clubs and ran straight to his car.

The next day, he signed for Liverpool for a second time.

'It went so quickly, and was almost unbelievable. I went to Anfield and signed the contract in [chief executive] Rick Parry's office. When I was back in my car, I screamed! I couldn't believe I was back. To be honest, I never thought I'd have a chance to come back – it just proves that anything can happen in football.'

Rafael Benítez was infamously in control of every aspect of his team. He was passionately concerned with the smallest details.

'Rafa's micro-management was quite scary. I went to see him around Christmas, to give him the recordings of some matches. He was home alone while his family was in Spain. The sight that met me made me realise the type of manager he is. He was in his room, and it was full of newspapers. He was studying recorded matches, analysing them. It was all brand new to me. He controlled every detail. He had the full overview of all players. But Rafa is Rafa. He was fantastic for the club, and I'll always be grateful that he brought me back.'

But all these new tools for analysis in football – what does it do to the sport?

'The simple answer is that the tools and analysing have taken away some of the spontaneity in football. But, people have different ideas and approaches. Too much analysing is not for me. I believe in a mix of modern analysis and good old spontaneity.'

When we meet, almost a decade has passed since Fowler made his Anfield comeback, when he scored twelve goals in twenty games. Since then, he has travelled the world and showed off his football talent in both Australia and Thailand, where he also tried his hand at management as player-manager.

Back in England he has started his own sports academy (Fowler Education and Football Academy, FEFA). He is a part-time coach with Liverpool's under-21s and he travels all over the world as an official ambassador for the club.

Despite still being close to football, he misses competing for trophies. The last few years he has worked on finishing his coaching education in top-level football. He wants to become a manager.

'I think a lot of people don't see my potential as a manager. And some probably think about how I was as a youngster, so they don't take me seriously. Yet. But I will be a manager one day.'

The football world is full of nicknames, and Robbie Fowler earned the title of God.

What's it like to have such a nickname?

'I must admit that sometimes that name is a little embarrassing. Still, compared to a lot of nicknames, I can't think of anything I'd rather be called. I've been called a lot of things through my life, and God is by far the best. It really is an honour. But I don't go around calling myself God.'

14

SAMI HYYPIÄ
THE SILENT FINN SPEAKS UP

'I think Liverpool was perfect for Sami and Sami was perfect for Liverpool.'
Steven Gerrard

IT WAS 1985. A GROUP OF ELEVEN- AND TWELVE-YEAR-OLD BOYS from the Finnish town of Kuusankoski, 100 miles northeast of Helsinki, travelled to the capital to compete in the country's most important junior cup competition. At six o'clock in the morning a regional television crew that had followed the team from the provinces woke the boys up. A camera lens was pointed at one of the kids, who stood relatively tall. He had a modest demeanour and was blond. And then they asked him: 'How many days a week do you train?'

'Two,' Sami Tuomas Hyypiä responded. Which was highly inaccurate.

Since then, the boy has grown up. He was a Liverpool fan as a kid, and went on to win the most sought-after trophy in club football with his favourite team, a team he captained before his greatest night.

I meet Hyypiä in June 2015 in East Grinstead outside London, a twenty-minute drive from Gatwick Airport. This is where he was living at the time with his wife Susanna Rissanen and their two boys, Rico Nestor and Kasper Erik. We rendezvous in a busy and surprisingly noisy coffee shop on the main street, sitting down at the back of the premises, against a mirrored wall set up to trick us into thinking the room is bigger than it is. We travel back in time to a happy and extremely active childhood.

'We played football at every chance we had and in our spare time,' he says. 'The football pitch was only a few hundred yards from our house. When we got home from school, it was all about racing through homework and then run out to play all afternoon and evening. Then home to catch some sleep before school next day. School was only four hundred yards from our house, and we played football in every break. Yes, we played football all the time. Not just twice a week.'

He smiles at me and shows off the characteristic gap between his front teeth in a face that reminds me of a warrior. He is still in his early forties, with clean-cut features that could have been chiselled. He looks like an archetypal Roman soldier: tall, slender and strong. But when he smiles, not just his mouth but his whole face lights up. He does not waste his smiles, but when they do appear, they are the real thing.

He very rarely gives personal interviews like this.

'I find it difficult to talk about myself,' he admits.

Does this have something to do with Finnish culture? I've spent a lot of holidays in Finland and met silent Finns. Across the border, Swedes talk non-stop, while Norwegians usually need a few drinks to talk, and Finns…

'. . . need a lot of drinks to talk!'

So it is a cultural thing?

'Yes, probably. Finns are pretty reserved and quiet in general. But my twenty years abroad have taught me to be more open. And achieving some of my goals in life has made me more confident. As the years have gone by I've become more open, which has helped me develop as a person. I don't feel any different to the guy who left a town in Finland twenty years ago, though.'

And that kid never aimed for a professional football career. He did not want to risk disappointing himself. He maintains that having an ambition and dreaming about something are entirely different.

'I attended a children's event the other day. We talked about sports, dreams and goals. I told them that my goal had always been to be the best possible version of me. My motivation was to work so hard that I reached my full potential. If you do the same, the level you play at will follow automatically. You shouldn't make the level in, say, Spanish or English top league your goal. You set yourself one target at a time. And once you reach that, you move on and set yourself another. You must always aim at getting better.'

It makes him happy to hear that people see him as no different from when he started out, even though he actually got to live out his dream.

But he has to admit that he has changed a little.

'People in Finland tell me it's nice I'm still the same person, and that I've kept my local dialect. It warms me, because I've seen a lot of people be changed by success, and I never wanted to be like them. But strictly speaking I'm not entirely the same person as that little boy who grew up in Kuusankoski; life experience from other places in the world has shaped me as well.'

But the down-to-earth Finn does not like to talk about himself, and does not think he is all that special.

'This is my life. It's how I am. In my eyes it's nothing special. But I've captained all the teams I've played on. That's probably proof I've got what it takes to lead a team.'

As well as being a club captain everywhere, he has also captained Finland a number of times. In fact, only football legend Jari Litmanen has captained Finland in more games than him. And when Hyypiä left Liverpool as a player, he was wanted on the coaching staff.

'Being appointed captain never changed the way I felt, or played. It might well be because I'm Finnish. The captain there is the most experienced player, most trained in handling various situations. It's basically a seniority thing. In England it's different, the captaincy is a very special thing; a big honour. This is one of the areas England is very different from other countries.'

Why is it like that? Is it about the hierarchy in England, the nobility, the working class?

'Yes! Definitely. And maybe Liverpool saw something in me that made them think I could be captain. I wasn't very vocal in the dressing room, it's not my style. If I'd tried to be, everyone would have understood I was trying to be something I'm not.'

But everyone I've talked to has said that if you had something to say, they all listened intently.

'Yes, that's true. I'm an observer first. If I go into a room, the dressing room even, I mostly listen to the others. So if I decide to speak, people know it's about something important.'

It is obvious that mental training, focus, concentration and leadership are topics that are close to Sami Hyypiä's heart.

'It's a matter of choosing captains who are professionals,' he insists. 'I was always professional, because I knew that professional behaviour and hard work was necessary to succeed. I wasn't among the biggest talents when I was little.'

Even though Sami wasn't from a big city, the local boys' team run by his father

Jouko managed to rear four players that ended up playing in the top flight of Finnish football.

'As I grew older, some of the players in my team were a lot better than me. We were in school together and played together. I always worked really hard to try and get on their level. I made a habit of pushing myself to the limit.'

Some supremely talented children are able to score freely in junior matches without needing to train much. Sometimes this results in players believing they do not need to work hard in order to improve.

'They only reach a certain level. Then their development stops, and they won't be mentally prepared to start the hard work as seniors or in a top club. Then their football career plummets. I've seen that happen many times in Finland.'

Just like in Norway, Denmark and Sweden, the Finns had live English football broadcast to their homes by public television in the 1970s and 1980s. At that time, Liverpool were the most successful side in the First Division, and one of the dominant teams in Europe. This recruited a lot of Scandinavian Liverpool hearts. The club also captured Sami Hyypiä's heart, despite the fact his football-playing dad and coach was a Manchester United fan.

So Liverpool became his favourite team, and Ian Rush his idol, since he kept banging in goals on the small television at the Hyypiä home.

'My first hero was Ian Rush. Obviously because he was a fantastic goal scorer. But the work he laid down for the entire team was incredible and unique. He worked over the whole pitch to help the team. That's why it was quite an experience when he came over to me many years later and talked to me as if I were a friend. It was fantastic.'

Again his face lights up in a big smile, his eyes shining with joy under the blond fringe.

'We shook hands and talked for a long time. It was such a privilege to meet him.'
And he knew who you were!
'Yes!'
His smile turns into a grin.

Ian Rush says he got a lot of help from his siblings, because his older brothers let him play with them. But you're an only child.

'It would have been nice to have somebody there, a sibling. But we've been fine like it was. I'm happy about my childhood and how life has turned out. My parents were fairly strict, but gave me a lot of freedom too. And I didn't do anything stupid. I wasn't spoiled, we were a working-class family and didn't have a lot of money. But we had a good life.'

The town they lived in existed because of the cellulose works. His father worked at the factory that gave the place its own peculiar, acrid smell, a smell that might burn the nose of a visitor, but that the locals were used to. And if the wind blew the right way, the smell was weaker. And you could not complain: after all, the factory sustained around 95 per cent of the families who lived there.

Hyypiä senior also played amateur football for Pallo-Peikot (PaPe), the club that would be the springboard for his son Sami into the big world as a football professional. His mother Irma worked in a bank. And in her spare time, she was the goalkeeper for an amateur football team.

'Mum was a goalie, and I went with her to matches since I was so little I was in a pram, and the substitutes looked after me. Football has always been my favourite sport. It was the summer activity for most kids. I played ice hockey too, it was the most common sport in my town in the winter. And then I went cross-country skiing. I had a normal and very active childhood. There were eight families side by side in a row of terraced houses, and there were a lot of boys and girls at my age, so we played together a lot. We didn't have PlayStation or Xbox. We'd always play outdoors, usually with a smile. It couldn't have been better.'

Hyypiä's father described his son as being short-tempered in Sami's autobiography. It seems unusual because he's so calm when he plays football.

'If you show too much emotion on the pitch it may destroy your focus, and focus is vital when you're playing. If you're very happy or very angry, it may influence your concentration and your game. Sometimes I'd be fuming because of something that happened or something that was said, but I always worked hard not to let my emotions show.'

How do you do that?

'The most important thing is that you're fully focused on the mission at hand. My advice would be to ask yourself, "Will it help me if I'm angry about the refereeing decision, or if I go ballistic after a bad tackle? No!" Don't let it disturb your game or your performance. It can ruin the rest of the game. If you're angry you may focus so much on that refereeing decision or the tackle that you're half a second late on the ball, and then your team concedes, or you go too hard into a tackle and get red-carded.

'You have to ask yourself the questions: "What is important? What can you do something about?" If you can't influence it, you have to let it go. It's trite saying that karma turns on you if you're upset on the pitch. But, maybe it helps to count to ten? Focus on the next challenge on the pitch? The same goes for any mistakes. Everybody makes mistakes, I made one too. Let it go. Put it behind you. Move on.

Focus on the job at hand again.'

And it is important that team-mates or the captain do not make bad matters worse if someone has made a mistake.

'It doesn't help that the captain or a fellow player shouts red-faced at the one who made a mistake, confronting him. That won't increase his focus or confidence ahead of the next challenge or the rest of the match. You need to know your team-mates. Some players need a kick in the behind to do their best. But most players usually need confidence more than anything. You should try and lift them up to be able to do their best. Captain or not, I would always be positive towards my fellow team-mates. It's the right way for me to solve situations if somebody made mistakes, or to try and improve my team-mates' performance. In football there is often a negative approach. Post-match analyses always focus on all the negatives, all the mistakes. Everything that could have been solved differently.

'Since working as a manager, I often refrain from commenting on one mistake. If the same thing happens again, I raise the issue. But I try to do it in a positive way. Encourage them to do things differently or better. I was the same with my team-mates when I wasn't captain. I think everyone who has played with me will confirm that I wasn't one to yell and shout on the pitch when someone made a mistake.'

Steven Gerrard said that Rafael Benítez would always bring up the negatives – never the positives – whether you won or not, and that it could be deflating.

'Rafa was a perfectionist. But of course it's hard to only be told about what you did wrong, after you've won 3–0. I think his intention of focusing on the negative was to keep everyone on their toes, and avoid complacency. He worked to make everyone improve. But it was sometimes tough on us players after a win. We felt we had done what we set out to do, and the next thing you know, you're presented with ten situations you could have solved better. Thinking back, I wonder if maybe it was actually smart to focus on improving, but possibly not all the time. But it's important to make your team aware of things that can easily be improved. It's often a question of simply keeping focus within the team.'

Hyypiä has adopted a different approach to his managerial career than Benítez.

'I might not mention it if it's an odd mistake. But if there's a structural flaw in the team, a collaboration failure between two to four players, and you could avoid the situation with better focus, then I'll talk about it. Even if we win.'

Could it drain energy from players, only being criticised and never praised?

'Yeah, it could. But then I was never the type of player who was on top of the world even if we won two games in a row. I would always analyse my matches afterwards and ask, "What could I have done better or differently?" So it wasn't that hard for me. I could relate to Rafael Benítez.'

After going the grades with MyPa in the Finnish top flight and four seasons with Willem II in the Netherlands, he was bought for Liverpool under Gérard Houllier's management in 1999. Rumour has it that it was a cameraman who tipped off chief executive Peter Robinson about a solid defender from Finland.

'Holland was a good step for me after Finland,' Hyypiä says. 'Willem II gave me a challenging environment where I had to play against good players for the same position. They also played a tactically different game of football than in Finland. My career would have looked different if I'd gone straight from Finland to Liverpool. I took small steps to get there instead of giant steps.

'When I came to England, nobody knew who I was, and that made it easier for me in my first season. In my second season it was more difficult to be mentally prepared, because expectations were much higher.'

During his first year, a lot of people asked Hyypiä what it felt like to have signed for Liverpool.

'It felt amazing, but it wasn't enough for me just to sign for Liverpool and train with the first team; I wanted to prove I could defend a place on the team. So I worked relentlessly from day one.'

Many would probably be content. Having signed for a big club, they'd be happy.

'Yes, and that's a big mistake. You have to maintain the right mentality even after you have the luck to be bought by a big club. Always focus on getting better.'

Three months into his Liverpool career he became the first Finn to have the honour of leading a Premier League team as captain.

'I was very surprised to be appointed,' he admits. 'Houllier only told me that I would be captain that day just before the game, just as we were leaving for the stadium.'

What did you feel walking onto the pitch?

'I was always very focused on my responsibilities. Focused on the game. I didn't just go around thinking, I'm the captain, I'm the captain! I probably wouldn't have played well if I did. But I certainly felt very proud.'

It was a huge honour. But it did not motivate him more than before.

'At such a high level you should find motivation in yourself. Nobody can help you give that little something extra if you're not enjoying what you're doing. I was so happy that my hobby became my job, that somebody paid me to do what I loved most. Nobody needed to motivate me to go out on the pitch and win games.'

How did you, as captain, think about motivating your team-mates?

'Sometimes you feel you need to say a few words in the dressing room to motivate your team-mates, and sometimes not. I wasn't the kind of captain who talks a lot before a match. I was calm, but some players would be quite nervous, and hopefully it helped them to see how calm and relaxed I was.'

By the time Sami Hyypiä came to Liverpool, the Premier League as a whole had become a cultural melting pot. The Liverpool players were from many different countries. And with the club's first ever manager from outside the United Kingdom – the Frenchman Gérard Houllier – the club was more continental than ever.

Hyypiä had been captain in the Finnish top flight, for the national team, in the Netherlands, and now was his chance to try his hand at captaining in England.

Which is the easier side to captain: the club team where you know your team-mates better, or on the national team, where you all speak the same language and are from the same culture?

'In my time on the national team the core of the team remained the same over many years, and then gradually a few lesser-known youngsters came in. So I felt I knew my team-mates on the national side almost as well as my club team-mates. I wasn't shouty in either team, but tried to help and guide the others, leading by example and by trying to be a good role model. Communication on the pitch is key, whether you're captain or not.'

But isn't communication easier when everybody has the same language and cultural background?

'No, I can't say captaining a team with the same language or culture made any difference. I would actually be in trouble on the first training at gatherings with the national team – I'd speak English instead of Finnish. It was so weird! Sometimes I almost had to slap myself to snap out of it, and stop talking English to my Finnish countrymen. But sometimes I let out automated short orders in English, no matter how hard I tried to talk Finnish: "Left! Wide!" You quickly get used to English.'

In modern football, players are rested for tactical reasons, or saved to spare key players from injuries ahead of important games. It has become one of the characteristic features of modern football: the constant juggling between league, cup, European and national team responsibilities. For that reason, there may be many who share the captaincy over a season. It was not the same in Ron Yeats' time. He played all the games when he was captain, unless injuries kept him out: then it would be anyone's guess or choice who was vice-captain, because the concept of a vice-captain had not yet been introduced. It would take a lot to keep the captain from playing.

When Sami started his captaincy in individual games, club captain Jamie Redknapp was out injured, but he was still an active voice in training and in the dressing room. Robbie Fowler was vice-captain and, in addition, Jamie Carragher had one or two games as captain too.

How do you keep focus when you've got the captain's responsibility in one match, and not in the next. Was it confusing?

'No, not really. It didn't feel like extra responsibility, because Jamie and Robbie were there and did everything that needed to be done off the pitch. And Robbie would often start on the bench when I was captain. He would contribute in the dressing room. So it didn't change anything for me. The only difference was I'd have to toss the coin and lead the team out for games. But I had no responsibilities outside the matches. Jamie and Robbie dealt with that.'

I am curious about the dynamics in a team. Does the captaincy influence the way your team-mates look at you? Did you feel that your team-mates respected you more when you became captain?

'I never felt there was a lack of respect in Liverpool. I was who I was, and it seemed everybody respected me. We had a few players at the time who gained a reputation as badly behaved and disrespectful, but I never experienced that people didn't respect each other on the team. And I never felt that they didn't respect me. We had discussions, we could see things differently, but that's the same in any relationship. If you're married, have a girlfriend, have a boyfriend or play on the same team: sometimes you see things differently.'

The more you dare discuss with your partner, colleague, boss or captain, the more confident you are, because you dare to be yourself. Dare to show all sides of yourself...

'Yes! Communication is very, very important. Now I've got experience as manager too. And if you believe your way and your opinion is the only way, you're wrong. You have to have a team around you that challenges you and that aren't afraid to speak their mind. That way you will develop as leader too. Other people's point of view will make you think. You may well end up doing things your way anyway, but at least you will have had the opportunity to solve matters differently. And this is important in all aspects of life: not to be stubborn. Don't walk around with blinkers, but be open to opinion and discussions.'

After retiring as player, Sami joined the coaching staff of Bayer Leverkusen, and later took over managerial responsibility there. Afterwards he went to the English Championship club Brighton and Hove Albion, as head coach, resigning in December 2014. (After this interview, he became the manager of FC Zürich in Switzerland in August 2015 but left again in May 2016 after they were relegated.)

'When I arrived at Brighton, I immediately said that my door is always open. I will always listen to everybody's opinion. Even if I don't share their views, I will listen. I wanted the players to come into my office and exchange ideas. It's extremely important in all kinds of leadership to exchange ideas and take time to listen. That's also how you develop your own ideas. Everything is under development, football too, and you have to be in on the race. You can't just stop, you need to develop along with how the game develops.'

As a leader in any level of football you get close to a lot of different people. And in life, we all have our problems or challenges that we struggle with. How much does a leader, a manager, a captain, angle for information when you see someone struggle, in the hope you may relieve the pressure on your team-mates?

'It's very important that people are brave enough to talk about their problems. Because nobody can help unless we know there's something wrong. If my team-mate was in trouble, with his partner or anything else, I couldn't help unless I knew. I want to listen to people's problems and help as well as I can. I may not have a solution, but it's always good to have someone else's view on something or someone you're in conflict with. It helps you to deal with the problem, and may give you new ideas on how to fix the situation. But in general, people involved in football aren't very good at sharing their problems.'

And sometimes, even when the problems are known, they are ignored, because the football teams often has had a very macho get-on-with-it-culture. David Fairclough was only twenty years old when he scored the decisive goal at Anfield against St Etienne, a goal that meant advancement in the European Cup, which in turn led to Liverpool's first European Cup triumph. People still come up to him every week to talk about a goal he scored in 1977.

Only a few months later, Fairclough's father died suddenly, and overnight the twenty-year-old, who still lived at home with his parents and a sister in their council house, was the breadwinner of the family on his modest football salary. He got a week off for the funeral arrangements, and then he was told to move on, get over it. Nobody offered him a shoulder to cry on, nobody put an arm around him or ask him how he felt. To this day, Fairclough is bitter that his manager, Bob Paisley, did not show him more compassion in what was a devastating time in his life. It was all very macho back in the 1970s. Get on with it.

Is it better today?

'No, I think footballers and leaders are still afraid to talk about their problems. You build a kind of friendship through playing together, but it isn't necessarily true friendship. I got along well with everybody during my playing career, but I wouldn't say many of them are my friends. And I wouldn't have talked about my problems in such superficial friendships. I had other friends to talk with, real friends.'

Besides, he feared sensitive or personal information might get publicised.

'I believe that people in general don't talk about their problems because they're ashamed of it. They don't want to be found out. And one thing I've discovered in football is that rumours spread rapidly.'

Footballers are not only afraid to talk about their mental problems. They are also afraid to open up about physical problems.

'In football, it's usually like that – you don't talk about your physical problems with your team-mates. But as a manager I have to know about them. Then it's up to me to decide if I use a player who is seventy per cent fit or someone else in that position who is a hundred per cent fit. If a player doesn't tell me about his injury, he takes that decision for me. That's not how I want it. But of course it's difficult for them to let me know about muscular problems when they want to play. That is a dilemma.

'When I was a player I also wanted to play all the games. But if I was struggling with injury I used to tell my manager about it and leave the decision up to him.'

Who were you closest to at Liverpool?

'Markus Babbel and Didi Hamann became close friends, but there were quite a few I could talk to. Luckily I didn't have any big problems.'

What should clubs do to help players open up and solve problems in the best possible way, both physical and mental issues?

'The clubs must encourage people to talk about their problems and to be honest. A lot of clubs now use a club psychologist who has a duty of confidentiality. This is no doubt a good development. Players can now talk without worrying about others hearing things they don't want to share. Depression will always be a problem, because as humans we are all different and solve things differently. Depression in football will never disappear, it's more common now than before. More money is involved, creating more pressure.'

Can you describe the pressure of playing for a top club?

'When we won matches with Liverpool, I used to think that was how it should be, it was normal. We didn't really celebrate, because the fans expected us to win. But when we lost, it was a disaster. The smaller teams I've played for were different. Winning would be the highlight of the week. And if we lost, it was just one of those things. But that wasn't the way in Liverpool. So I think some players might have problems when they come from a smaller club where there is less expectations and pressure. And when they go to a bigger club, like Manchester United, Manchester

City or Liverpool, they fail to reach the same level of performance because the pressure of expectation is so much higher. When you win a match, it's just the way it should be. But when you lose, it's a crisis, and people immediately start criticising both team and manager. So I'm glad we won more matches than we lost.'

Many matches won. Ten trophies in ten years at Liverpool is a fine record. Hyypiä played during the most successful period in Liverpool's Premier League history. What was his proudest moment as a player?

'Everybody wants to win the Champions League in their career. But I have many moments that I'm very proud of for various reasons. Sometimes I'm the only one who knows what made me proud. But Istanbul is the biggest match I've won, even though I've had better moments personally. I'm not the type who...'

He searches for the right words.

'When I win, I feel like I've won something, but I continue where I left off, move on to win something else. I put the triumph behind me and concentrate on day one of the next season. That's why I still haven't quite managed to take in what we achieved at the Atatürk Stadium.

'Nothing can change that we and I won in Istanbul. But I prefer the here and now. In ten years' time maybe I can think about being a Champions League winner. Because so much happens all the time. I live in the moment. In twenty or twenty-five years when I think back, I'll probably be even prouder that we won the Champions League. There won't be another match like it. It was very special, and a lot of people, even those who aren't fans of Liverpool or Milan, will always remember it.'

After he finished at Liverpool in 2009 at the age of 35 Hyypiä chose to continue his playing career in the Bundesliga with Bayer Leverkusen, rather than stay for a possible place on Liverpool's coaching staff. He played over fifty games in Germany before he became assistant manager and later manager of the same club. Now, a few years later, while queueing for coffee, he reveals that he would love to return to Liverpool one day and become part of the training team. Assistant manager or, maybe one day, manager of his favourite club; a club that helped make him popular and gave him an unforgettable football career.

Why is Liverpool a special club for you, and what did you learn from your time at Anfield?

'The fans make the club special. I thought about it when we celebrated the tenth anniversary of Istanbul: this couldn't have happened to any other club.'

There were ten thousand people in the hall who had bought tickets and filled the Echo Arena in Liverpool to relive the match and pay tribute to the players, and an almost complete team from Istanbul was reunited.

'Yes, the supporters make Liverpool special. There was a great atmosphere in the club in my ten years there. You could really feel the warmth. I felt that they took care of me. It was a great time.'

Players come and go, but you're still very popular with the Liverpool fans. Why do you think that is?

'No idea!'

Sami Hyypiä goes modest again.

Hard-working?

'Yes, I suppose the Liverpool fans like players who work as hard as they possibly can for the team. And maybe they saw that I was someone who always gave everything I had. Sometimes I didn't do well, sometimes I didn't feel well, and we didn't win all our matches. But at least I tried my utmost. I think fans appreciate that. Maybe that's why they liked me? But I hope that my playing ability wasn't half bad either...'

There it is again. The smile that cracks up the warrior mask and gives us a piece of Finnish sunshine.

During ten years with Liverpool there were many unforgettable moments. One of the most vivid is a less happy one: the day he lost the captaincy to Steven Gerrard.

When Hyypiä had shared what was in practice a joint captaincy with Robbie Fowler, the sidelined Jamie Redknapp remained club captain. Hyypiä had not felt that being captain changed anything in his performance or game. But when Fowler and Redknapp were sold in 2001 and 2002 respectively, Sami was appointed new club captain.

That meant he now had to do what was formerly split between three people. All the duties that were expected of the captain, also off the pitch: sponsor meetings, press conferences and representation. And all these duties outside the game influenced Hyypiä's performance. He was not as solid as he had been in his first years at the club. Something was not quite right. That is why Gérard Houllier and his assistant Phil Thompson made the tactical change of captain, and gave the responsibility to a young Steven Gerrard. Thompson had recognised the signs from his own time of taking on too much responsibility as captain and not playing up to his potential.

Thompson had been through the experience of having the captaincy taken off him in 1981 so he was better placed to speak to Sami about it in the weeks that followed.

'From that day, my performance improved. Because when you're captain there are so many things that need organising and fixing outside matches and training. There are sponsor events where the captain usually has to come and say a few words. And when the team meets for a meal, you have to arrange everything. To me, that was the downside of being a captain. It would be an exaggeration to say it was a relief Stevie took over, but it gave me less to do. So I could concentrate on the important part: play good football and win.'

The day after Sami's difficult talk with the assistant manager about losing the captaincy, it was time to meet the new captain in training at Melwood. Steven Gerrard was only 23 years old and felt a little uncomfortable about succeeding a team-mate he valued highly.

'I came into training in the morning, and Stevie avoided contact with me. I went up to him and said: "Congratulations, you deserve it. I know this means a lot to you. And if you need help, I'm always here for you."'

Gerrard took his hand, smiled at him and thanked the Finn – who once again had put the team before himself.

15

JAMIE CARRAGHER
THE BOY WHO DID NOT NEED RECOGNITION

'I don't know how these foreign players understood Carra at all, his Scouse accent is even stronger than mine!'
Phil Thompson

AFTER TWENTY YEARS OF WAITING, AND LONGING, HOW DO you prepare to play the Champions League final, as the underdog?

'Fifth in the league, lost to Burnley in the FA Cup. There was nothing about our season saying we were even going to feature in the Champions League final,' Jamie Carragher reflects on Liverpool's 2004/05 campaign. 'Just think about some of the sides we'd met along the way. We'd beaten Juventus. Chelsea had an incredibly strong team too, but we'd knocked them out. We'd had some fantastic nights at Anfield. Of course we were ready to win it, but we actually thought more about enjoying the experience. I was sure I'd never play a Champions League final again, and just getting there was totally unexpected.'

Less than a minute into the sizzling match, Milan scored the opening goal.

'The game hadn't even started. You're still hazy – a lot of players hadn't even touched the ball yet – and then it's like the match starts all over again, but this time you start 1–0 down. And with a goal against you, it's easy to forget tactics. Maybe that's why we went 3–0 down.

'I felt it was all over. We left the pitch at half-time thinking, This proves we're not on the same level. Before the match we thought about all the great teams we'd knocked out of the competition, and it left us feeling we had a chance. Half-time was a reality check: 3–0. I was thinking, that's probably the level of difference between AC Milan and Liverpool.'

In the dressing room, Rafael Benítez reorganised the team. He told Djimi Traoré to hit the shower, and Didi Hamann to get warmed up. Then the physio came out saying Steve Finnan could not play on, even though Finnan tried to convince them he could. Traoré was told to come back out of the shower and put his boots back on. Finnan was none too pleased. Djibril Cissé got kitted out; he thought he was coming on.

'Rafa reorganised the team, and all of a sudden there were twelve of us. He might have thought that was the only way to win! Then he told Cissé to sit down again, but it wasn't easy getting through to him because he was wearing headphones.'

What did Rafael Benítez say?

'Now, we were all beside ourselves, so we all have different versions of what he said. But Rafa isn't a manager who lifts you and motivates you vocally. Tactically he's very good, though. He changed the formation to three at the back – I think that was crucial.'

But didn't he say two important things at half-time: 'If we get an early goal, we still have a chance,' and 'Listen to the fans!'

'We could hear the singing like an echo through the tunnel and into the dressing room. And the fans' chanting lifted us. I feel the supporters played just as important a part as anyone on the team that night. Second half was coming up, and I thought: At least we have to go out there and fight.'

Every time Carragher watches clips from the second half he smiles. Suddenly 3–0 became 3–3. In the penalty shoot-out that followed, Carragher told Jerzy Dudek, Liverpool's Polish goalkeeper, to mimic Bruce Grobbelaar. Twenty-one years earlier, the Zimbabwean turned his legs to spaghetti when facing Roma's penalty-takers in Europe's grandest final and it was enough to put them off as Liverpool prevailed. For Dudek, it worked again.

'It's more than a football match and more than a Champions League final,' Carragher says. 'People still talk about it. When I see pictures of the supporters and their joy, I would have loved to go back to that moment. It's very rare in life as a player, or supporter, to experience anything like that. It was a very special night. Not just for Liverpool, but for football. One of the best Champions League finals ever. Nobody who loves football will ever forget that night. And for us players who had the chance to be involved, it's a fantastic privilege. The supporters will always remember where they were when Liverpool won the European Cup for the fifth time.'

Ten years later, Jamie and I are on the top floor of the Hilton Hotel in Liverpool.
We rewind to the day when he was appointed vice-captain two months after Istanbul
in a friendly match at Wrexham.

'I guess it was done in the wrong way, really. Sami Hyypiä was the captain, and
then Stevie became captain, so we automatically thought Sami was vice-captain.
But before this pre-season match I was suddenly told that I was the vice-captain.
It took me by surprise. And I wondered if Sami was OK with it. I think we were
considering bringing in a centre-back at the time, and maybe the manager thought
that Sami wouldn't play every week. But I honestly don't know if Rafa Benítez had
told Sami. So the two of us, Stevie and me, carried the trophy out onto the pitch
before the game to show the fans. But that was Rafa for you. He wasn't great at
communication. There was still some shock, though.'

Carragher had tried his hand at captaining already a few years earlier. Benítez was
not the only one who had seen leadership potential in him. He had led the team out
on a couple of occasions during the treble season under Gérard Houllier.

'Jamie and Robbie were out, and maybe Sami was on the sideline. We didn't
know who would be captain until Houllier told us, in front of everyone, that Friday.
Then he declared that I was going to be captain the next day. It was a massive
moment for me.'

How did the match go?

'We beat Manchester City 3–2. In the second game I led, we won away in Europe,
1–0. I think Nick Barmby scored. And then we played away against West Ham, and
drew, 1–1.'

So you didn't lose any of your matches as captain first time around?

Jamie Carragher grins.

'No!' he says, breaking into his characteristic laugh, light and trilling.

Do you know how many matches you captained through your career?

'No, honestly no idea, do you? Maybe fifty? Stevie's been out injured a few times
over the years… my dad guesses it's around forty.'

Jamie messages Liverpool's statistics expert, Ged Rea, and shortly after the answer
arrives: 'I was actually captain ninety times!'

Almost twice as many as he had thought. That corresponds to two full seasons as
leader on the pitch for Liverpool. And Rea only counted matches where Carragher

started as captain. Games where he took over captaincy mid-match were not even considered.

James Lee Duncan Carragher, born in 1978, was a die-hard Everton supporter growing up. Not that he had much of a choice, born into the blue part of a completely football-mad city. He takes his middle names from the then Everton manager Gordon Lee and star player Duncan McKenzie.

'It was a special time, I was lucky to grow up in the middle of the 1980s,' he remembers. 'I don't think there's ever been better football on Merseyside than back then. Liverpool and Everton were the two best teams in the country, maybe even two of the best teams in Europe. The whole decade, up until Liverpool won the league for the last time in 1990, Merseyside football was dominant. I was an Evertonian, but I played for Liverpool from 1989, so it was a fantastic time.'

As the oldest of three brothers, he was allowed to travel to matches in Europe with his father Philly at the age of seven. This was in an era when the terraces of English football grounds held dubious reputations.

'In 1985 Everton won the league and the Cup Winners' Cup, and my dad and I went to the semi-final away against Bayern Munich. At this time there was a lot of talk about hooligans and supporter trouble. When we got off the plane in Germany, a TV presenter showed up, and asked me if I were a hooligan – and I was only seven!'

He smiles thinking back to the absurdity of the situation, but also recalling such a great memory from his childhood as a football fan.

'Being successful in Europe was new to Everton. Liverpool had been doing it for years, of course. So making it to the Olympic Stadium, Bayern Munich's old ground, was a fantastic experience. (I later returned with England to that stadium, and won 5–1.) As a first-timer on a European away match, I got to meet the Everton players after the match. That was really nice. They remind me of it to this day, if I bump into one of them. That's an experience I'll never forget, even if Liverpool are my team now.'

Philly Carragher, Jamie's father, also ran a Sunday league football team. He often took his boys with him to training.

What would you have been without your dad?

'I might not have been part of football, to be honest. My passion for football comes from my dad. He was manager for various teams when I was a kid, and he got me into football. At that time you weren't allowed into organised football before the age of eleven. I was only seven. He lied about my age to get me in. I didn't play much – a lot of them were three or four years older than me. But that's certainly where I got my passion for football.'

Ever since childhood, Jamie Carragher has been a proper football geek. As a young boy he would devour anything he could find about football. He would be glued to the television set if football was on. He read match programmes and football magazines from cover to cover. And he and his family were frequent visitors to Goodison Park.

On away trips, Jamie learned a lot about the relationship between players and fans. The Everton players were great at taking care of their supporters when they were on the continent.

'I admired the footballers, they were my heroes. It's still like that with quite a few Liverpool players too. I admired a lot of them even though I wasn't a Liverpool fan. I followed the team that had Barnes and Beardsley very closely – and I ended up playing with Barnes and Rush at the beginning of my career. I'm still just a fan when I meet players of that [era]. So I really get what it's like to be a fan. When you think about football stars as heroes, you don't consider them normal people. You think there's something extraordinary about them, that they're different than everybody else. But they're really just normal guys. They have a knack for playing football, that's all. But to a die-hard football fan, that's hard to see.'

He admired a lot of captains through his childhood and youth. For an Evertonian, Kevin Ratcliffe was the obvious favourite. He captained the Blues from Merseyside from 1984 to 1991 and also the Welsh national team. For Liverpool, Jamie looked up to Alan Hansen. Graeme Souness was the perfect captain, he reckons, and anyone would have wanted him as the leader of their team.

Carragher says central midfield often has had the most inspiring captains.

'Robson, Gerrard and Souness were all central midfielders. The midfield is so important. That's where duels are fought and matches often won. The three were perfect captain types as far as I'm concerned.'

You picked out three midfielders. What do you think is the ideal position on the pitch for a captain?

'I would say a central defender is slightly better than central midfield. Wherever in the world you watch football, if it's in a park, at top level or in lower divisions, the captain is usually in central defence or midfield.'

Carragher grew up to be a responsible player – and a responsible person. Whether he was captain or not, he took on a lot of responsibility. He has continued to do so through his own charity, the 23 Foundation.

He has had a lot of role models in football, and he highlights Steve Heighway as one of the most important. When Carragher started, Heighway was responsible for developing young talents at Liverpool's centre of excellence. Heighway is afforded the main credit for Jamie Carragher's return to Liverpool after he had been given a chance to train and develop for a year with his favourite team, Everton. Carragher's father recognised Liverpool's youth set-up was stronger at the time. Indeed, his son would follow a number of boyhood Evertonians through the Liverpool youth ranks during the 1990s: Steve McManaman, Robbie Fowler, Michael Owen, David Thompson. Gradually, Carragher switched his allegiances.

Jamie also had important role models outside football.

'Growing up, there wasn't much that was not about football, but my parents and some of my teachers were crucial. There are always a few teachers who play an important part. For me, it was John Rourke, the headmaster at my comprehensive school, and later Mike Dickinson, my PE teacher, who still works for Everton, actually. He was a former PE teacher and physiotherapist for the English schoolboys team. The teachers you're a little afraid of, but at the same time admire, they have a special charisma and power of influence.'

Jamie says he received the most important guidance from his parents, though.

'My dad was the strict one, and Mum was the soft-hearted and caring one, who looked after us three boys, took care of the house and cooked for us all. I guess it was a little old-fashioned. She took care of everything at the house, and Dad took us to football. My mum was never much involved in the football side of my life, but she made sure we were fine.'

You appear to be a balanced, safe and confident type, with no need to draw attention to yourself or crave recognition. Were your parents good at complimenting you, lifting you up?

'No, and I don't think constantly being told how fantastic you are is necessarily the best way. My dad wasn't like that, and I'm not going to be that way with my kids. In fact, a lot of players say that: "My parents were my biggest critics. Mine just let me play."

'I wasn't stuck up. I was just intensely focused on football, and on winning. When I was ten years old, I was so much harder on myself than anyone else could be. I didn't need anyone to tell me how good I was.

'My dad was supportive. He'd give me a little praise when I played well, and gave me a few tips when I hadn't. But you know from when you're quite little if you haven't played a good match. You don't need anyone to tell you that.

'In other words, you don't have to make it worse as parents, if your children don't perform to their fullest capability in sports, but you also need to be careful going in the opposite direction.

'Parents should be there and support their kids, but not blow their horns or brag unrestrictedly, because that will make kids forget that they need to work to get better.'

Do you think that, as parents, we give our children too much praise?

'That is a concern, yes. It's important to give them some praise when they've done well, and assure them that they can do better next time, if things didn't go their way. That's my recipe for my son James after football training or matches. But I don't say anything straight after a match if it didn't go well, he'd be ever so disappointed. I might bring it up before the next match instead: "Come on, you can do better than last time!" And then I give him some advice on how he can improve, and I cheer him on.'

Jamie's son plays football, and his daughter, Mia, wants to be a dancer.

'They are both very competitive. If Mia has a dance performance and isn't best pleased with herself, she knows. She'll be feeling down and in need of support. But we're all different. Some kids might not have that sense of reality, and think they're a lot better than they are, and in that case maybe it's a parent's job to hold back on the praise a little.'

✦

Carragher played under two different captains during his first two years as a Liverpool senior-team player. John Barnes was his first.

'John Barnes isn't your typical captain,' he says. 'It's rare that a creative player like him gets the captaincy, especially in England. But he was the oldest player in a young squad, and the most respected player. Respected by all. Still very technical, although his legs weren't quite what they had been. But we all knew that Barnes five or six years earlier had probably been the best in the world, and one of the best players who ever played for Liverpool. So I had massive respect for him.

'At that time, Barnes was contemplating becoming a manager, so he had more of a say on the team than a lot of other captains. He talked more and became the voice of a team who didn't have many like him. He was definitely the most vocal of us all.'

John says he was very frustrated back then, he felt he was trying to lead a team that wasn't really interested in being led. Do you get his drift?

'Yes. The Premier League had exploded, money was pouring in. It was like a new world had just started. I'd just gotten into the squad, and could see John Barnes' frustration. His career was coming to an end, he wouldn't have that many chances left to win trophies. And with the team he was playing for, it could be difficult to reach new triumphs. It was very frustrating for him.'

After Barnes, there was Paul Ince.

'Paul Ince was a great, bubbling personality. He didn't stand back from anything. A big personality with a strong presence. Big mouth. He helped me tremendously. We played central midfield together in his first year. Ince didn't like playing defensive midfield. He wanted to go forward and score goals, and he did score a few in his first season, eight of them. He was also a typical captain in the way he played and led matches. I played in his position for England Under-21, and he played in that position for the seniors. Paul could use both legs, was dauntless, always took the ball. He was the same kind as Steven Gerrard, only a level or two below by the time he played for Liverpool.'

Jamie Redknapp became captain after Ince was sold to Middlesbrough a couple of years later.

'Jamie Redknapp was a good captain. He was just really unlucky to be in a suit and tie when we were winning trophies. He'd lift the trophies, but all the injuries kept him from playing. He didn't just focus on himself if the team didn't do well. He was passionate about the club. He paid a lot of attention to young and new players who arrived to the team, always kind and good to people. He was given the honour of the captaincy from Houllier, and it was a pity that he didn't really get to show just how good he was. But he knew he had it in him.'

With Redknapp out injured, the captaincy rotated.

What was it like, having a rotating captaincy? Was it confusing?

'Not really, it was more that Gérard Houllier changed so many things on the team. Usually the captain is guaranteed a place in the starting eleven. Jamie was injured, and Robbie was competing with Emile Heskey and Michael Owen for a spot on the team, so he didn't play every week. But Sami Hyypiä played every week. I think it was something of the same with Alex Ferguson at Manchester United a few years back. Nobody really knew who was captain.'

The year following the treble season, Sami Hyypiä was chosen captain after Redknapp left for Tottenham Hotspur and Fowler was sold to Leeds United.

'Sami Hyypiä was a tremendous player, someone people respected, and he looked like a captain. He wasn't the type of person who took a lot of space, or tried to organise everything. He was a quiet type. But he earned respect from his achievements on the pitch. You could feel he was captain in the way he led the team on the pitch too. The first three seasons he was at the club, he was absolutely outstanding. There was a big commotion if Sami had a bad game, because it was so unusual: "What's wrong with him?" Because he played well over such a long period.'

Then, some way into his captaincy, Hyypiä started to experience problems on the pitch.

'We all go through bad patches, and Sami had a two-month period where he didn't do so well. And I think we all knew that Stevie [Gerrard] would become captain at some point. He'd gone through the grades, he was twenty-three, it was just a matter of time before he'd get the captain's armband.'

Why was it only a question of time?

'Stevie was our best player, and the right type to become captain. He's such an inspirational fella. And I think the timing was right, considering Sami was having a bit of a down period. In addition, Stevie had reached that age when other clubs, in a year or two, would start looking at him.'

You're a little older than Steven. Were you disappointed that you didn't get the captaincy before him?

'Not really. I played every week under Gérard Houllier, but I don't think I was among the best on the team. And I wasn't guaranteed to play every week, like a captain should be. Stevie was a better player than me, and I think they imagined he could be captain for the next ten years. And that's what happened.'

How did he develop as a captain, do you think, from that time and until you saw him walk off the pitch after his last Anfield match as captain?

'Incredibly! He came in as very young, and was looked on as a role model. As he developed, he helped other players more and more, not least those who were new in the club, and the youngsters. The last few years he's sent a lot of texts to players, called them, followed up on them and checked if they needed anything. He also talked to potential new signings.'

He was more active behind the scenes than most people imagine then?

'Oh, absolutely. He grew a lot with the responsibility. Steve wanted to contribute as much as he could for the club to succeed.'

At the beginning of their Liverpool careers, Carragher spent more time with Michael Owen while Gerrard was closer to Danny Murphy. When Owen and Murphy left the club in the same summer, Carragher and Gerrard's friendship began to blossom. But Carragher says they are very different to one another, certainly as players.

'We were two different personalities on the pitch. Steven was the one who could get us out of trouble and score goals. The best player, an iconic player of our time.

He led by example. Everybody respected him and looked up to him.

'My role in it was organising. Maybe I did more of what you'd think a captain would normally do, while Stevie was more of an attacking type. An attacker needs to think of himself, be on the ball, try to score, whereas I was part of the back four. We needed to be structured, and I would always be organising, talking, yelling commands.'

Phil Thompson says he thought of his fellow players as chess pieces, that he would move around. Did Steven and you do the same?

'Yes, I did, no doubt about that. Stevie, no, because he was an attacker in a freer role, where you think more about scoring goals, while a defensive midfielder or centre-back thinks more about the team. So I'd say it was more my role to make sure the five or six at the back were in the right positions, while Stevie concentrated on getting the attackers to work forward. But I didn't care if I wore the armband or not. To be quite honest, I didn't want it, because that would mean Stevie wasn't playing. And that would be a loss for the team, because he was that good.'

Carragher did not change, captain or not. He was always the leader in defence.

'But don't get me wrong, I was proud to lead the team out at the big stadiums. I had the honour of captaining in the Santiago Bernabéu against Real Madrid in the Champions League in 2009. It was great to be able to shake Raúl's hand before the match, and exchange pennants. Raúl may not be a captain type, but he was an icon for Real Madrid, and it was incredible just to be on the pitch and shake hands with such a legend.'

That match is beyond doubt Carragher's proudest moment as captain.

'We were under a lot of pressure during the entire match, as we often were when we were out playing in Europe back then. I remember these matches best of all. They were truly special. We won the match 1–0 against the most successful team in European football history. I can't think of a bigger match I've captained.'

It may not have changed his game directly, being the vice-captain for almost ten years. But what was it like, having the responsibility for so long in such a world-famous club?

'You just have to jump at the opportunity. I've never been to a smaller club than Liverpool. I've always been there, so I don't know anything else. I'm sure Stevie will say the same. From the outside it may look like a massive role to be captain, but the vice-captaincy is slightly different. Stevie's been captain and role model for such a long time. But having local lads as vice-captain and captain makes results even more personal. After a victory you get to celebrate with family and friends. Terrific! People all around you are happy. But setbacks and losses feel worse, because you'll hear it on every street corner and in every house, from your own. So responsibility did weigh a little heavier as a local vice-captain. A heavy and personal responsibility towards the supporters, your team-mates and your family.'

Roy Evans gave Carragher his chance in the first team in January 1997, shortly before his nineteenth birthday. He was a 75th-minute substitute for Rob Jones in a League Cup quarter-final defeat to Middlesbrough. His full debut came ten days later in a Premier League match against Aston Villa. Carragher was told the night before that he would play but then Liverpool signed Bjørn Tore Kvarme, leaving his place in doubt – not that he knew. The next morning, Evans told him he was not playing in defence, but midfield, because Patrik Berger was ill.

'I scored a goal, and that's the kind of luck you need to succeed in this game. If Berger hadn't been ill, I might have stayed on the bench.'

There is often a connection between the biggest football profiles and how well they did in their debut.

'If you get a chance, you've got to grab it. I was just eighteen, that's young. Robbie Fowler, Steve McManaman, Michael Owen and Steven Gerrard also had their debuts at a young age, and during their first two games they were either man of the match or they scored. As a kid you won't get ten matches to prove your worth, you need to show it quickly, or the manager won't dare to go for you.'

He thinks Gérard Houllier treated the role of the captain with greater seriousness than any of his other managers.

'He put a lot into the captaincy. In addition, Houllier chose five or six players for a committee that he could consult with and talk to a few times a year. He told us that we were the leaders of the squad, and had to set the standard for the team.'

What did you discuss in those meetings?

'At the beginning of a season we would plot a course: what were we going to do, what should we concentrate on. We also shared responsibility and roles when new players came in. When things weren't going our way, he gave us responsibility both in the dressing room and on the pitch. He valued the captain's role very highly.'

In his first years with Liverpool, Carragher proved he was a man of many talents. An extremely useful player who could play a variety of positions: central defence, midfield, right--back and left-back.

'Gérard Houllier would say to me: "There will always be a place for you on the team. But I don't know where you will play." That was good enough for me. If I hadn't accepted playing different positions, I'd have had to either sit on the bench or changed clubs. I give credit to the people who trained me at Liverpool when I was young that I could play in many different positions. We were always told that a good player can play anywhere. In Liverpool we were drilled with passing and moving – regardless of where we were playing. If I hadn't been able to play so many positions, I don't think I would have spent my entire career at Liverpool.'

In 2004, Rafael Benítez was introduced as the new Liverpool manager.

Benítez seems like a manager who wanted more control – how did he compare to Houllier and Evans?

'I don't think any of our managers would have let us players change tactics in a game. Every now and then I could make a few twists, but no big changes. Do players from earlier decades say they could change the game as they were playing?'

Yes, some of them do…

'OK, but what did they do? Back then they all played 4–4–2, so what did they really change? It wasn't like they radically changed the structure. They probably made the same type of changes I did. I told the defensive midfielder to stay back, or I'd shout to Steven, who was often playing behind Torres, that he needed to go deeper for ten minutes. Little things, during play.

'It's not like you would run to the sideline and ask if it's OK that Stevie pulls back a little. You make those decisions, and I think being a centre-back helps you make such decisions. Or maybe you tell the right-back to move up, because the opposition put on a different type player. You make plans ahead of the game, but as the match evolves and changes, you can make a few adjustments.'

In 2010, Roy Hodgson took over. It was a turbulent time at the club, with supporters opposing the owners Tom Hicks and George Gillett.

What was Hodgson like, in his relation to captain and vice-captain?

'He wasn't there long enough for me to say much about it, plus I dislocated my shoulder, so I wasn't playing for half the time Roy was there. It was disappointing. We were just starting to get on to something. Then we lost 2–1 to Tottenham, in a match we should have won easily. Stevie was out with a long-term injury too, so I would have led the team for a while there if I hadn't been out injured.'

What type of manager was Hodgson at Liverpool?

'Roy was a coach, he'd put us through our training sessions. It was a shame for all parties that it ended like it did. He'd had a couple of very good seasons at Fulham before he came to us. He took them to the UEFA Cup final, and they grabbed four points in their meetings with us in 2009–10. His Fulham team was difficult to play against. But for some reason, he just didn't work at Liverpool.'

It was a turbulent time at the club too.

'Yes, it was a difficult time in more than one way. Both the ownership and a new manager. The supporters got heavily involved, and it wasn't an easy time for Roy Hodgson to be manager. But he went on to manage England, he's done OK for himself.'

In October 2010 the club changed owners again, and the American sports investment company Fenway Sports Group took over. In an attempt to raise enthusiasm and team spirit again, in early 2011 they hired Kenny Dalglish as a temporary manager. He had once been a leader on the pitch, and now made a very popular comeback at the club.

'Kenny was both a manager and a giant figure in Liverpool. Steve Clarke would put us through our training sessions, but Kenny was always on the field. He was quite simply the role model. He picked the team. Besides, we all knew that we were working with a manager who had won three or four titles with different clubs. He was a top manager and very special. It was simply incredible for us to work with him, especially for me and Stevie. Kenny was someone we looked up to. We brought back one trophy from two Wembley finals. I honestly think it was pretty unfortunate that he lost his job after a season like that.'

Graeme Souness feels it was wrong that he lost the job.

'Yes, I thought it was too harsh. You couldn't really say we'd had a bad season, considering we played two cup finals and won one of them. We started the season off well, and were on the road to top four, but it ended disappointingly. You've got to remember that when you play cups for that long there's an extra number of midweek matches, focus on cup matches – like the semi-final against Everton – and all of this is added to the mix, and influences the league. It's not that simple, if we hadn't done so well in the cups, we would have made top four.'

Carragher's last season as a professional football was under yet another manager, the Northern Irishman, Brendan Rodgers.

'He communicated a lot with his players. He talked a lot to me as a senior player, even though I didn't often start during his first months as boss. But I think he realised how much the club meant to Stevie and me. He talked to us to learn what Liverpool were all about, he learned about the traditions of the club, and he talked even more to Stevie, since he was captain and played regularly. But even when I wasn't playing, he wanted to have a chat about how the team were doing, and where we could improve. '

Carragher played his way back into the team again at the end of his final season, and once again he stood strong in defence and was invaluable for many matches. But as the 2012/13 campaign was coming to an end, he decided to hang up his boots, aged 35.

His time is now divided in four broad parts: between ferrying his kids to and from football and dance practice; the boxing gym where he keeps fit; the Sky television studios; as well as events around his charity, the 23 Foundation.

Not everyone knows how much charity work you've done...

'. . . but you don't have to write about that in your book,' he replies, modestly.

It's part of the leadership responsibility, isn't it?

'Well, yes, both Steven Gerrard and I have set up charities, trying to help as we may. We both come from areas where we are reminded not to forget about our background. Stevie and I grew up in working-class areas, like most people in Liverpool. Bootle and Huyton. We've been very lucky with our careers, financially too. So the least we can do is give something back and try to help.

'I don't think our families would have let us forget the areas we came from.'

16

STEVEN GERRARD
ICON

'He could have been captain when he was eighteen, he was that good.'
Jamie Redknapp

IT IS 16 MAY 2015. THE SUN IS SHINING AND THE SKY IS CLEAR and blue. There are no clouds over Anfield. Outside the stadium supporters have assembled earlier than usual before the game. Every souvenir stall is covered in Steven Gerrard flags, and there is a continuous stream of arriving supporters with Gerrard cardboard masks. Outside the supporters' shop under the world-famous Kop stand, there is a massive photo of a celebrating Gerrard in the red home kit. In capitals on the photo it reads: 'Red. For life.'

Inside the dressing room, which until the Main Stand's redevelopment in the summer of 2016 was virtually identical to how it was when Ron Yeats last got changed there over forty years before, captain Steven Gerrard pulls on the red shirt for the very last time at his beloved Anfield. He says that whenever he does this, he thinks about his cousin, Jon-Paul Gilhooley, who went off to watch Liverpool play Nottingham Forest in the FA Cup semi-final at Hillsborough Stadium, and never returned. Aged ten, he became the youngest victim of the crush in the Leppings Lane terrace. Gerrard was only eight when his cousin was cruelly torn away from his family, and says he has played every one of his games for Liverpool first team through the previous seventeen years with his cousin in his thoughts.

In Gerrard's penultimate game as captain for Liverpool, he is not leading his team onto the pitch. The Crystal Palace and Liverpool players have lined up in two rows facing each other, making a guard of honour for the man who has served the team as captain for the past twelve years of his life. Today he is the last man out of the players' tunnel; he is carrying his youngest daughter while the two older ones lead the way out in front of their dad. They walk like this past all the players. Gerrard high-fives all the Palace players, to a deafening cheer from both home and away supporters. He is met by an impressive mosaic that covers two stands, as the fans hold up sheets of coloured paper: 'Captain' is written in large red letters on a white background on the Centenary Stand, while the Kop spells out 'S 8 G' on a white background. Today there are nothing but Gerrard banners flying from the legendary stand. The entire stadium is singing: 'Steven Gerrard is our captain, Steven Gerrard is a Red, Steven Gerrard plays for Liverpool, Scouser born and bred.'

He was born into a football-mad family, just like so many others in Liverpool. Growing up, he always dreamed about playing for Liverpool. He had so many idols.

'When I was little and played amateur football, most of my heroes were Liverpool players: John Barnes, Peter Beardsley – and Ronnie Whelan and Steve McMahon, because they played in similar positions to myself,' he tells me when we meet on the top floor of the Liverpool Hilton three weeks later. 'But I didn't dream about becoming captain at that time. That dream came further down the line.'

In a few days' time Gerrard will move to the United States to start his new life as a Los Angeles Galaxy player. We meet at a unique time: between two different eras of his life. It's the perfect time to reflect over his own career with Liverpool and his leadership through as many as 470 games as captain, over a period of 12 years. No one in the club's rich history has served longer as captain. Only Ron Yeats comes close – he had 417 matches over close to a decade. They have both carried so much responsibility on their shoulders, on behalf of millions of fans.

Gerrard arrives straight from the hairdresser, in a black bomber jacket over a grey T-shirt and casual black trousers. On his feet there are trendy white Adidas trainers. He leans back in his chair and talks with a soft, quiet voice. He is present, passionate and personal, and takes time to reflect on the topic. It is his first days as a non-Liverpool player, his first days without being part of the football club he has trained with and played for since he joined its centre of excellence at the age of eight. Two weeks after his final match, and after a month of touching tributes and thank-yous in the press, on social media, at events, in the stadium and in meeting with fans, he is starting to take in that his football career with Liverpool is over.

'My whole family loves football, they're obsessed with football, whether they are red or blue,' he says. 'Early on I just wanted to play football, and Liverpool were my team. I grew up watching a lot of cup finals, my dad had a lot of tapes of Liverpool. So when I wasn't playing football in the streets or with my amateur team, I sat at home watching these tapes. I was obsessed with watching great goals, good playing and match highlights. And my dad would constantly talk about the Liverpool players he loved: Dalglish, Souness, Phil Thompson, Emlyn Hughes. And he always said to me, "Watch how they do it. Look at how they solve this. See how he moves. Look at how he dribbles and shoots." So from the age of seven or eight I was becoming aware of Liverpool. How massive the club was.'

Your dad must have had an important influence on you and your career. Could you have done this without him?

'He's the key. I come from a family where both my parents were without a set job, so they went out and took on casual work to try and bring money into the house. But anything I asked for – kits, balls, football boots – they did everything they could to try and get it for me. When I was eight or nine years old I often had to take two or three bus rides at night to get to the Liverpool training. My dad was always on the next seat – and even now, at thirty-five playing my final game, my dad is with me.'

He grew up in the bustling working-class Bluebell Estate, in Huyton in Liverpool, on Ironside Street, together with his older brother Paul, his parents and his grandad. His other grandad lived across the street. His dad was the boss at home, and the one to keep Steven out of trouble. Steven did not want to break any rules because he did not want to ruin his good relationship with his dad.

When Steven was eleven years old he fell for the temptation to steal some stationery in downtown Liverpool with a mate. He thought it was a good idea, as it would let him spend a five-pound note burning in his pocket on a burger and drinks at the train station. But he was caught, and back home his dad gave it to him straight: if Steve Heighway, Liverpool's youth development boss, found out about this, he risked getting kicked out of Liverpool. Theft was completely unacceptable in the family.

The incident taught Gerrard a valuable lesson. The only thing he wanted was to become a footballer and to play for Liverpool. If there were two parties he never wanted to let down, it was Liverpool and his dad.

'My dad has been my most important adviser in all my years as a player. When I've been down or lost interest a little, he's spurred me on. So yes, he's the key to my career.'

But did he ever try to push you harder than you wanted him to when you were in your teens?

'Where we grew up, on a council estate, there was lots of opportunities to get into trouble. You could easily lose interest in football. There's a lot of things to watch out for on a council estate: gangs on street corners getting involved in drinking, smoking, motor bikes, stuff like that.

'My brother at times came off the path and did stuff that probably wasn't so good. But my dad saw that I had some talent, and wouldn't allow me to go down that road. He'd always pull me away from my mates. My brother did too. So it was my big brother and my dad who kept me focused and on the path, especially from when I was about fourteen to eighteen.'

Paul Ince has told me about his childhood. He was in one of those gangs who always ended up in trouble, but he made it out. What do you think, since you know him, that he's got that made him succeed despite his background?

'He's got incredible talent, and could use both feet near enough the same. But I think what made Paul Ince the player he was, was his inner hunger, inner drive, inner passion. That's what got him through the system and to the top, and made him stay on top for longevity. He was certainly one I looked up to, when I started following the England team and dreamed about playing there. And when he came to Liverpool, I'd finished school and started training with the club full time.

'And Paul Ince won't know this, but I used to watch him. I watched a lot of what he did both on and off the pitch. I picked up little things and took with me what I loved about him, but I also noticed some things that he could have done differently. I watched a lot of players that way. Those I didn't like so much too. The ones who didn't give a hundred per cent in training, things like that. Because you don't just look at what's good, you look at what's wrong too. That's not the way to do it, I'd be thinking. In that way I developed and learned a lot, both as a player and a person.'

The team you were breaking into had some players that had achieved already what you wanted to do: Robbie Fowler, Steve McManaman, Jamie Redknapp…

'Yeah, I was really lucky, because I grew up with a core of local players at Liverpool. Having the local lads in the first team to look up to, playing your way into the same team as them. They'd been where I'd been. So they'd put their arm around me and help me. Jamie Redknapp helped me massively, and he was practically a local lad since he was there for such a long time.

'Redknapp was my hero. I love him as a guy, and I loved him as a player. He went out of his way to help me. I was sixteen and an apprentice on forty-seven pounds a week. And he was a national star who played for England and LFC and was vice-captain under Paul Ince. Every day he'd call me over and check on me if I was all right, if I had the football boots and the equipment that I needed. And he'd tell me where he was off to after training and ask me to join him. He didn't have to do that. When someone behaves like that to you at sixteen, it does something important to you. So when I was twenty-six and I was captain, I'd treat younger players the way Jamie had. He was very kind to people who'd been in the same situation as himself. He came to Liverpool at around sixteen and almost became a Scouser during the ten years he was here. He wasn't just a top player, he was also a top guy who'd go out of his way to help – not just me, but many of my friends at that time. He looked after us and protected us. Jamie showed great leadership.'

He was bullied in school because his dad was a well-known football manager. And you're a massive character in this city. You've had to put up with a lot through the years. What's it been like?

Gerrard looks at me across the small hotel table and nods in confirmation.

'Up until I made my debut, I was left alone. Nobody knew who I was. I had a lot of injuries when I was about sixteen or seventeen. All the attention was on Michael Owen, and it suited me just fine. Michael progressed through the system a lot quicker than me, so no one was really aware of me. But from the moment I made it into the first team, it had such a big impact. That's when the stick and the aggression, especially in this city, started to come my way. But we've all had it. Robbie Fowler, Jamie Carragher, me. It's just the way it is. It's part of the game. You've got to take the rough with the smooth, especially when you're playing in a football city like this, with two big football teams.'

Aged eighteen, Gerrard made his debut for Liverpool's first team, when he was introduced as substitute for right-back Vegard Heggem in the final minutes at home against Blackburn. It was 29 November 1998. The boy with the close-cropped hair and wintery-white skin took a deep breath, and ran onto the green pitch. It was the dream come true.

Since Jamie Redknapp was out with injury, Gerrard got a few games in midfield and then right-wing, playing a total of thirteen games in his first season.

The next year he started playing regularly with Redknapp in midfield. That was also when he scored his first goal, in the 4–1 victory against Sheffield Wednesday. But then he had to pay the price for a body that grew too quickly, and for playing a few games too many when he was younger. He had back trouble and later groin trouble, and was out of action for a while.

In the 2000/01 treble season his physical problems eased, and Gerrard played all fifty games and scored ten goals, led by the captains Hyypiä and Fowler, the two of them taking turns wearing the armband.

'I think Robbie was made captain because of who he was: an icon in the dressing room, and possibly the best striker in England at that time,' says Gerrard. 'We had a natural respect for Robbie. He was a bubbly character in the dressing room, very easy to like, and he got along well with every single player. He didn't talk much. But when he did, we listened. He wasn't a very vocal or aggressive captain, but what he said made good sense. He led by example. I enjoyed so much playing with him, and we're still good friends. He's a top guy. It's a shame he struggled with injuries, or I think he would have shattered every record there was in the club. He's the best finisher I've ever played with.'

Both Rush and Fowler were captains and strikers. Is it ideal for an attacker to be captain?

'No, I don't think it's an ideal position for a captain. But when you've got two players like Fowler and Rush, with that kind of respect, you understand why they were appointed captains. It's almost like the Alan Shearer scenario. You understand why they're leaders based on their character and the respect they enjoy – not just from the players in the dressing room, but from the supporters and the staff at the club. But for me, the ideal position to be captain is in central defence or central midfield, where you can see the whole pitch. That being said, I've got no problem with the two of them as captains, they're both heroes of mine.'

And then a tall Finn entered the scene as captain. What was Sami Hyypiä like as a leader?

'He was a very likable fella, and very quiet to begin with. You couldn't pick on anything in his daily work, he was professional: his diet and nutrition was spot on, as was his gym work. He was always perfectly prepared. He was the best man in training, made very few mistakes. Often you won't quite know what quality you get when you buy a player for two and half million pounds. That wasn't a problem with Sami – a player of his abilities today would cost around thirty-five to forty million.

'He didn't arrive in Liverpool as a leader or a captain, but he developed into a leader type. The fans loved him and the players loved him. He'd talk quite a lot, but softly, and usually what he said made a lot of sense. I think Liverpool was perfect for Sami and Sami was perfect for Liverpool.'

Gerrard served as Hyypiä's vice-captain for a while. It was a time when the captain's performance was not quite up to standard – the responsibility seemed to be weighing Hyypiä down. There were too many duties outside of training and matches for him. Redknapp had experienced the same, he had also felt that the armband was like an extra weight on rough days.

Can people take on too much responsibility as a captain, so their performance as a player is affected?

'You need to be thick-skinned to be captain. Before you accept the responsibility of being captain for Liverpool Football Club you've got to tell yourself: "There will be good days and bad days." On good days you'll feel on top of the world. On bad days you'll feel sad and lonely. If you can't handle the low days, when the shit hits the fan and everyone's out to get you, if you can't handle those days mentally, don't take the job.

'I think Sami was one of the best defenders in Europe when he arrived. He played very, very well. Then he got the armband, and he had a few games where he wasn't quite himself. I think he took it to heart, because he's such a nice guy. I think he felt that it was his fault the team didn't play well, and it probably affected him a little. And I think the staff noticed. He was still a terrific captain, but maybe not for the long term. But certainly a top player.'

Did you feel that pressure when you were a captain?

'Every day! Every single day, even when I wasn't playing badly, I felt that pressure. But I loved it, even on bad days. When we'd had a bad game, or if I'd played badly, I used to tell myself: "I'm the captain. I need to put this right, and I'll have another chance to do that in three or four days."

'I dreamed about wearing the captain's armband from when I was about ten. So when I got it, I wanted to enjoy it, even on bad days.'

That dream came true a little sooner than he really felt prepared for when Gérard Houllier called him into his office. The year was 2003.

'Are you ready to become captain full time?' he asked.

'I was a bit shocked, I didn't feel ready to become Liverpool captain. I was only twenty-three, I felt I was too young to be. But I thought: This might be my only chance. And I was desperate to become captain.'

That day, Steven Gerrard accepted the enormous responsibility it is to captain one of English football's most successful club, a job and a responsibility he ended up having for a record twelve years.

It still felt uncomfortable to take the armband off Hyypiä, and it was difficult to know how to greet his former captain, who all of a sudden had been demoted. Yet the Finn broke the ice with his new captain, wisely offering his congratulations and support.

'I learned a lot from that transition as regards to how Sami handled it and what he said to me. He helped me a lot, especially the first two years. I was lucky to have Sami and Jamie Carragher behind me in defence. It was like having two vice-captains covering my back. I could lead from my position, but if anyone got past me, I had the two of them to put things right.'

What type of captain were you? What did you focus on?

'For me it was about keeping the standards and doing things right. Not about being aggressive, making anyone uncomfortable. If I had a problem with someone, or needed to confront them about something, I always tried to do it one-on-one, away from the traffic. I've seen captains do it differently, by going for someone in front of everybody else. That's not right. And if you're not doing things right, there's got to be room for the team to take it up with you too.'

When did you address the team the most: during the game, at half-time or in training?

'Everywhere. As captain for Liverpool the responsibility isn't just on the pitch. Every single day – from when you get into your car and drive to training – you need to be focused, and make sure you do the right things. Kids come up to you, kids from the academy, and when they're around you, they're watching what you're doing, and how you do it. So the leader of the pack has to make sure he does what's right.'

Gerrard's role as captain developed with time. He became involved in the contact of players that the club wanted to sign, and he also communicated with the players that were considering leaving the Liverpool, but the club was eager to keep. He also had good communications with new signings and upcoming talents.

Just like the club captains that preceded him, he met at press conferences on behalf of the team, and at sponsorship events. He has been a popular interviewee, and the player who topped almost everyone's wish lists whenever the club has promised to bring some of their first-team players. Gerrard developed into one of the greatest players in Premier League history, and as England captain the demands on him increased even more.

In addition, he has done so much to brighten the days for fans young and old who find themselves in difficult situations. He has made innumerable visits to hospitals and children's wards, around Christmas and at other times, and quite a few privately made visits to terminally ill children – to make a tiny difference in an extreme situation of immeasurable sorrow. The fact these football icons do things like this shows not only their social responsibility, but human compassion, and great leadership at work. 'It's the least they could do,' some may say, 'considering how much money they make.' But it is not for everyone to endure the strain it is to repeatedly, throughout one's career, visit and try and cheer up dying children and their families. I think only people who have been at a child's deathbed can understand how tough that is.'

In 2011, Gerrard established his own charitable foundation to help and support children in need. He decided to set it up after meeting a lot of children in difficult situations. The goal is to make a lasting change for the children he helps. His testimonial match at a sold-out Anfield in 2013 and the corresponding gala dinner at the Echo Arena attracted more than one thousand people; they were two of the biggest events to date where proceeds went partly to his own charity, as well as other charity projects.

In his long Liverpool career Gerrard has played under Gérard Houllier, Rafael Benítez, Roy Hodgson, Kenny Dalglish and Brendan Rodgers.

Which managers have given you most space to influence the game as captain?

'All of them have given me the space, given me the chance to express myself. But from a captaining point of view, Houllier was the most important, because he gave me that responsibility, and he gave me the confidence by telling me why he wanted me to be captain – why I deserved to be captain.

'When I became captain, I still had a lot to learn. There was much room for improvement. But he gave me the self-confidence and belief that I could become a captain for a long time.'

He was like a father figure too, wasn't he?

'Yes, he was. He wasn't just interested in what I did on the pitch or what I did as a player. He was interested in the life I led outside football and matches too. He made sure I lived the right kind of life, that I was eating right and all that. He helped me stay focused and become even more professional.'

Rafael Benítez was his next Liverpool manager. How did he deal with the Spaniard's way of mostly giving feedback on mistakes and observations on potential for improvement?

'Things changed a little with Benítez. I'd been so close to Houllier. He talked to me almost every single day and gave me loads of positive feedback, but Benítez was a different type. He kept more distance to his players. But Rafa managed to get more respect out of us. He demanded our best efforts in a way that made us want to impress him. That way he got even more out of us.'

But it must have been frustrating…

'Every player wants a pat on the back. But Benítez has a different approach.

There were times when I felt I had deserved a little more praise than I got. But I still think some of my best performances happened under Benítez, because I was so determined to do my absolute best. In an attempt to get that recognition from him, to make him like me, I went that extra mile.'

In the space of twelve months, Steven Gerrard scored three of the most important goals in modern Liverpool history. Two of them came against West Ham United in the FA Cup final of 2006, contributing towards a 3–3 draw which Liverpool ended up winning on penalties.

Before that, there was Istanbul. He was the captain. Liverpool were 3–0 down at half-time. His goal made it 3–1: a platform for Liverpool to build on. From there, an improbable recovery was mounted and arguably the greatest Champions League final in history unravelled.

'The pinnacle will always be the Champions League final in Istanbul,' he says.

Before the match, Gerrard huddled his team-mates on the pitch. He was desperate to tell them, especially the foreign lads, just how much the Champions League final means to Liverpool. In his autobiography, he recalls shouting at them in the huddle; the words flying out of him:

We are Liverpool. Liverpool belong in the European Cup final. Just look at the fans. Look at how much this means to them. It means the world. Don't let them down. You don't realise the reaction you will get from these fans if you win. You will be a hero for the rest of your life. This is our chance, our moment. Don't let it slip. We have come this far, let's not fucking give it up tonight. Let's start well, get into them, show them we're Liverpool. Lads, no regrets. Make every challenge count, every run count, every shot count, otherwise you will regret it for the rest of your life. No regrets. Let's win it.

Gerrard squints across the table and smiles at the mere thought of that warm night at the Atatürk stadium.

'We were playing the best team in Europe: AC Milan. I often go through their team, from the keeper to the front men, and they probably had five or six of the best twenty players in Europe at the time. We were certainly the underdogs.

'Every time I watch the highlights from the game, I see something new. A couple of weeks ago I noticed Djimi Traoré made a clearance off the line in extra time. No one ever mentions that. People look at the goals and the slides by Jamie and Sami.

But I look at the eleven who started the match, and the subs who came on and had a great impact on the game. Everybody played an important role. There was a lot of leadership on the night.

'But as captain, of course, I was very proud of my own contribution. At half-time I thought: We just need a bit of respect. We have to at least try to give our fans something. A moment to cheer about. They've travelled far, and we're 3–0 down. We were battered in the first half, it could've easily been worse, maybe 6–0. After the first half, most of us were concerned. But at the start of the second half we were more positive. We created a little more. I think that first goal gave us the glimmer of hope and confidence that we needed.'

Yes, your goal was certainly essential to the turnaround.

'Looking back at the game now, Milan had a ten-minute period where they fell apart, and luckily we managed to capitalise on that. But there were other periods after 3–3 where it could have gone the other way.

'I think the key moral from that game is – whichever role you had in the game: captain, team player, supporter – it's never over. No matter how badly you're playing, no matter how bad your injury is, there's always a chance. A game of football can turn at any moment. That's a quite inspirational message to send to young players, don't you think! Never give up. Even if you're trailing 2–0 or 3–0. There's still time. Just dig in your heels and hang on, there's still a chance.'

One of Gerrard's worst moments came in the near fairy-tale spring of 2014, when Liverpool were eyeing what would have been their first league title in 24 years.

Everyone remembers how he, the captain, huddled up the players, heads against each other, to celebrate what seemed a key victory against Manchester City towards the end of the season. They were on a long winning streak. They thrashed the top teams with red goals galore. In the huddle Gerrard shouted the words that are now both famous and infamous: 'We do not let this fucking slip!'

And then he did just that: He slipped and fell, defending against Chelsea, who went on to score the goal that was a fatal turning point in the battle for the title.

In the car after the game Steven Gerrard cried. It was years since he had cried. Now he could not hold back his tears and he did not notice anything in the outside world. Sitting in the backseat he felt numb, as if he had lost a family member. He had dreamed of winning the league since he had watched captain Alan Hansen and his team, managed by Kenny Dalglish, win it in May 1990.

His wife Alex and one of his best mates were in the car too. They tried to comfort him, tell him the season was not over yet, but Steven just knew that the ultimate dream of a league title had vanished when he let Demba Ba pass him.

'I believe the lows help you to focus, and keep you grounded, they drive you onwards and make you want to achieve more in football,' is his grim appraisal when I ask him about this incident. The brevity of his utterance tells me everything I need to know.

✦

Steven Gerrard's final home game as captain is over. His team-mates have been and changed in the dressing room, where he has time and again given them encouragement and instructions for inspiration and team-building. Now they all come out on the Anfield pitch with 'Gerrard 8' on their back. It is time for the annual end-of-season lap of honour around the pitch. But this year it is also a thank you to their captain – the club captain for an unprecedented twelve years.

When all his team-mates are out on the green mat, the captain is called back onto the pitch. His three daughters, Lexie, Lilly and Lourdes – in peach-coloured jackets and white ra-ra skirts, like Daddy's glamorous little soldiers – are all with him. Again the youngest, Lourdes, is on his arm as he goes down the steps of the players' tunnel, and touches the red and white 'This Is Anfield' sign one last time. He has touched it hundreds of times before. It is meant to bring luck, as it has done for decades in the club, for generations of players. Bill Shankly started the tradition; he had it hung there as a warning to their opponents. For one last time as the leader of the team, Gerrard's fingertips touch the lower edge of the sign.

The time has come to take his final farewell with the home fans. Their chant 'Steven Gerrard is our captain, Steven Gerrard is a Red, Steven Gerrard plays for Liverpool, Scouser born and bred' is on repeat, and so loud it echoes off the tin roof. I'm on the Kop singing with my husband and our nine-year-old son. And then something unexpected happens. My son starts crying, so vigorously his narrow shoulders with the 'Gerrard 8' shirt is shaking. He is sobbing. That is too much for his parents. We look at him, at each other, and we well up. A few of the big, burly guys on the Kop look at the little blond kid crying, and it spreads. It catches on almost like a forest fire, and more and more of us let our tears flow. It is so final. An era is over in Liverpool's proud history of captains.

Gerrard applauds the fans, hugs the man who gave him the chance as first-team player, and then appointed him captain – Gérard Houllier. He has been waiting on the pitch outside the tunnel. A stadium mike is directed at the captain.

'It felt very strange playing my last game here. I've been dreading this moment. I've loved every minute I've played here, and I'm absolutely devastated I'm never gonna play in front of these supporters again.'

After a short interview about his time at the club, he is met with a deafening cheer as a thank you, so loud his daughter covers her ears. On the front row of the directors' box, Kenny Dalglish is seen biting his lip. It is an emotional moment for everyone. The fans start singing their tribute again: 'Steven Gerrard is our captain, Steven Gerrard is a Red…' Gerrard looks down, seemingly moved; he moistens his lip before he looks out over the crowd and continues:

'Just before I go, before the tears come, as I say: I've played in front of most supporters around the world, but let me tell you – you are the best. Thank you very much, all the best!'

The fans reply with a loud 'You'll Never Walk Alone'. He starts his lap of honour around the pitch but stops in the first corner, between the Main Stand and the Kop. Jamie Redknapp and Jamie Carragher are waiting, live on *Sky Sports*. They both give him a big hug before they have a short chat with him. Three former Liverpool captains. No matter how unreal it sounds, Steven will be in that category too now.

ACKNOWLEDGEMENTS

My most heartfelt thanks

I AM SO INCREDIBLY GRATEFUL FOR THE CONFIDENCE, THE insight and the time that Liverpool FC's captains have given me: Ron Yeats, Tommy Smith, Phil Thompson, Graeme Souness, Ronnie Whelan, Mark Wright, Ian Rush, John Barnes, Paul Ince, Glenn Hysén, Sami Hyypiä and Steven Gerrard. And a special thank you to Phil Neal, Robbie Fowler, Jamie Redknapp and Jamie Carragher, captains who all opened many doors for me. I am also grateful that Ian St. John, Chris Lawler and Roy Evans have contributed to the time travel and the insight into this row of captaincies. (Alan Hansen and Kenny Dalglish have not been forgotten, but unfortunately they were not available for interviews for this project.)

Deep respect and thank you to Ole Magne Ansnes who has worked untiringly as a consultant and soundboard, to Kathrine Hake-Steffensen, translator from the original language Norwegian to English, and also fact checker and enthusiastic supporter.

Also a big thank you to deCoubertin Books. I couldn't have chosen a better publisher for this English version. Simon Hughes, James Corbett and Ian Allen who have all worked on the editorial and lifted this book with their professionalism and knowledge. Megan Pollard for overseeing publicity and events in the UK and

Thomas Regan for the design.

I don't know anyone who knows so much about, or who lives and breathes so unceasingly for LFC, as Christopher Wood – my Liverpool oracle. This book would not have been the same without Chris on my team.

It has been a privilege to team up with one of Britain's best rock photographers, Tony Woolliscroft. Also a big thank you to Bernt Dag Ravnevand, Lars Steinar Ansnes, Rolf Martin Krey, maestro of player facts; Jonny Stokkeland, Lars Gisnås, Sport Media, the publisher who – years ago – took a chance on me, an outsider in the football world, Tore Larsen, Einar Byrkjedal, Anita Iren Vassli, Johan Ivar Ansnes, Odd Inge Hovd, Joakim Sørensen, Pia Jacobsen and DuoDu's Rita Nylander and Anne Grut Sørum. Ged Rea for statistics about the captains; Arnie Baldursson and Gudmundur Magnusson from lfchistory.net, Morten Gulliksen, Tage Herstad, Kamilla Herstad, Karen Elizabeth Gill, Kaya and Chris Herstad Carney, Haakon Forren, Synøve Asplund, Thor-Kenneth Maarnes, Tomas Håkki Eriksson, Ann Yeats, Janette Simpson, Anna Matthews, Sue Griffins, Richard Thompson, Katie Lydon, Olivia Cole, Craig Duffy, David Hillyard, Hilton Hotel, The Boot Room Anfield, Liverpool FC, Don Jones and Peter McDowell from LFCTV,

A special thank you to Liverpool FC Supporters' Club Norway; Tore Hansen, Secretary of the club, Torbjørn Flatin and Pål Christian Møller; André Øien, Thomas Larsen Bergheim, Bertil Holen, Tore Karlsen and Nils Jacob Førli. I would also like to thank Fredrik Lund and Nina Felløy at Kaare Lund Agenturer, who have dressed me in lovely Replay clothes; Ståle Gjersvold from TrønderEnergi, Eli Flakne and Cathrine Tronstad, Eli Arnstad, Ann Marit Ansnes; and Magic, the 23 Foundation represented by Philly and Gery Carragher, Mike and Gayner Lepic, John Connors and Lunch with legends, Helen Ainscough, Yaukan and the rest of the staff from one of my favourite spots in Liverpool: the Racquet Club, who let us use their premises for interviews and photos, and Robin Grime and 5Times.

Thank you ever so much to my mother-in-law, Gudrun Ansnes, and my mother Synnøve Beldo Lund (the latter, also the queen of comma rules!) – amazing women of resource and our children's beloved grandmothers.

And I would never have written this book without the help of my best friend, sparring partner and husband, Jostein Ansnes, editor and the one who pulled me into this football madness years ago.

The biggest thanks are for my children, my biggest source of inspiration, and someone it is worth working very hard for: Elias and Elvira Lund Ansnes.

Ragnhild Lund Ansnes (1nil)

BIBLIOGRAPHY

Books for inspiration, research and background

Anderson, Jeff, *'The Official Liverpool FC Illustrated History'* (Charlton, 2004)

Ansnes, Ragnhild Lund *'Liverpool FC Heroes'* (Trinity Sports Media, 2010)

Ansnes, Ragnhild Lund *'Liverpool Hearts'* (Sport Media, 2010)

Baldursson, Arnie & Magnusson, Gudmundur *'Liverpool: the Complete Record'* (deCoubertin, 2011)

Barnes, John *'The Autobiography'* (Headline, 1999)

Callaghan, Ian *'On the Ball'* (Sport Media, 2010)

Carragher, Jamie *'My Autobiography'* (Corgi, 2008)

Dalglish, Kenny, *'My Liverpool Home'* (Hodder & Stoughton, 2011)

Fowler, Robbie *'My Autobiography'* (Macmillan, 2005)

Gerrard, Steven *'Gerrard'* (Bantam, 2007)

Gerrard, Steven *'My Story'* (Penguin, 2015)

Gill, Karen *'The Real Bill Shankly'* (Sport Media, 2008)

Hansen, Alan, *'A Matter of Opinion'* (Bantam, 1999)

Hyypiä, Sami *'From Voikkaa to the Premiership'* (Mainstream, 2003)

Keith, John *'The Essential Shankly'* (Robson, 2011)

Rush, Ian *'The Autobiography'* (Ebury, 2008)

Smith, Tommy *'Anfield Iron'* (Bantam, 2008)

Thompson, Phil *'Stand Up Pinocchio'* (Trinity Sports Media, 2005)

Whelan, Ronnie *'Walk On'* (Simon & Schuster, 2011)

Yeats, Ron *'Soccer with a Mersey Beat'* (Pelham, 1966)